MOUNTAIN CLIMBING

# A TRAMP ABROAD

BY

## MARK TWAIN

(SAMUEL L. CLEMENS)

IN TWO VOLUMES

VOL. II

HARPER & BROTHERS PUBLISHERS

NEW YORK AND LONDON

L–Q

17513

# ILLUSTRATIONS

# CONTENTS

# Contents

## CHAPTER XV.

## CHAPTER XVI.

## CHAPTER XVII.

## CHAPTER XVIII.

## CHAPTER XIX.

## CHAPTER XX.

## CHAPTER XXI.

viii                          Contents

### APPENDIX.

# A TRAMP ABROAD

# CHAPTER I.

AN hour's sail brought us to Lucerne again. I judged it best to go to bed and rest several days, for I knew that the man who undertakes to make the tour of Europe on foot must take care of himself.

Thinking over my plans, as mapped out, I perceived that they did not take in the Furka Pass, the Rhone Glacier, the Finsteraarhorn, the Wetterhorn, etc. I immediately examined the guide-book to see if these were important, and found they were; in fact, a pedestrian tour of Europe could not be complete without them. Of course that decided me at once to see them, for I never allow myself to do things by halves, or in a slurring, slipshod way.

I called in my agent and instructed him to go without delay and make a careful examination of these noted places, on foot, and bring me back a written report of the result, for insertion in my book. I instructed him to go to Hospenthal as quickly as possible, and make his grand start from there; to extend his foot expedition as far as the Giesbach fall, and return to me from thence by diligence or mule. I told him to take the courier with him.

He objected to the courier, and with some show of reason, since he was about to venture upon new and untried ground; but I thought he might as well learn how to take care of the courier now as later, therefore I enforced my point. I said that the trouble, delay, and inconvenience of traveling with a courier were balanced by the deep respect which a courier's presence commands, and I must insist that as much style be thrown into my journeys as possible.

So the two assumed complete mountaineering costumes and departed. A week later they returned, pretty well used up, and my agent handed me the following

### OFFICIAL REPORT
*Of a Visit to the Furka Region. By H. Harris, Agent.*

About seven o'clock in the morning, with perfectly fine weather, we started from Hospenthal, and arrived at the *maison* on the Furka in a little under *quatre* hours. The want of variety in the scenery from Hospenthal made the *kahkahponeeka* wearisome; but let none be discouraged; no one can fail to be completely *recompensée* for his fatigue, when he sees, for the first time, the monarch of the Oberland, the tremendous Finsteraarhorn. A moment before all was dullness, but a *pas* further has placed us on the summit of the Furka; and exactly in

front of us, at a *hopow* of only fifteen miles, this
magnificent mountain lifts its snow-wreathed precipices into the deep blue sky. The inferior mountains on each side of the pass form a sort of frame
for the picture of their dread lord, and close in the
view so completely that no other prominent feature
in the Oberland is visible from this *bong-a-bong ;*
nothing withdraws the attention from the solitary
grandeur of the Finsteraarhorn and the dependent
spurs which form the abutments of the central peak.

With the addition of some others, who were also
bound for the Grimsel, we formed a large *xhvloj* as
we descended the *steg* which winds round the
shoulder of a mountain toward the Rhone glacier.
We soon left the path and took to the ice; and after
wandering amongst the crevasses *un peu*, to admire
the wonders of these deep blue caverns, and hear
the rushing of waters through their subglacial chan-
nels, we struck out a course toward *l'autre côté* and
crossed the glacier successfully, a little above the
cave from which the infant Rhone takes its first
bound from under the grand precipice of ice. Half
a mile below this we began to climb the flowery side
of the Meienwand. One of our party started before
the rest, but the *Hitze* was so great, that we found
*ihm* quite exhausted, and lying at full length in the
shade of a large *Gestein*. We sat down with him
for a time, for all felt the heat exceedingly in the
climb up this very steep *bolwoggoly*, and then we set
out again together, and arrived at last near the Dead

Man's Lake, at the foot of the Sidelhorn. This
lonely spot, once used for an extempore burying
place, after a sanguinary *battue* between the French
and Austrians, is the perfection of desolation; there
is nothing in sight to mark the hand of man, except
the line of weather-beaten whitened posts, set up to
indicate the direction of the pass in the *owdawakk*
of winter. Near this point the footpath joins the
wider track, which connects the Grimsel with the
head of the Rhone *schnawp;* this has been carefully
constructed, and leads with a tortuous course among
and over *les pierres*, down to the bank of the gloomy
little *swosh-swosh*, which almost washes against the
walls of the Grimsel Hospice. We arrived a little
before four o'clock at the end of our day's journey,
hot enough to justify the step, taken by most of the
*partie*, of plunging into the crystal water of the
snow-fed lake.

The next afternoon we started for a walk up the
Unteraar glacier, with the intention of, at all events,
getting as far as the *Hütte* which is used as a sleeping place by most of those who cross the Strahleck
Pass to Grindelwald. We got over the tedious collection of stones and *débris* which covers the *pied* of
the *Gletcher*, and had walked nearly three hours
from the Grimsel, when, just as we were thinking of
crossing over to the right, to climb the cliffs at the
foot of the hut, the clouds, which had for some
time assumed a threatening appearance, suddenly
dropped, and a huge mass of them, driving toward

us from the Finsteraarhorn, poured down a deluge of *haboolong* and hail. Fortunately, we were not far from a very large glacier table; it was a huge rock balanced on a pedestal of ice high enough to admit of our all creeping under it for *gowkarak*. A stream of *puckittypukk* had furrowed a course for itself in the ice at its base, and we were obliged to stand with one *Fuss* on each side of this, and endeavor to keep ourselves *chaud* by cutting steps in the steep bank of the pedestal, so as to get a higher place for standing on, as the *wasser* rose rapidly in its trench. A very cold *bzzzzzzzzeeeee* accompanied the storm, and made our position far from pleasant; and presently came a flash of *Blitzen*, apparently in the middle of our little party, with an instantaneous clap of *yokky*, sounding like a large gun fired close to our ears; the effect was startling; but in a few seconds our attention was fixed by the roaring echoes of the thunder against the tremendous mountains which completely surrounded us. This was followed by many more bursts, none of *welche*, however, was so dangerously near; and after waiting a long *demi*-hour in our icy prison, we sallied out to walk through a *haboolong* which, though not so heavy as before, was quite enough to give us a thorough soaking before our arrival at the Hospice.

The Grimsel is *certainement* a wonderful place; situated at the bottom of a sort of huge crater, the sides of which are utterly savage *Gebirge*, composed of barren rocks which cannot even support a single

2**

pine *arbre*, and afford only scanty food for a herd
of *gmwkwllolp*, it looks as if it must be completely
*begraben* in the winter snows. Enormous avalanches
fall against it every spring, sometimes covering
everything to the depth of thirty or forty feet; and,
in spite of walls four feet thick, and furnished with
outside iron shutters, the two men who stay here
when the *voyageurs* are snugly quartered in their
distant homes can tell you that the snow sometimes
shakes the house to its foundations.

Next morning the *hogglebumgullup* still continued
bad, but we made up our minds to go on, and make
the best of it. Half an hour after we started, the
*Regen* thickened unpleasantly, and we attempted to
get shelter under a projecting rock, but being far
too *nass* already to make standing at all *agréable*,
we pushed on for the Handeck, consoling ourselves
with the reflection that from the furious rushing of
the river Aar at our side, we should at all events see
the celebrated *Wasserfall* in *grande perfection*.
Nor were we *nappersocket* in our expectation; the
water was roaring down its leap of 250 feet in a
most magnificent frenzy, while the trees which cling
to its rocky sides swayed to and fro in the violence
of the hurricane which it brought down with it;
even the stream, which falls into the main cascade
at right angles, and *toutefois* forms a beautiful feature
in the scene, was now swollen into a raging torrent;
and the violence of this " meeting of the waters,"
about fifty feet below the frail bridge where we

stood, was fearfully grand. While we were looking at it, *glücklicheweise* a gleam of sunshine came out, and instantly a beautiful rainbow was formed by the spray, and hung in mid air suspended over the awful gorge.

On going into the *châlet* above the fall, we were informed that a *Brücke* had broken down near Guttanen, and that it would be impossible to proceed for some time; accordingly we were kept in our drenched condition for *eine Stunde*, when some *voyageurs* arrived from Meiringen, and told us that there had been a trifling accident, *aber* that we could now cross. On arriving at the spot, I was much inclined to suspect that the whole story was a ruse to make us *slowwk* and drink the more in the Handeck Inn, for only a few planks had been carried away, and though there might perhaps have been some difficulty with mules, the gap was certainly not larger than a *mmbglx* might cross with a very slight leap. Near Guttanen the *haboolong* happily ceased, and we had time to walk ourselves tolerably dry before arriving at Reichenbach, *wo* we enjoyed a good *dîné* at the Hotel des Alps.

Next morning we walked to Rosenlaui, the *beau idéal* of Swiss scenery, where we spent the middle of the day in an excursion to the glacier. This was more beautiful than words can describe, for in the constant progress of the ice it has changed the form of its extremity and formed a vast cavern, as blue as the sky above, and rippled like a frozen ocean.

A few steps cut in the *whoopjamboreehoo* enabled us to walk completely under this, and feast our eyes upon one of the loveliest objects in creation. The glacier was all around divided by numberless fissures of the same exquisite color, and the finest wood-*Erdbeeren* were growing in abundance but a few yards from the ice. The inn stands in a *charmant* spot close to the *côté de la rivière*, which, lower down, forms the Reichenbach fall, and embosomed in the richest of pinewoods, while the fine form of the Wellhorn looking down upon it completes the enchanting *bopple*. In the afternoon we walked over the Great Scheideck to Grindelwald, stopping to pay a visit to the Upper glacier by the way; but we were again overtaken by bad *hogglebumgullup* and arrived at the hotel in *solche* a state that the landlord's wardrobe was in great request.

The clouds by this time seemed to have done their worst, for a lovely day succeeded, which we determined to devote to an ascent of the Faulhorn. We left Grindelwald just as a thunderstorm was dying away, and we hoped to find *guten Wetter* up above; but the rain, which had nearly ceased, began again, and we were struck by the rapidly increasing *froid* as we ascended. Two-thirds of the way up were completed when the rain was exchanged for *gnillic*, with which the *Boden* was thickly covered, and before we arrived at the top the *gnillic* and mist became so thick that we could not see one another at more than twenty *poopoo* distance, and it became difficult to pick our way over the rough and thickly covered ground. Shivering with cold we turned into bed with a double allowance of clothes, and slept comfortably while the wind howled *autour de la maison;* when I awoke, the wall and the window looked equally dark, but in another hour I found I could just see the form of the latter; so I jumped out of bed, and forced it open, though with difficulty from the frost and the quantities of *gnillic* heaped up against it.

A row of huge icicles hung down from the edge of the roof, and anything more wintry than the whole *Anblick* could not well be imagined; but the sudden appearance of the great mountains in front was so startling that I felt no inclination to move toward bed again. The snow which had collected upon *la fenêtre* had increased the *Finsterniss oder der Dunkelheit*, so that when I looked out I was surprised to find that the daylight was considerable, and that the *balragoomah* would evidently rise before long. Only the brightest of *les étoile*s were still shining; the sky was cloudless overhead, though small curling mists lay thousands of feet below us in the valleys, wreathed around the feet of the mountains, and adding to the splendor of their lofty summits. We were soon dressed and out of the house, watching the gradual appoach of dawn, thoroughly absorbed in the first near view of the Oberland giants, which broke upon us unexpectedly after the intense obscurity of the evening before.

2**

"*Kabaugwakko    songwashee    Kum    Wetterhorn
snawpo !*" cried some one, as that grand summit
gleamed with the first rose of dawn; and in a few
moments the double crest of the Schreckhorn followed its example; peak after peak seemed warmed
with life, the Jungfrau blushed even more beautifully
than her neighbors, and soon, from the Wetterhorn
in the east to the Wildstrubel in the west, a long
row of fires glowed upon mighty altars, truly worthy
of the gods. The *wlgw* was very severe; our sleeping place could hardly be *distinguee* from the snow
around it, which had fallen to the depth of a *flirk*
during the past evening, and we heartily enjoyed a
rough scramble *en bas* to the Giesbach falls, where
we soon found a warm climate. At noon the day
before at Grindelwald the thermometer could not
have stood at less than 100 degrees Fahr. in the
sun; and in the evening, judging from the icicles
formed, and the state of the windows, there must
have been at least twelve *dingblatter* of frost, thus
giving a change of 80 degrees during a few hours.

I said:

"You have done well, Harris; this report is
concise, compact, well expressed; the language is
crisp, the descriptions are vivid and not needlessly
elaborated; your report goes straight to the point,
attends strictly to business, and doesn't fool around.
It is in many ways an excellent document. But it
has a fault,— it is too learned, it is much too
learned. What is ' *dingblatter* ' ? "

"'Dingblatter' is a Fiji word meaning 'degrees'."

"You knew the English of it, then?"

"Oh, yes."

"What is 'gnillic'?"

"That is the Esquimaux term for 'snow'."

"So you knew the English for that, too?"

"Why, certainly."

"What does 'mmbglx' stand for?'

"That is Zulu for 'pedestrian'."

"'While the form of the Wellhorn looking down upon it completes the enchanting bopple.' What is 'bopple'?"

"'Picture.' It's Choctaw."

"What is 'schnawp'?"

"'Valley.' That is Choctaw, also."

"What is 'bolwoggoly'?"

"That is Chinese for 'hill'."

"'Kahkahponeeka'?"

"'Ascent.' Choctaw."

"'But we were again overtaken by bad hogglebumgullup.' What does 'hogglebumgullup' mean?"

"That is Chinese for 'weather'."

"Is 'hogglebumgullup' better than the English word? Is it any more descriptive?"

"No, it means just the same."

"And 'dingblatter' and 'gnillic,' and 'bopple,' and 'schnawp,'— are they better than the English words?"

"No, they mean just what the English ones do."

"Then why do you use them? Why have you used all this Chinese and Choctaw and Zulu rubbish?"

"Because I didn't know any French but two or three words, and I didn't know any Latin or Greek at all."

"That is nothing. Why should you want to use foreign words, anyhow?"

"To adorn my page. They all do it."

"Who is 'all'?"

"Everybody. Everybody that writes elegantly. Anybody has a right to that wants to."

"I think you are mistaken." I then proceeded in the following scathing manner. "When really learned men write books for other learned men to read, they are justified in using as many learned words as they please — their audience will understand them; but a man who writes a book for the general public to read is not justified in disfiguring his pages with untranslated foreign expressions. It is an insolence toward the majority of the purchasers, for it is a very frank and impudent way of saying, 'Get the translations made yourself if you want them, this book is not written for the ignorant classes.' There are men who know a foreign language so well and have used it so long in their daily life that they seem to discharge whole volleys of it into their English writings unconsciously, and so they omit to translate, as much as half the time. That is a great cruelty to nine out of ten of the man's readers. What is the excuse for this? The writer would say he only uses the foreign language where the delicacy of his point cannot be conveyed in English. Very

well, then he writes his best things for the tenth
man, and he ought to warn the other nine not to
buy his book. However, the excuse he offers is at
least an excuse; but there is another set of men
who are like *you;* they know a *word* here and there,
of a foreign language, or a few beggarly little three-
word phrases, filcned from the back of the Dictionary, and these they are continually peppering into
their literature, with a pretense of knowing that
language,— what excuse can they offer? The foreign
words and phrases which they use have their exact
equivalents in a nobler language,— English; yet
they think they " adorn their page " when they say
*Strasse* for street, and *Bahnhof* for railway station,
and so on,— flaunting these fluttering rags of poverty in the reader's face and imagining he will be
ass enough to take them for the sign of untold riches
held in reserve. I will let your ' learning ' remain in
your report; you have as much right, I suppose, to
' adorn your page ' with Zulu and Chinese and
Choctaw rubbish as others of your sort have to
adorn theirs with insolent odds and ends smouched
from half a dozen learned tongues whose *a-b abs*
they don't even know."

When the musing spider steps upon the red-hot
shovel, he first exhibits a wild surprise, then he
shrivels up. Similar was the effect of these blistering words upon the tranquil and unsuspecting Agent.
I can be dreadfully rough on a person when the
mood takes me.

# CHAPTER II.

WE now prepared for a considerable walk,—from Lucerne to Interlaken, over the Brünig Pass. But at the last moment the weather was so good that I changed my mind and hired a four-horse carriage. It was a huge vehicle, roomy, as easy in its motion as a palanquin, and exceedingly comfortable.

We got away pretty early in the morning, after a hot breakfast, and went bowling along over a hard, smooth road, through the summer loveliness of Switzerland, with near and distant lakes and mountains before and about us for the entertainment of the eye, and the music of multitudinous birds to charm the ear. Sometimes there was only the width of the road between the imposing precipices on the right and the clear cool water on the left with its shoals of uncatchable fishes skimming about through the bars of sun and shadow; and sometimes, in place of the precipices, the grassy land stretched away, in an apparently endless upward slant, and was dotted everywhere with snug little chalets, the peculiarly captivating cottage of Switzerland.

The ordinary chalet turns a broad, honest gable

end to the road, and its ample roof hovers over the home in a protecting, caressing way, projecting its sheltering eaves far outward. The quaint windows are filled with little panes, and garnished with white muslin curtains, and brightened with boxes of blooming flowers. Across the front of the house, and up the spreading eaves and along the fanciful railings of the shallow porch, are elaborate carvings, — wreaths, fruits, arabesques, verses from Scripture, names, dates, etc. The building is wholly of wood, reddish brown in tint, a very pleasing color. It generally has vines climbing over it. Set such a house against the fresh green of the hillside, and it looks ever so cosy and inviting and picturesque, and is a decidedly graceful addition to the landscape.

One does not find out what a hold the chalet has taken upon him, until he presently comes upon a new house,— a house which is aping the town fashions of Germany and France, a prim, hideous, straight-up-and-down thing, plastered all over on the outside to look like stone, and altogether so stiff, and formal, and ugly, and forbidding, and so out of tune with the gracious landscape, and so deaf and dumb and dead to the poetry of its surroundings, that it suggests an undertaker at a picnic, a corpse at a wedding, a puritan in Paradise.

In the course of the morning we passed the spot where Pontius Pilate is said to have thrown himself into the lake. The legend goes that after the Crucifixion his conscience troubled him, and he fled from Jerusalem and wandered about the earth, weary of life and a prey to tortures of the mind. Eventually, he hid himself away, on the heights of Mount Pilatus, and dwelt alone among the clouds and crags for years; but rest and peace were still denied him, so he finally put an end to his misery by drowning himself.

Presently we passed the place where a man of better odor was born. This was the children's friend, Santa Claus, or St. Nicholas. There are some unaccountable reputations in the world. This saint's is an instance. He has ranked for ages as the peculiar friend of children, yet it appears he was not much of a friend to his own. He had ten of them, and when fifty years old he left them, and sought out as dismal a refuge from the world as possible, and became a hermit in order that he might reflect upon pious themes without being disturbed by the joyous and other noises from the nursery, doubtless.

Judging by Pilate and St. Nicholas, there exists no rule for the construction of hermits; they seem made out of all kinds of material. But Pilate attended to the matter of expiating his sin while he was alive, whereas St. Nicholas will probably have to go on climbing down sooty chimneys, Christmas eve, forever, and conferring kindness on other people's children, to make up for deserting his own. His bones are kept in a church in a village (Sachseln), which we visited, and are naturally held in great reverence. His portrait is common in the farmhouses of the region, but is believed by many to be but an indifferent likeness. During his hermit life, according to the legend, he partook of the bread and wine of the communion once a month, but all the rest of the month he fasted.

A constant marvel with us, as we sped along the bases of the steep mountains on this journey, was, not that avalanches occur, but that they are not occurring all the time. One does not understand why rocks and landslides do not plunge down these declivities daily. A landslip occurred three quarters of a century ago, on the route from Arth to Brunnen, which was a formidable thing. A mass of conglomerate two miles long, a thousand feet broad, and a hundred feet thick, broke away from a cliff three thousand feet high and hurled itself into the valley below, burying four villages and five hundred people, as in a grave.

We had such a beautiful day, and such endless pictures of limpid lakes, and green hills and valleys, and majestic mountains, and milky cataracts dancing down the steeps and gleaming in the sun, that we could not help feeling sweet toward all the world; so we tried to drink all the milk, and eat all the grapes and apricots and berries, and buy all the bouquets of wild flowers which the little peasant boys and girls offered for sale; but we had to retire from this contract, for it was too heavy. At short distances,—and they were entirely too short,—all

along the road, were groups of neat and comely
children, with their wares nicely and temptingly set
forth in the grass under the shade trees, and as soon
as we approached they swarmed into the road, holding out their baskets and milk bottles, and ran
beside the carriage, barefoot and bareheaded, and
importuned us to buy. They seldom desisted early,
but continued to run and insist,—beside the wagon
while they could, and behind it until they lost
breath. Then they turned and chased a returning
carriage back to their trading post again. After
several hours of this, without any intermission, it
becomes almost annoying. I do not know what we
should have done without the returning carriages to
draw off the pursuit. However, there were plenty
of these, loaded with dusty tourists and piled high
with luggage. Indeed, from Lucerne to Interlaken
we had the spectacle, among other scenery, of an
unbroken procession of fruit peddlers and tourist
carriages.

Our talk was mostly anticipatory of what we
should see on the down grade of the Brünig, by and
by, after we should pass the summit. All our
friends in Lucerne had said that to look down upon
Meiringen, and the rushing blue-gray river Aar, and
the broad level green valley; and across at the
mighty Alpine precipices that rise straight up to the
clouds out of that valley; and up at the microscopic
chalets perched upon the dizzy eaves of those
precipices and winking dimly and fitfully through

the drifting veil of vapor; and still up and up, at the superb *Oltschibach* and the other beautiful cascades that leap from those rugged heights, robed in powdery spray, ruffled with foam, and girdled with rainbows — to look upon these things, they said, was to look upon the last possibility of the sublime and the enchanting. Therefore, as I say, we talked mainly of these coming wonders; if we were conscious of any impatience, it was to get there in favorable season; if we felt any anxiety, it was that the day might remain perfect, and enable us to see those marvels at their best.

As we approached the Kaiserstuhl, a part of the harness gave way. We were in distress for a moment, but only a moment. It was the fore-and-aft gear that was broken,— the thing that leads aft from the forward part of the horse and is made fast to the thing that pulls the wagon. In America this would have been a heavy leathern strap; but, all over the continent it is nothing but a piece of rope the size of your little finger,— clothes-line is what it is. Cabs use it, private carriages, freight carts and wagons, all sorts of vehicles have it. In Munich I afterward saw it used on a long wagon laden with fifty-four half barrels of beer; I had before noticed that the cabs in Heidelberg used it; — not new rope, but rope that had been in use since Abraham's time, — and I had felt nervous, sometimes, behind it when the cab was tearing down a hill. But I had long been accustomed to it now, and had even become afraid of the leather strap which belonged in its place. Our driver got a fresh piece of clothes-line out of his locker and repaired the break in two minutes.

So much for one European fashion. Every country has its own ways. It may interest the reader to know how they " put horses to " on the continent. The man stands up the horses on each side of the thing that projects from the front end of the wagon, and then throws the tangled mess of gear on top of the horses, and passes the thing that goes forward through a ring, and hauls it aft, and passes the other thing through the other ' ng and hauls it aft on the other side of the other horse, opposite to the first one, after crossing them and bringing the loose end back, and then buckles the other thing underneath the horse, and takes another thing and wraps it around the thing I spoke of before, and puts another thing over each horse's head, with broad flappers to it to keep the dust out of his eyes, and puts the iron thing in his mouth for him to grit his teeth on, up hill, and brings the ends of these things aft over his back, after buckling another one around under his neck to hold his head up, and hitching another thing on a thing that goes over his shoulders to keep his head up when he is climbing a hill, and then takes the slack of the thing which I mentioned a while ago, and fetches it aft and makes it fast to the thing that pulls the wagon, and hands the other things up to the driver to steer

with. I never have buckled up a horse myself, but
I do not think we do it that way.

We had four very handsome horses, and the driver
was very proud of his turnout. He would bowl
along on a reasonable trot, on the highway, but
when he entered a village he did it on a furious run,
and accompanied it with a frenzy of ceaseless whip
crackings that sounded like volleys of musketry.
He tore through the narrow streets and around the
sharp curves like a moving earthquake, showering
his volleys as he went, and before him swept a continuous tidal wave of scampering children, ducks,
cats, and mothers clasping babies which they had
snatched out of the way of the coming destruction;
and as this living wave washed aside, along the
walls, its elements, being safe, forgot their fears and
turned their admiring gaze upon that gallant driver
till he thundered around the next curve and was lost
to sight.

He was a great man to those villagers, with his
gaudy clothes and his terrific ways. Whenever he
stopped to have his cattle watered and fed with
loaves of bread, the villagers stood around admiring
him while he swaggered about, the little boys gazed
up at his face with humble homage, and the landlord
brought out foaming mugs of beer and conversed
proudly with him while he drank. Then he mounted
his lofty box, swung his explosive whip, and away
he went again, like a storm. I had not seen anything like this before since I was a boy, and the

3**

stage used to flourish through the village with the
dust flying and the horn tooting.

When we reached the base of the Kaiserstuhl, we
took two more horses; we had to toil along with
difficulty for an hour and a half or two hours, for
the ascent was not very gradual, but when we passed
the backbone and approached the station, the driver
surpassed all his previous efforts in the way of rush
and clatter.  He could not have six horses all the
time, so he made the most of his chance while he
had it.

Up to this point we had been in the heart of the
William Tell region.  The hero is not forgotten, by
any means, or held in doubtful veneration.  His
wooden image, with his bow drawn, above the doors
of taverns, was a frequent feature of the scenery.

About noon we arrived at the foot of the Brünig
Pass, and made a two-hour stop at the village hotel,
another of those clean, pretty, and thoroughly well
kept inns which are such an astonishment to people
who are accustomed to hotels of a dismally different
pattern in remote country towns.  There was a
lake here, in the lap of the great mountains, the
green slopes that rose toward the lower crags were
graced with scattered Swiss cottages nestling among
miniature farms and gardens, and from out a leafy
ambuscade in the upper heights tumbled a brawling
cataract.

Carriage after carriage, laden with tourists and
trunks, arrived, and the quiet hotel was soon popu-

lous  We were early at the table d'hote and saw
the people all come in. There were twenty-five,
perhaps. They were of various nationalities, but
we were the only Americans. Next to me sat an
English bride, and next to her sat her new husband,
whom she called "Neddy," though he was big
enough and stalwart enough to be entitled to his
full name. They had a pretty little lovers' quarrel
over what wine they should have. Neddy was for
obeying the guide-book and taking the wine of the
country; but the bride said:

"What, that nahsty stuff!"

"It isn't nahsty, pet, it's quite good."

"It *is* nahsty."

"No, it *isn't* nahsty."

"It's *o*ful nahsty, Neddy, and I shanh't drink it."

Then the question was, what she must have. She
said he knew very well that she never drank anything
but champagne. She added:

"You know very well papa always has champagne
on his table, and I've always been used to it."

Neddy made a playful pretense of being dis-
tressed about the expense, and this amused her so
much that she nearly exhausted herself with laughter,— and this pleased *him* so much that he repeated
his jest a couple of times, and added new and killing
varieties to it. When the bride finally recovered,
she gave Neddy a love-box on the arm with her fan,
and said with arch severity:

"Well, you would *have* me,— nothing else would

do,— so you'll have to make the best of a bad
bargain.  *Do* order the champagne, I'm oful dry."

So with a mock groan which made her laugh
again, Neddy ordered the champagne.

The fact that this young woman had never mois-
tened the selvedge edge of her soul with a less
plebeian tipple than champagne, had a marked and
subduing effect upon Harris.  He believed she belonged to the royal family.  But I had my doubts.

We heard two or three different languages spoken
by people at the table and guessed out the nationalities of most of the guests to our satisfaction, but
we failed with an elderly gentleman and his wife and
a young girl who sat opposite us, and with a gentleman of about thirty-five who sat three seats beyond
Harris.  We did not hear any of these speak.  But
finally the last-named gentleman left while we were
not noticing, but we looked up as he reached the far
end of the table.  He stopped there a moment, and
made his toilet with a pocket comb.  So he was a
German; or else he had lived in German hotels long
enough to catch the fashion.  When the elderly
couple and the young girl rose to leave, they bowed
respectfully to us.  So they were Germans, too.
This national custom is worth six of the other one,
for export.

After dinner we talked with several Englishmen,
and they inflamed our desire to a hotter degree than
ever, to see the sights of Meiringen from the heights
of the Brünig Pass.  They said the view was marvel-

ous, and that one who had seen it once could never forget it. They also spoke of the romantic nature of the road over the pass, and how in one place it had been cut through a flank of the solid rock, in such a way that the mountain overhung the tourist as he passed by; and they furthermore said that the sharp turns in the road and the abruptness of the descent would afford us a thrilling experience, for we should go down in a flying gallop and seem to be spinning around the rings of a whirlwind, like a drop of whisky descending the spirals of a corkscrew. I got all the information out of these gentlemen that we could need; and then, to make everything complete, I asked them if a body could get hold of a little fruit and milk here and there, in case of necessity. They threw up their hands in speechless intimation that the road was simply paved with refreshment peddlers. We were impatient to get away, now, and the rest of our two-hour stop rather dragged. But finally the set time arrived and we began the ascent. Indeed it was a wonderful road. It was smooth, and compact, and clean, and the side next the precipices was guarded all along by dressed stone posts about three feet high, placed at short distances apart. The road could not have been better built if Napoleon the First had built it. He seems to have been the introducer of the sort of roads which Europe now uses. All literature which describes life as it existed in England, France, and Germany up to the close of the last century, is filled

3**

with pictures of coaches and carriages wallowing through these three countries in mud and slush half-wheel deep; but after Napoleon had floundered through a conquered kingdom he generally arranged things so that the rest of the world could follow dry shod.

We went on climbing, higher and higher, and curving hither and thither, in the shade of noble woods, and with a rich variety and profusion of wild flowers all about us; and glimpses of rounded grassy backbones below us occupied by trim chalets and nibbling sheep, and other glimpses of far lower altitudes, where distance diminished the chalets to toys and obliterated the sheep altogether; and every now and then some ermined monarch of the Alps swung magnificently into view for a moment, then drifted past an intervening spur and disappeared again.

It was an intoxicating trip altogether; the exceeding sense of satisfaction that follows a good dinner added largely to the enjoyment; the having something especial to look forward to and muse about, like the approaching grandeurs of Meiringen, sharpened the zest. Smoking was never so good before, solid comfort was never solider; we lay back against the thick cushions, silent, meditative, steeped in felicity.

    .    .    .    .    .    .    .    .

I rubbed my eyes, opened them, and started. I had been dreaming I was at sea, and it was a thrill-

ing surprise to wake up and find land all around
me. It took me a couple of seconds to "come
to," as you may say; then I took in the situation.
The horses were drinking at a trough in the edge of
a town, the driver was taking beer, Harris was
snoring at my side, the courier, with folded arms
and bowed head, was sleeping on the box, two
dozen barefooted and bareheaded children were
gathered about the carriage, with their hands crossed
behind, gazing up with serious and innocent admiration at the dozing tourists baking there in the sun.
Several small girls held night-capped babies nearly
as big as themselves in their arms, and even these
fat babies seemed to take a sort of sluggish interest
in us.

We had slept an hour and a half and missed all
the scenery! I did not need anybody to tell me
that. If I had been a girl, I could have cursed for
vexation. As it was, I woke up the agent and gave
him a piece of my mind. Instead of being humili-
ated, he only upbraided me for being so wanting in
vigilance. He said he had expected to improve his
mind by coming to Europe, but a man might travel
to the ends of the earth with me and never see anything, for I was manifestly endowed with the very
genius of ill luck. He even tried to get up some
emotion about that poor courier, who never got a
chance to see anything, on account of my heedlessness. But when I thought I had borne about enough
of this kind of talk, I threatened to make Harris

tramp back to the summit and make a report on that scenery, and this suggestion spiked his battery.

We drove sullenly through Brienz, dead to the seductions of its bewildering array of Swiss carvings and the clamorous *hoo*-hooing of its cuckoo clocks, and had not entirely recovered our spirits when we rattled across the bridge over the rushing blue river and entered the pretty town of Interlaken. It was just about sunset, and we had made the trip from Lucerne in ten hours.

## CHAPTER III.

WE located ourselves at the Jungfrau Hotel, one of those huge establishments which the needs of modern travel have created in every attractive spot on the continent. There was a great gathering at dinner, and, as usual, one heard all sorts of languages.

The table d'hôte was served by waitresses dressed in the quaint and comely costume of the Swiss peasants. This consists of a simple gros de laine, trimmed with ashes of roses, with overskirt of sacre bleu ventre saint gris, cut bias on the off side, with facings of petit polonaise and narrow insertions of pâté de foie gras backstitched to the mise en scène in the form of a jeu d'esprit. It gives to the wearer a singularly piquant and alluring aspect.

One of these waitresses, a woman of forty, had side whiskers reaching half way down her jaw. They were two fingers broad, dark in color, pretty thick, and the hairs were an inch long. One sees many women on the continent with quite conspicuous moustaches, but this was the only woman I saw who had reached the dignity of whiskers.

After dinner the guests of both sexes distributed themselves about the front porches and the ornamental grounds belonging to the hotel, to enjoy the cool air; but, as the twilight deepened toward darkness, they gathered themselves together in that saddest and solemnest and most constrained of all places, the great blank drawing-room which is the chief feature of all continental summer hotels. There they grouped themselves about, in couples and threes, and mumbled in bated voices, and looked timid and homeless and forlorn.

There was a small piano in this room, a clattery, wheezy, asthmatic thing, certainly the very worst miscarriage in the way of a piano that the world has seen. In turn, five or six dejected and homesick ladies approached it doubtingly, gave it a single inquiring thump, and retired with the lockjaw. But the boss of that instrument was to come, nevertheless; and from my own country,— from Arkansaw.

She was a brand new bride, innocent, girlish, happy in herself and her grave and worshiping stripling of a husband; she was about eighteen, just out of school, free from affectations, unconscious of that passionless multitude around her; and the very first time she smote that old wreck one recognized that it had met its destiny. Her stripling brought an armful of aged sheet music from their room,— for this bride went "heeled," as you might say,— and bent himself lovingly over and got ready to turn the pages.

The bride fetched a swoop with her fingers from one end of the keyboard to the other, just to get her bearings, as it were, and you could see the congregation set their teeth with the agony of it. Then, without any more preliminaries, she turned on all the horrors of the "Battle of Prague," that venerable shivaree, and waded chin deep in the blood of the slain. She made a fair and honorable average of two false notes in every five, but her soul was in arms and she never stopped to correct. The audience stood it with pretty fair grit for a while, but when the cannonade waxed hotter and fiercer, and the discord average rose to four in five, the procession began to move. A few stragglers held their ground ten minutes longer, but when the girl began to wring the true inwardness out of the "cries of the wounded," they struck their colors and retired in a kind of panic.

There never was a completer victory; I was the only non-combatant left on the field. I would not have deserted my countrywoman anyhow, but indeed I had no desires in that direction. None of us like mediocrity, but we all reverence perfection. This girl's music was perfection in its way; it was the worst music that had ever been achieved on our planet by a mere human being.

I moved up close, and never lost a strain. When she got through, I asked her to play it again. She did it with a pleased alacrity and a heightened enthusiasm. She made it *all* discords, this time. She got an amount of anguish into the cries of the wounded that shed a new light on human suffering. She was on the warpath all the evening. All the time, crowds of people gathered on the porches and pressed their noses against the windows to look and marvel, but the bravest never ventured in. The bride went off satisfied and happy with her young fellow, when her appetite was finally gorged, and the tourists swarmed in again.

What a change has come over Switzerland, and in fact all Europe, during this century. Seventy or eighty years ago Napoleon was the only man in Europe who could really be called a traveler; he was the only man who had devoted his attention to it and taken a powerful interest in it; he was the only man who had traveled extensively; but now everybody goes everywhere; and Switzerland, and many other regions which were unvisited and unknown remotenesses a hundred years ago, are in our days a buzzing hive of restless strangers every summer. But I digress.

In the morning, when we looked out of our windows, we saw a wonderful sight. Across the valley, and apparently quite neighborly and close at hand, the giant form of the Jungfrau rose cold and white into the clear sky, beyond a gateway in the nearer highlands. It reminded me, somehow, of one of those colossal billows which swells suddenly up beside one's ship, at sea, sometimes, with its crest and shoulders snowy white, and the rest of its noble proportions streaked downward with creamy foam.

I took out my sketch book and made a little picture of the Jungfrau, merely to get the shape.

I do not regard this as one of my finished works, in fact I do not rank it among my Works at all; it is only a study; it is hardly more than what one might call a sketch. Other artists have done me the grace to admire it; but I am severe in my judgments of my own pictures, and this one does not move me.

It was hard to believe that that lofty wooded rampart on the left which so overtops the Jungfrau was not actually the higher of the two, but it was not, of course. It is only 2,000 or 3,000 feet high, and of

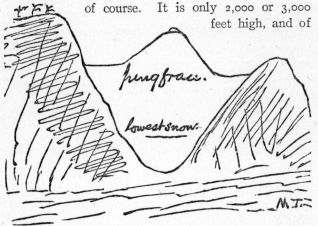

course has no snow upon it in summer, whereas the Jungfrau is not much short of 14,000 feet high and therefore that lowest verge of snow on her side, which seems nearly down to the valley, is really

about seven thousand feet higher up in the air than
the summit of that wooded rampart. It is the distance that makes the deception. The wooded height
is but four or five miles removed from us, but the
Jungfrau is four or five times that distance away.

Walking down the street of shops, in the forenoon, I was attracted by a large picture, carved,
frame and all, from a single block of chocolate-
colored wood. There are people who know everything. Some of these had told us that continental
shop-keepers always raise their prices on English
and Americans. Many people had told us it was
expensive to buy things through a courier, whereas
I had supposed it was just the reverse. When I saw
this picture, I conjectured that it was worth more
than the friend I proposed to buy it for would like to
pay, but still it was worth while to inquire; so
I told the courier to step in and ask the price, as if
he wanted it for himself; I told him not to speak in
English, and above all not to reveal the fact that he
was a courier. Then I moved on a few yards, and
waited.

The courier came presently and reported the price.
I said to myself, " It is a hundred francs too much,"
and so dismissed the matter from my mind. But in
the afternoon I was passing that place with Harris,
and the picture attracted me again. We stepped
in, to see how much higher broken German would
raise the price. The shopwoman named a figure
just a hundred francs lower than the courier had

named. This was a pleasant surprise. I said I would take it. After I had given directions as to where it was to be shipped, the shopwoman said, appealingly:

"If you please, do not let your courier know you bought it."

This was an unexpected remark. I said:

"What makes you think I have a courier?"

"Ah, that is very simple; he told me himself."

"He was very thoughtful. But tell me,—why did you charge him more than you are charging me?"

"That is very simple, also: I do not have to pay you a percentage."

"O, I begin to see. You would have had to pay the courier a percentage."

"Undoubtedly. The courier always has his percentage. In this case it would have been a hundred francs."

"Then the tradesman does not pay a part of it,—the purchaser pays all of it?"

"There are occasions when the tradesman and the courier agree upon a price which is twice or thrice the value of the article, then the two divide, and both get a percentage."

"I see. But it seems to me that the purchaser does all the paying, even then."

"Oh, to be sure! It goes without saying."

"But I have bought this picture myself; therefore why shouldn't the courier know it?"

The woman exclaimed, in distress:

"Ah, indeed it would take all my little profit! He would come and demand his hundred francs, and I should have to pay."

"He has not done the buying. You could refuse."

"I could not dare to refuse. He would never bring travelers here again. More than that, he would denounce me to the other couriers, they would divert custom from me, and my business would be injured."

I went away in a thoughtful frame of mind. I began to see why a courier could afford to work for $55 a month and his fares. A month or two later I was able to understand why a courier did not have to pay any board and lodging, and why my hotel bills were always larger when I had him with me than when I left him behind, somewhere, for a few days.

Another thing was also explained, now, apparently. In one town I had taken the courier to the bank to do the translating when I drew some money. I had sat in the reading room till the transaction was finished. Then a clerk had brought the money to me in person, and had been exceedingly polite, even going so far as to precede me to the door and hold it open for me and bow me out as if I had been a distinguished personage. It was a new experience. Exchange had been in my favor ever since I had been in Europe, but just that one time. I got simply the face of my draft, and no extra francs, whereas I had expected to get quite a number of them. This was the first time I had ever used the courier at a bank. I had suspected something then, and as long as he remained with me afterward I managed bank matters by myself.

Still, if I felt that I could afford the tax, I would never travel without a courier, for a good courier is a convenience whose value cannot be estimated in dollars and cents. Without him, travel is a bitter harassment, a purgatory of little exasperating annoyances, a ceaseless and pitiless punishment,— I mean to an irascible man who has no business capacity and is confused by details.

Without a courier, travel hasn't a ray of pleasure in it, anywhere; but with him it is a continuous and unruffled delight. He is always at hand, never has to be sent for; if your bell is not answered promptly,— and it seldom is,— you have only to open the door and speak, the courier will hear, and he will have the order attended to or raise an insurrection. You tell him what day you will start, and whither you are going,— leave all the rest to him. You need not inquire about trains, or fares, or car changes, or hotels, or anything else. At the proper time he will put you in a cab or an omnibus, and drive you to the train or the boat; he has packed your luggage and transferred it, he has paid all the bills. Other people have preceded you half an hour to scramble for impossible places and lose their tempers, but you can take your time; the

4**

courier has secured your seats for you, and you can occupy them at your leisure.

At the station, the crowd mash one another to pulp in the effort to get the weigher's attention to their trunks; they dispute hotly with these tyrants, who are cool and indifferent; they get their baggage billets, at last, and then have another squeeze and another rage over the disheartening business of trying to get them recorded and paid for, and still another over the equally disheartening business of trying to get near enough to the ticket office to buy a ticket; and now, with their tempers gone to the dogs, they must stand penned up and packed together, laden with wraps and satchels and shawl-straps, with the weary wife and babies, in the waiting room, till the doors are thrown open — and then all hands make a grand final rush to the train, find it full, and have to stand on the platform and fret until some more cars are put on. They are in a condition to kill somebody by this time. Meantime, you have been sitting in your car, smoking, and observing all this misery in the extremest comfort.

On the journey the guard is polite and watchful, — won't allow anybody to get into your compartment, — tells them you are just recovering from the small-pox and do not like to be disturbed. For the courier has made everything right with the guard. At way stations the courier comes to your compartment to see if you want a glass of water, or a newspaper, or anything; at eating stations he sends luncheon out to you, while the other people scramble and worry in the dining-rooms. If anything breaks about the car you are in, and a station master proposes to pack you and your agent into a compartment with strangers, the courier reveals to him confidentially that you are a French duke born deaf and dumb, and the official comes and makes affable signs that he has ordered a choice car to be added to the train for you.

At custom houses the multitude file tediously through, hot and irritated, and look on while the officers burrow into the trunks and make a mess of everything; but you hand your keys to the courier and sit still. Perhaps you arrive at your destination in a rainstorm at ten at night,— you generally do. The multitude spend half an hour verifying their baggage and getting it transferred to the omnibuses; but the courier puts you into a vehicle without a moment's loss of time, and when you reach your hotel you find your rooms have been secured two or three days in advance, everything is ready, you can go at once to bed. Some of those other people will have to drift around to two or three hotels, in the rain, before they find accommodations.

I have not set down half of the virtues that are vested in a good courier, but I think I have set down a sufficiency of them to show that an irritable man who can afford one and does not employ him is not a wise economist. My courier was the worst one in Europe, yet he was a good deal better than none at all. It could not pay him to be a better one than he was, because I could not afford to buy things through him. He was a good enough courier for the small amount he got out of his service. Yes, to travel with a courier is bliss, to travel without one is the reverse.

I have had dealings with some very bad couriers; but I have also had dealings with one who might fairly be called perfection. He was a young Polander, named Joseph N. Verey. He spoke eight languages, and seemed to be equally at home in all of them; he was shrewd, prompt, posted, and punctual; he was fertile in resources, and singularly gifted in the matter of overcoming difficulties; he not only knew how to do everything in his line, but he knew the best ways and the quickest; he was handy with children and invalids; all his employer needed to do was to take life easy and leave everything to the courier. His address is, care of Messrs. Gay & Son, Strand, London; he was formerly a conductor of Gay's tourist parties. Excellent couriers are somewhat rare; if the reader is about to travel, he will find it to his advantage to make a note of this one.

# CHAPTER IV.

THE beautiful Giesbach Fall is near Interlaken, on the other side of the lake of Brienz, and is illuminated every night with those gorgeous theatrical fires whose name I cannot call just at this moment. This was said to be a spectacle which the tourist ought by no means to miss. I was strongly tempted, but I could not go there with propriety, because one goes in a boat. The task which I had set myself was to walk over Europe on foot, not skim over it in a boat. I had made a tacit contract with myself; it was my duty to abide by it. I was willing to make boat trips for pleasure, but I could not conscientiously make them in the way of business.

It cost me something of a pang to lose that fine sight, but I lived down the desire, and gained in my self-respect through the triumph. I had a finer and a grander sight, however, where I was. This was the mighty dome of the Jungfrau softly outlined against the sky and faintly silvered by the starlight. There was something subduing in the influence of that silent and solemn and awful presence; one seemed to meet the immutable, the indestructible, the eternal, face to face, and to feel the trivial and fleeting nature of his own existence the more sharply by the contrast. One had the sense of being under the brooding contemplation of a spirit, not an inert mass of rocks and ice,— a spirit which had looked down, through the slow drift of the ages, upon a million vanished races of men, and judged them; and would judge a million more,— and still be there, watching, unchanged and unchangeable, after all life should be gone and the earth have become a vacant desolation.

While I was feeling these things, I was groping, without knowing it, toward an understanding of what the spell is which people find in the Alps, and in no other mountains,— that strange, deep, nameless influence, which, once felt, cannot be forgotten,— once felt, leaves always behind it a restless longing to feel it again,— a longing which is like homesickness; a grieving, haunting yearning, which will plead, implore, and persecute till it has its will. I met dozens of people, imaginative and unimaginative, cultivated and uncultivated, who had come from far countries and roamed through the Swiss Alps year after year,— they could not explain why. They had come first, they said, out of idle curiosity, because everybody talked about it; they had come since because they could not help it, and they should keep on coming, while they lived, for the same reason; they had tried to break their chains and stay away, but it was futile; now, they had no desire to break them. Others came nearer formulating what they felt: they said they could find perfect rest and peace nowhere else when they were troubled: all frets and worries and chafings sank to sleep in the presence of the benignant serenity of the Alps; the Great Spirit of the Mountain breathed his own peace upon their hurt minds and sore hearts, and healed them; they could not think base thoughts or do mean and sordid things here, before the visible throne of God.

Down the road a piece was a Kursaal,—whatever that may be,—and we joined the human tide to see what sort of enjoyment it might afford. It was the usual open-air concert, in an ornamental garden, with wines, beer, milk, whey, grapes, etc.,—the whey and the grapes being necessaries of life to certain invalids whom physicians cannot repair, and who only continue to exist by the grace of whey or grapes. One of these departed spirits told me, in a sad and lifeless way, that there was no way for him to live but by whey; never drank anything, now, but whey, and dearly, dearly loved whey, he didn't know whey he did, but he did. After making this pun he died,—that is the whey it served him.

Some other remains, preserved from decomposition by the grape system, told me that the grapes were of a peculiar breed, highly medicinal in their nature, and that they were counted out and administered by the grape-doctors as methodically as if they

were pills.  The new patient, if very feeble, began
with one grape before breakfast, took three during
breakfast, a couple between meals, five at luncheon,
three in the afternoon, seven at dinner, four for
supper, and part of a grape just before going to
bed, by way of a general regulator.  The quantity
was gradually and regularly increased, according to
the needs and capacities of the patient, until by and
by you would find him disposing of his one grape
per second all the day long, and his regular barrel
per day.

He said that men cured in this way, and enabled
to discard the grape system, never afterward got
over the habit of talking as if they were dictating to
a slow amanuensis, because they always made a
pause between each two words while they sucked
the substance out of an imaginary grape.  He said
these were tedious people to talk with.  He said
that men who had been cured by the other process
were easily distinguished from the rest of mankind
because they always tilted their heads back, between
every two words, and swallowed a swig of imaginary
whey.  He said it was an impressive thing to observe two men, who had been cured by the two pro-
cesses, engaged in conversation,— said their pauses
and accompanying movements were so continuous
and regular that a stranger would think himself in
the presence of a couple of automatic machines.
One finds out a great many wonderful things, by
traveling, if he stumbles upon the right person.

I did not remain long at the Kursaal; the music was good enough, but it seemed rather tame after the cyclone of that Arkansaw expert. Besides, my adventurous spirit had conceived a formidable enterprise — nothing less than a trip from Interlaken, by the Gemmi and Visp, clear to Zermatt, on foot! So it was necessary to plan the details, and get ready for an early start. The courier (this was not the one I have just been speaking of) thought that the portier of the hotel would be able to tell us how to find our way. And so it turned out. He showed us the whole thing, on a relief-map, and we could see our route, with all its elevations and depressions, its villages and its rivers, as clearly as if we were sailing over it in a balloon. A relief-map is a great thing. The portier also wrote down each day's journey and the nightly hotel on a piece of paper, and made our course so plain that we should never be able to get lost without high-priced outside help.

I put the courier in the care of a gentleman who was going to Lausanne, and then we went to bed, after laying out the walking costumes and putting them into condition for instant occupation in the morning.

However, when we came down to breakfast at 8 A. M., it looked so much like rain that I hired a two-horse top-buggy for the first third of the journey. For two or three hours we jogged along the level road which skirts the beautiful lake of Thun, with a dim and dreamlike picture of watery expanses

and spectral Alpine forms always before us, veiled
in a mellowing mist. Then a steady downpour set
in, and hid everything but the nearest objects. We
kept the rain out of our faces with umbrellas, and
away from our bodies with the leather apron of the
buggy; but the driver sat unsheltered and placidly
soaked the weather in and seemed to like it. We
had the road all to ourselves, and I never had a
pleasanter excursion.

The weather began to clear while we were driving
up a valley called the Kienthal, and presently a vast
black cloud bank in front of us dissolved away and
uncurtained the grand proportions and the soaring
loftinesses of the Blumis Alp. It was a sort of breath-
taking surprise; for we had not supposed there was
anything behind that low-hung blanket of sable
cloud but level valley. What we had been mistaking for fleeting glimpses of sky away aloft there,
were really patches of the Blumis' snowy crest
caught through shredded rents in the drifting pall
of vapor.

We dined in the inn at Frutigen, and our driver
ought to have dined there, too, but he would not
have had time to dine and get drunk both, so he
gave his mind to making a masterpiece of the latter,
and succeeded. A German gentleman and his two
young lady daughters had been taking their nooning
at the inn, and when they left, just ahead of us, it
was plain that their driver was as drunk as ours, and
as happy and good natured, too, which was saying

a good deal. These rascals overflowed with attentions and information for their guests, and with
brotherly love for each other. They tied their reins,
and took off their coats and hats, so that they might
be able to give unencumbered attention to conversation and to the gestures necessary for its
illustration.

The road was smooth; it led up and over and
down a continual succession of hills; but it was
narrow, the horses were used to it, and could not
well get out of it anyhow; so why shouldn't the
drivers entertain themselves and us? The noses of
our horses projected sociably into the rear of the
forward carriage, and as we toiled up the long hills
our driver stood up and talked to his friend, and his
friend stood up and talked back to him, with his
rear to the scenery. When the top was reached
and we went flying down the other side, there was
no change in the programme. I carry in my memory yet the picture of that forward driver, on his
knees on his high seat, resting his elbows on its
back, and beaming down on his passengers, with
happy eye, and flying hair, and jolly red face, and
offering his card to the old German gentleman while
he praised his hack and horses, and both teams were
whizzing down a long hill with nobody in a position
to tell whether we were bound to destruction or an
undeserved safety.

Toward sunset we entered a beautiful green valley
dotted with chalets, a cosy little domain hidden

away from the busy world in a cloistered nook among giant precipices topped with snowy peaks that seemed to float like islands above the curling surf of the sea of vapor that severed them from the lower world. Down from vague and vaporous heights, little ruffled zigzag milky currents came crawling, and found their way to the verge of one of those tremendous overhanging walls, whence they plunged, a shaft of silver, shivered to atoms in mid-descent and turned to an airy puff of luminous dust. Here and there, in grooved depressions among the snowy desolations of the upper altitudes, one glimpsed the extremity of a glacier, with its sea-green and honeycombed battlements of ice.

Up the valley, under a dizzy precipice, nestled the village of Kandersteg, our halting place for the night. We were soon there, and housed in the hotel. But the waning day had such an inviting influence that we did not remain housed many moments, but struck out and followed a roaring torrent of ice water up to its far source in a sort of little grass-carpeted parlor, walled in all around by vast precipices and overlooked by clustering summits of ice. This was the snuggest little croquet ground imaginable; it was perfectly level, and not more than a mile long by half a mile wide. The walls around it were so gigantic, and everything about it was on so mighty a scale that it was belittled, by contrast, to what I have likened it to,— a cosy and carpeted parlor. It was so high above the Kandersteg valley that there was nothing between it and the snow peaks. I had never been in such intimate relations with the high altitudes before; the snow peaks had always been remote and unapproachable grandeurs, hitherto, but now we were hob-a-nob,— if one may use such a seemingly irreverent expression about creations so august as these.

We could see the streams which fed the torrent we had followed issuing from under the greenish ramparts of glaciers; but two or three of these, instead of flowing over the precipices, sank down into the rock and sprang in big jets out of holes in the mid-face of the walls.

The green nook which I have been describing is called the Gasternthal. The glacier streams gather and flow through it in a broad and rushing brook to a narrow cleft between lofty precipices; here the rushing brook becomes a mad torrent and goes booming and thundering down toward Kandersteg, lashing and thrashing its way over and among monster bowlders, and hurling chance roots and logs about like straws. There was no lack of cascades along this route. The path by the side of the torrent was so narrow that one had to look sharp, when he heard a cow bell, and hunt for a place that was wide enough to accommodate a cow and a Christian side by side, and such places were not always to be had at an instant's notice. The cows wear church bells, and that is a good idea in the cows, for where that torrent is, you couldn't hear an ordinary cow-bell any further than you could hear the ticking of a watch.

I needed exercise, so I employed my agent in setting stranded logs and dead trees adrift, and I sat on a bowlder and watched them go whirling and leaping head over heels down the boiling torrent. It was a wonderfully exhilarating spectacle. When I had had exercise enough, I made the agent take some, by running a race with one of those logs. I made a trifle by betting on the log.

After dinner we had a walk up and down the quiet Kandersteg valley, in the soft gloaming, with the spectacle of the dying lights of day playing about the crests and pinnacles of the still and solemn upper realm for contrast, and text for talk. There were no sounds but the dulled complaining of the torrent and the occasional tinkling of a distant bell. The spirit of the place was a sense of deep, pervading peace; one might dream his life tranquilly away there, and not miss it or mind it when it was gone.

The summer departed with the sun, and winter came with the stars. It grew to be a bitter night in that little hotel, backed up against a precipice that had no visible top to it, but we kept warm, and woke in time in the morning to find that everybody else had left for the Gemmi three hours before,— so our little plan of helping that German family (principally the old man) over the pass, was a blocked generosity.

# CHAPTER V.

WE hired the only guide left, to lead us on our way. He was over seventy, but he could have given me nine-tenths of his strength and still had all his age entitled him to. He shouldered our satchels, overcoats, and alpenstocks, and we set out up the steep path. It was hot work. The old man soon begged us to hand over our coats and waistcoats to him to carry, too, and we did it; one could not refuse so little a thing to a poor old man like that; he should have had them if he had been a hundred and fifty.

When we began that ascent, we could see a microscopic chalet perched away up against heaven on what seemed to be the highest mountain near us. It was on our right, across the narrow head of the valley. But when we got up abreast it on its own level, mountains were towering high above on every hand, and we saw that its altitude was just about that of the little Gasternthal which we had visited the evening before. Still it seemed a long way up in the air, in that waste and lonely wilderness of rocks. It had an unfenced grass-plot in front of it

(59)

which seemed about as big as a billiard table, and this grass plot slanted so sharply downwards, and was so brief, and ended so exceedingly soon at the verge of the absolute precipice, that it was a shuddery thing to think of a person's venturing to trust his foot on an incline so situated at all. Suppose a man stepped on an orange peel in that yard; there would be nothing for him to seize; nothing could keep him from rolling; five revolutions would bring him to the edge, and over he would go. What a frightful distance he would fall! — for there are very few birds that fly as high as his starting-point. He would strike and bounce, two or three times, on his way down, but this would be no advantage to him. I would as soon take an airing on the slant of a rainbow as in such a front yard. I would rather, in fact, for the distance down would be about the same, and it is pleasanter to slide than to bounce. I could not see how the peasants got up to that chalet,— the region seemed too steep for anything but a balloon.

As we strolled on climbing up higher and higher, we were continually bringing neighboring peaks into view and lofty prominence which had been hidden behind lower peaks before; so by and by, while standing before a group of these giants, we looked around for the chalet again; there it was, away down below us, apparently on an inconspicuous ridge in the valley! It was as far below us, now, as it had been above us when we were beginning the ascent.

After a while the path led us along a railed precipice, and we looked over — far beneath us was the
snug parlor again, the little Gasternthal, with its
water jets spouting from the face of its rock walls.
We could have dropped a stone into it. We had
been finding the top of the world all along — and
always finding a still higher top stealing into view in
a disappointing way just ahead; when we looked
down into the Gasternthal we felt pretty sure that
we had reached the genuine top at last, but it was
not so; there were much higher altitudes to be
scaled yet. We were still in the pleasant shade of
forest trees, we were still in a region which was
cushioned with beautiful mosses and aglow with the
many-tinted luster of innumerable wild flowers.

We found, indeed, more interest in the wild
flowers than in anything else. We gathered a
specimen or two of every kind which we were unac-
quainted with; so we had sumptuous bouquets. But
one of the chief interests lay in chasing the seasons
of the year up the mountain, and determining them
by the presence of flowers and berries which we
were acquainted with. For instance, it was the end
of August at the level of the sea; in the Kandersteg
valley at the base of the pass, we found flowers
which would not be due at the sea level for two or
three weeks; higher up, we entered October, and
gathered fringed gentians. I made no notes, and have
forgotten the details, but the construction of the
floral calendar was very entertaining while it lasted.

5**

In the high regions we found rich store of the splendid red flower called the Alpine rose, but we did not find any examples of the ugly Swiss favorite called *Edelweiss*. Its name seems to indicate that it is a noble flower and that it is white. It may be noble enough, but it is not attractive, and it is not white. The fuzzy blossom is the color of bad cigar ashes, and appears to be made of a cheap quality of gray plush. It has a noble and distant way of confining itself to the high altitudes, but that is probably on account of its looks; it apparently has no monopoly of those upper altitudes, however, for they are sometimes intruded upon by some of the loveliest of the valley families of wild flowers. Everybody in the Alps wears a sprig of Edelweiss in his hat. It is the native's pet, and also the tourist's.

All the morning, as we loafed along, having a good time, other pedestrians went staving by us with vigorous strides, and with the intent and determined look of men who were walking for a wager. These wore loose knee-breeches, long yarn stockings, and hob-nailed high-laced walking shoes. They were gentlemen who would go home to England or Germany and tell how many miles they had beaten the guide-book every day. But I doubted if they ever had much real fun, outside of the mere magnificent exhilaration of the tramp through the green valleys and the breezy heights; for they were almost always alone, and even the finest scenery loses incalculably when there is no one to enjoy it with.

All the morning an endless double procession of mule-mounted tourists filed past us along the narrow path,—the one procession going, the other coming. We had taken a good deal of trouble to teach ourselves the kindly German custom of saluting all strangers with doffed hat, and we resolutely clung to it, that morning, although it kept us bareheaded most of the time and was not always responded to. Still we found an interest in the thing, because we naturally liked to know who were English and Americans among the passers-by. All continental natives responded of course; so did some of the English and Americans, but, as a general thing, these two races gave no sign. Whenever a man or a woman showed us cold neglect, we spoke up confidently in our own tongue and asked for such information as we happened to need, and we always got a reply in the same language. The English and American folk are not less kindly than other races, they are only more reserved, and that comes of habit and education. In one dreary, rocky waste, away above the line of vegetation, we met a procession of twenty-five mounted young men, all from America. We got answering bows enough from these, of course, for they were of an age to learn to do in Rome as Rome does, without much effort.

At one extremity of this patch of desolation, overhung by bare and forbidding crags which husbanded drifts of everlasting snow in their shaded cavities, was a small stretch of thin and discouraged grass, and a man and a family of pigs were actually living here in some shanties. Consequently this place could be really reckoned as " property"; it had a money value, and was doubtless taxed. I think it must have marked the limit of real estate in this world. It would be hard to set a money value upon any piece of earth that lies between that spot and the empty realm of space. That man may claim the distinction of owning the end of the world, for if there is any definite end to the world he has certainly found it.

From here forward we moved through a storm-swept and smileless desolation. All about us rose gigantic masses, crags, and ramparts of bare and dreary rock, with not a vestige or semblance of plant or tree or flower anywhere, or glimpse of any creature that had life. The frost and the tempests of unnumbered ages had battered and hacked at these cliffs, with a deathless energy, destroying them piecemeal; so all the region about their bases was a tumbled chaos of great fragments which had been split off and hurled to the ground. Soiled and aged banks of snow lay close about our path. The ghastly desolation of the place was as tremendously complete as if Doré had furnished the working plans for it. But every now and then, through the stern gateways around us we caught a view of some neighboring majestic dome, sheathed with glittering ice, and displaying its white purity at an elevation compared to which ours was groveling and plebeian.

and this spectacle always chained one's interest and admiration at once, and made him forget there was anything ugly in the world.

I have just said that there was nothing but death and desolation in these hideous places, but I forgot. In the most forlorn and arid and dismal one of all, where the racked and splintered débris was thickest, where the ancient patches of snow lay against the very path, where the winds blew bitterest and the general aspect was mournfulest and dreariest, and furthest from any suggestion of cheer or hope, I found a solitary wee forget-me-not flourishing away, not a droop about it anywhere, but holding its bright blue star up with the prettiest and gallantest air in the world, the only happy spirit, the only smiling thing, in all that grisly desert. She seemed to say, "Cheer up! — as long as we are here, let us make the best of it." I judged she had earned a right to a more hospitable place; so I plucked her up and sent her to America to a friend who would respect her for the fight she had made, all by her small self, to make a whole vast despondent Alpine desolation stop breaking its heart over the unalterable, and hold up its head and look at the bright side of things for once.

We stopped for a nooning at a strongly built little inn called the Schwarenbach. It sits in a lonely spot among the peaks, where it is swept by the trailing fringes of the cloud rack, and is rained on, snowed on, and pelted and persecuted by the

5**

storms, nearly every day of its life. It was the only habitation in the whole Gemmi Pass.

Close at hand, now, was a chance for a blood-curdling Alpine adventure. Close at hand was the snowy mass of the Great Altels cooling its topknot in the sky and daring us to an ascent. I was fired with the idea, and immediately made up my mind to procure the necessary guides, ropes, etc., and undertake it. I instructed Harris to go to the landlord of the inn and set him about our preparations. Meantime, I went diligently to work to read up and find out what this much-talked-of mountain-climbing was like, and how one should go about it, —for in these matters I was ignorant. I opened Mr. Hinchliff's "Summer Months among the Alps" (published 1857), and selected his account of his ascent of Monte Rosa. It began:

"It is very difficult to free the mind from excitement on the evening before a grand expedition——"

I saw that I was too calm; so I walked the room a while and worked myself into a high excitement; but the book's next remark,—that the adventurer must get up at two in the morning,—came as near as anything to flatting it all out again. However, I reinforced it, and read on, about how Mr. Hinchliff dressed by candle-light and was "soon down among the guides, who were bustling about in the passage, packing provisions, and making every preparation for the start;" and how he glanced out into the cold clear night and saw that—

"The whole sky was blazing with stars, larger and brighter than they appear through the dense atmosphere breathed by inhabitants of the lower parts of the earth. They seemed actually suspended from the dark vault of heaven, and their gentle light shed a fairy-like gleam over the snow-fields around the foot of the Matterhorn, which raised its stupendous pinnacle on high, penetrating to the heart of the Great Bear, and crowning itself with a diadem of his magnificent stars. Not a sound disturbed the deep tranquillity of the night, except the distant roar of streams which rush from the high plateau of the St. Theodule glacier, and fall headlong over precipitous rocks till they lose themselves in the mazes of the Gorner glacier."

He took his hot toast and coffee, and then about half past three his caravan of ten men filed away from the Riffel Hotel, and began the steep climb. At half past five he happened to turn around, and "beheld the glorious spectacle of the Matterhorn, just touched by the rosy-fingered morning, and looking like a huge pyramid of fire rising out of the barren ocean of ice and rock around it." Then the Breithorn and the Dent Blanche caught the radiant glow; but "the intervening mass of Monte Rosa made it necessary for us to climb many hours before we could hope to see the sun himself, yet the whole air soon grew warmer after the splendid birth of day."

He gazed at the lofty crown of Monte Rosa and

E**

the wastes of snow that guarded its steep ap-
proaches, and the chief guide delivered the opinion
that no man could conquer their awful heights and
put his foot upon that summit. But the adventurers
moved steadily on, nevertheless.

They toiled up, and up, and still up; they passed
the Grand Plateau; then toiled up a steep shoulder
of the mountain, clinging like flies to its rugged
face; and now they were confronted by a tremendous wall from which great blocks of ice and snow
were evidently in the habit of falling. They turned
aside to skirt this wall, and gradually ascended until
their way was barred by a "maze of gigantic snow
crevasses,"— so they turned aside again, and "began a long climb of sufficient steepness to make a
zigzag course necessary."

Fatigue compelled them to halt frequently, for a
moment or two. At one of these halts somebody
called out, "Look at Mont Blanc!" and "we were
at once made aware of the very great height we had
attained by actually seeing the monarch of the Alps
and his attendant satellites right over the top of the
Breithorn, itself at least 14,000 feet high!"

These people moved in single file, and were all
tied to a strong rope, at regular distances apart, so
that if one of them slipped on those giddy heights,
the others could brace themselves on their alpenstocks and save him from darting into the valley,
thousands of feet below. By and by they came to
an ice-coated ridge which was tilted up at a sharp

angle, and had a precipice on one side of it. They had to climb this, so the guide in the lead cut steps in the ice with his hatchet, and as fast as he took his toes out of one of these slight holes, the toes of the man behind him occupied it.

"Slowly and steadily we kept on our way over this dangerous part of the ascent, and I daresay it was fortunate for some of us that attention was distracted from the head by the paramount necessity of looking after the feet; *for, while on the left the incline of ice was so steep that it would be impossible for any man to save himself in case of a slip, unless the others could hold him up, on the right we might drop a pebble from the hand over precipices of unknown extent down upon the tremendous glacier below.*

"Great caution, therefore, was absolutely necessary, and in this exposed situation we were attacked by all the fury of that grand enemy of aspirants to Monte Rosa — a severe and bitterly cold wind from the north. The fine powdery snow was driven past us in clouds, penetrating the interstices of our clothes, and the pieces of ice which flew from the blows of Peter's axe were whisked into the air, and then dashed over the precipice. We had quite enough to do to prevent ourselves from being served in the same ruthless fashion, and now and then, in the more violent gusts of wind, were glad to stick our alpenstocks into the ice and hold on hard."

Having surmounted this perilous steep, they sat

down and took a brief rest with their backs against a
sheltering rock and their heels dangling over a
bottomless abyss; then they climbed to the base of
another ridge,— a more difficult and dangerous one
still:

"The whole of the ridge was exceedingly narrow,
and the fall on each side desperately steep, but the
ice in some of these intervals between the masses of
rock assumed the form of a mere sharp edge,
almost like a knife; these places, though not more
than three or four short paces in length, looked un-
commonly awkward; but, like the sword leading
true believers to the gates of Paradise, they must
needs be passed before we could attain to the summit of our ambition. These were in one or two
places so narrow, that in stepping over them with
toes well turned out for greater security, *one end of
the foot projected over the awful precipice on the right,
while the other was on the beginning of the icy slope
on the left, which was scarcely less steep than the
rocks.* On these occasions Peter would take my
hand, and each of us stretching as far as we could,
he was thus enabled to get a firm footing two paces
or rather more from me, whence a spring would
probably bring him to the rock on the other side;
then, turning round, he called to me to come, and,
taking a couple of steps carefully, I was met at the
third by his outstretched hand ready to clasp mine,
and in a moment stood by his side. The others followed in much the same fashion. Once my right

foot slipped on the side toward the precipice, but I threw out my left arm in a moment so that it caught the icy edge under my armpit as I fell, and supported me considerably; at the same instant I cast my eyes down the side on which I had slipped, and contrived to plant my right foot on a piece of rock as large as a cricket ball, which chanced to protrude through the ice, on the very edge of the precipice. Being thus anchored fore and aft, as it were, I believe I could easily have recovered myself, even if I had been alone, though it must be confessed the situation would have been an awful one; as it was, however, a jerk from Peter settled the matter very soon, and I was on my legs all right in an instant. The rope is an immense help in places of this kind.''

Now they arrived at the base of a great knob or dome veneered with ice and powdered with snow — the utmost summit, the last bit of solidity between them and the hollow vault of heaven. They set to work with their hatchets, and were soon creeping, insect-like, up its surface, with their heels projecting over the thinnest kind of nothingness, thickened up a little with a few wandering shreds and films of cloud moving in lazy procession far below. Presently, one man's toe-hold broke and he fell! There he dangled in mid-air at the end of the rope, like a spider, till his friends above hauled him into place again.

A little bit later, the party stood upon the wee pedestal of the very summit, in a driving wind, and looked out upon the vast green expanses of Italy and a shoreless ocean of billowy Alps.

When I had read thus far, Harris burst into the room in a noble excitement and said the ropes and the guides were secured, and asked if I was ready. I said I believed I wouldn't ascend the Altels this time. I said Alp-climbing was a different thing from what I had supposed it was, and so I judged we had better study its points a little more before we went definitely into it. But I told him to retain the guides and order them to follow us to Zermatt, because I meant to use them there. I said I could feel the spirit of adventure beginning to stir in me, and was sure that the fell fascination of Alp-climbing would soon be upon me. I said he could make up his mind to it that we would do a deed before we were a week older which would make the hair of the timid curl with fright.

This made Harris happy, and filled him with ambitious anticipations. He went at once to tell the guides to follow us to Zermatt and bring all their paraphernalia with them.

# CHAPTER VI.

A GREAT and priceless thing is a new interest!
How it takes possession of a man! how it clings
to him, how it rides him! I strode onward from
the Schwarenbach hostelry a changed man, a reor-
ganized personality. I walked in a new world, I saw
with new eyes. I had been looking aloft at the
giant snow-peaks only as things to be worshiped
for their grandeur and magnitude, and their unspeakable grace of form; I looked up at them now, as
also things to be conquered and climbed. My sense
of their grandeur and their noble beauty was neither
lost nor impaired; I had gained a new interest in the
mountains without losing the old ones. I followed
the steep lines up, inch by inch, with my eye, and
noted the possibility or impossibility of following
them with my feet. When I saw a shining helmet
of ice projecting above the clouds, I tried to imagine
I saw files of black specks toiling up it roped together
with a gossamer thread.

We skirted the lonely little lake called the
Daubensee, and presently passed close by a
glacier on the right, — a thing like a great river

frozen solid in its flow and broken square off like a wall at its mouth. I had never been so near a glacier before.

Here we came upon a new board shanty, and found some men engaged in building a stone house; so the Schwarenbach was soon to have a rival. We bought a bottle or so of beer here; at any rate they called it beer, but I knew by the price that it was dissolved jewelry, and I perceived by the taste that dissolved jewelry is not good stuff to drink.

We were surrounded by a hideous desolation. We stepped forward to a sort of jumping-off place, and were confronted by a startling contrast: we seemed to look down into fairyland. Two or three thousand feet below us was a bright green level, with a pretty town in its midst, and a silvery stream winding among the meadows; the charming spot was walled in on all sides by gigantic precipices clothed with pines; and over the pines, out of the softened distances, rose the snowy domes and peaks of the Monte Rosa region. How exquisitely green and beautiful that little valley down there was! The distance was not great enough to obliterate details, it only made them little, and mellow, and dainty, like landscapes and towns seen through the wrong end of a spyglass.

Right under us a narrow ledge rose up out of the valley, with a green, slanting, bench-shaped top, and grouped about upon this green-baize bench were a lot of black and white sheep which looked merely like oversized worms. The bench seemed lifted well up into our neighborhood, but that was a deception, — it was a long way down to it.

We began our descent, now, by the most remarkable road I have ever seen. It wound in corkscrew curves down the face of the colossal precipice, — a narrow way, with always the solid rock wall at one elbow, and perpendicular nothingness at the other. We met an everlasting procession of guides, porters, mules, litters, and tourists climbing up this steep and muddy path, and there was no room to spare when you had to pass a tolerably fat mule. I always took the inside, when I heard or saw the mule coming, and flattened myself against the wall. I preferred the inside, of course, but I should have had to take it anyhow, because the mule prefers the outside. A mule's preference — on a precipice — is a thing to be respected. Well, his choice is always the outside. His life is mostly devoted to carrying bulky paniers and packages which rest against his body, — therefore he is habituated to taking the outside edge of mountain paths, to keep his bundles from rubbing against rocks or banks on the other. When he goes into the passenger business he absurdly clings to his old habit, and keeps one leg of his passenger always dangling over the great deeps of the lower world while that passenger's heart is in the highlands, so to speak. More than once I saw a mule's hind foot cave over the outer edge and send earth and rubbish into the bottomless abyss; and I noticed that upon these occasions the rider, whether male or female, looked tolerably unwell.

There was one place where an 18-inch breadth of light masonry had been added to the verge of the path, and as there was a very sharp turn, here, a panel of fencing had been set up there at some ancient time, as a protection. This panel was old and gray and feeble, and the light masonry had been loosened by recent rains. A young American girl came along on a mule, and in making the turn the mule's hind foot caved all the loose masonry and one of the fence posts overboard; the mule gave a violent lurch inboard to save himself, and succeeded in the effort, but that girl turned as white as the snows of Mont Blanc for a moment.

The path here was simply a groove cut into the face of the precipice; there was a four-foot breadth of solid rock under the traveler, and a four-foot breadth of solid rock just above his head, like the roof of a narrow porch; he could look out from this gallery and see a sheer summitless and bottomless wall of rock before him, across a gorge or crack a biscuit's toss in width,— but he could not see the bottom of his own precipice unless he lay down and projected his nose over the edge. I did not do this, because I did not wish to soil my clothes.

Every few hundred yards, at particularly bad places, one came across a panel or so of plank fencing; but they were always old and weak, and they generally leaned out over the chasm and did not make any rash promises to hold up people who might need support. There was one of these panels which had only its upper board left; a pedestrianizing English youth came tearing down the path, was seized with an impulse to look over the precipice, and without an instant's thought he threw his weight upon that crazy board. It bent outward a foot! I never made a gasp before that came so near suffocating me. The English youth's face simply showed a lively surprise, but nothing more. He went swinging along valleywards again, as if he did not know he had just swindled a coroner by the closest kind of a shave.

The Alpine litter is sometimes like a cushioned box made fast between the middles of two long poles, and sometimes it is a chair with a back to it and a support for the feet. It is carried by relays of strong porters. The motion is easier than that of any other conveyance. We met a few men and a great many ladies in litters; it seemed to me that most of the ladies looked pale and nauseated; their general aspect gave me the idea that they were patiently enduring a horrible suffering. As a rule, they looked at their laps, and left the scenery to take care of itself.

But the most frightened creature I saw, was a led horse that overtook us. Poor fellow, he had been born and reared in the grassy levels of the Kandersteg valley and had never seen anything like this hideous place before. Every few steps he would

6**

stop short, glance wildly out from the dizzy height, and then spread his red nostrils wide and pant as violently as if he had been running a race; and all the while he quaked from head to heel as with a palsy. He was a handsome fellow, and he made a fine statuesque picture of terror, but it was pitiful to see him suffer so.

This dreadful path has had its tragedy. Baedeker, with his customary overterseness, begins and ends the tale thus:

"The descent on horseback should be avoided. In 1861 a Comtesse d'Herlincourt fell from her saddle over the precipice and was killed on the spot."

We looked over the precipice there, and saw the monument which commemorates the event. It stands in the bottom of the gorge, in a place which has been hollowed out of the rock to protect it from the torrent and the storms. Our old guide never spoke but when spoken to, and then limited himself to a syllable or two, but when we asked him about this tragedy he showed a strong interest in the matter. He said the Countess was very pretty, and very young,— hardly out of her girlhood, in fact. She was newly married, and was on her bridal tour. The young husband was riding a little in advance; one guide was leading the husband's horse, another was leading the bride's. The old man continued:

"The guide that was leading the husband's horse

happened to glance back, and there was that poor young thing sitting up staring out over the precipice; and her face began to bend downward a little, and she put up her two hands slowly and met it,—so, —and put them flat against her eyes,—so,—and then she sunk out of the saddle, with a sharp shriek, and one caught only the flash of a dress, and it was all over."

Then after a pause:

"Ah, yes, that guide saw these things,—yes, he saw them all. He saw them all, just as I have told you."

After another pause:

"Ah, yes, he saw them all. My God, that was *me*. I was that guide!"

This had been the one event of the old man's life; so one may be sure he had forgotten no detail connected with it. We listened to all he had to say about what was done and what happened and what was said after the sorrowful occurrence, and a painful story it was.

When we had wound down toward the valley until we were about on the last spiral of the corkscrew, Harris's hat blew over the last remaining bit of precipice,—a small cliff a hundred or hundred and fifty feet high,—and sailed down towards a steep slant composed of rough chips and fragments which the weather had flaked away from the precipices. We went leisurely down there, expecting to find it without any trouble, but we had made a mistake, as to that. We hunted during a couple of hours,— not because the old straw hat was valuable, but out of curiosity to find out how such a thing could manage to conceal itself in open ground where there was nothing left for it to hide behind. When one is reading in bed, and lays his paper-knife down, he cannot find it again if it is smaller than a sabre; that hat was as stubborn as any paper-knife could have been, and we finally had to give it up; but we found a fragment that had once belonged to an opera-glass, and by digging around and turning over the rocks we gradually collected all the lenses and the cylinders and the various odds and ends that go to make up a complete opera-glass. We afterwards had the thing reconstructed, and the owner can have his adventurous long-lost property by submitting proofs and paying costs of rehabilitation. We had hopes of finding the owner there, distributed around amongst the rocks, for it would have made an elegant paragraph; but we were disappointed. Still, we were far from being disheartened, for there was a considerable area which we had not thoroughly searched; we were satisfied he was there, somewhere, so we resolved to wait over a day at Leuk and come back and get him.

Then we sat down to polish off the perspiration and arrange about what we would do with him when we got him. Harris was for contributing him to the British Museum; but I was for mailing him to his widow. That is the difference between Harris and me: Harris is all for display, I am all for the simple right, even though I lose money by it. Harris argued in favor of his proposition and against mine, I argued in favor of mine and against his. The discussion warmed into a dispute; the dispute warmed into a quarrel. I finally said, very decidedly:

" My mind is made up. He goes to the widow."

Harris answered sharply:

"And *my* mind is made up. He goes to the Museum."

I said, calmly:

" The Museum may whistle when it gets him."

Harris retorted:

" The widow may save herself the trouble of whistling, for I will see that she never gets him."

After some angry bandying of epithets, I said:

" It seems to me that you are taking on a good many airs about these remains. I don't quite see what *you've* got to say about them?"

"*I?* I've got *all* to say about them. They'd never have been thought of if I hadn't found their opera-glass. The corpse belongs to me, and I'll do as I please with him."

I was leader of the Expedition, and all discoveries achieved by it naturally belonged to me. I was entitled to these remains, and could have enforced my right; but rather than have bad blood about the matter, I said we would toss up for them. I threw heads and won, but it was a barren victory, for although we spent all the next day searching, we

6**

never found a bone. I cannot imagine what could ever have become of that fellow.

The town in the valley is called Leuk or Leukerbad. We pointed our course toward it, down a verdant slope which was adorned with fringed gentians and other flowers, and presently entered the narrow alleys of the outskirts and waded toward the middle of the town through liquid "fertilizer." They ought to either pave that village or organize a ferry.

Harris's body was simply a chamois-pasture; his person was populous with the little hungry pests; his skin, when he stripped, was splotched like a scarlet fever patient's; so, when we were about to enter one of the Leukerbad inns, and he noticed its sign, "Chamois Hotel," he refused to stop there. He said the chamois was plentiful enough, without hunting up hotels where they made a specialty of it. I was indifferent, for the chamois is a creature that will neither bite me nor abide with me: but to calm Harris, we went to the Hôtel des Alpes.

At the table d'hôte we had this, for an incident. A very grave man,— in fact his gravity amounted to solemnity, and almost to austerity,— sat opposite us and he was "tight," but doing his best to appear sober. He took up a *corked* bottle of wine, tilted it over his glass awhile, then sat it out of the way, with a contented look, and went on with his dinner.

Presently he put his glass to his mouth, and of course found it empty. He looked puzzled, and

glanced furtively and suspiciously out of the corner
of his eye at a benignant and unconscious old lady
who sat at his right. Shook his head, as much as to
say, "No, she couldn't have done it." He tilted
the corked bottle over his glass again, meantime
searching around with his watery eye to see if anybody was watching him. He ate a few mouthfuls,
raised his glass to his lips, and of course it was still
empty. He bent an injured and accusing side gaze
upon that unconscious old lady, which was a study
to see. She went on eating and gave no sign. He
took up his glass and his bottle, with a wise private
nod of his head, and set them gravely on the left
hand side of his plate,— poured himself another
imaginary drink, — went to work with his knife and
fork once more,— presently lifted his glass with
good confidence, and found it empty, as usual.

This was almost a petrifying surprise. He straightened himself up in his chair and deliberately and sor-
rowfully inspected the busy old ladies at his elbows,
first one and then the other. At last he softly pushed
his plate away, set his glass directly in front of him,
held on to it with his left hand, and proceeded to
pour with his right. This time he observed that
nothing came. He turned the bottle clear upside
down; still nothing issued from it; a plaintive look
came into his face, and he said, as if to himself,
"*'ic! They've got it all!*" Then he set the bottle
down, resignedly, and took the rest of his dinner
dry.

F **

It was at that table d'hôte, too, that I had under inspection the largest lady I have ever seen in private life. She was over seven feet high, and magnificently proportioned. What had first called my attention to her, was my stepping on an outlying flange of her foot, and hearing, from up toward the ceiling, a deep " Pardon, m'sieu, but you encroach ! "

That was when we were coming through the hall, and the place was dim, and I could see her only vaguely. The thing which called my attention to her the second time was, that at a table beyond ours were two very pretty girls, and this great lady came in and sat down between them and me and blotted out the view. She had a handsome face, and she was very finely formed,— perfectly formed, I should say. But she made everybody around her look trivial and commonplace. Ladies near her looked like children, and the men about her looked mean. They looked like failures; and they looked as if they felt so, too. She sat with her back to us. I never saw such a back in my life. I would have so liked to see the moon rise over it. The whole congregation waited, under one pretext or another, till she finished her dinner and went out; they wanted to see her at her full altitude, and they found it worth tarrying for. She filled one's idea of what an empress ought to be, when she rose up in her unapproachable grandeur and moved superbly out of that place.

We were not at Leuk in time to see her at her

heaviest weight. She had suffered from corpulence and had come there to get rid of her extra flesh in the baths. Five weeks of soaking,— five uninterrupted hours of it every day,— had accomplished her purpose and reduced her to the right proportions.

Those baths remove fat, and also skin diseases. The patients remain in the great tanks for hours at a time. A dozen gentlemen and ladies occupy a tank together, and amuse themselves with rompings and various games. They have floating desks and tables, and they read or lunch or play chess in water that is breast deep. The tourist can step in and view this novel spectacle if he chooses. There's a poor-box, and he will have to contribute. There are several of these big bathing houses, and you can always tell when you are near one of them by the romping noises and shouts of laughter that proceed from it. The water is running water, and changes all the time, else a patient with a ringworm might take the bath with only a partial success, since, while he was ridding himself of his ringworm, he might catch the itch.

The next morning we wandered back up the green valley, leisurely, with the curving walls of those bare and stupendous precipices rising into the clouds before us. I had never seen a clean, bare precipice stretching up five thousand feet above me before, and I never shall expect to see another one. They exist, perhaps, but not in places where one can easily get close to them. This pile of stone is peculiar

From its base to the soaring tops of its mighty towers, all its lines and all its details vaguely suggest human architecture. There are rudimentary bow windows, cornices, chimneys, demarcations of stories, etc. One could sit and stare up there and study the features and exquisite graces of this grand structure, bit by bit, and day after day, and never weary his interest. The termination, toward the town, observed in profile, is the perfection of shape. It comes down out of the clouds in a succession of rounded, colossal, terrace-like projections,— a stairway for the gods; at its head spring several lofty storm-scarred towers, one above another, with faint films of vapor curling always about them like spectral banners. If there were a king whose realms included the whole world, here would be the palace meet and proper for such a monarch. He would only need to hollow it out and put in the electric light. He could give audience to a nation at a time under its roof.

Our search for those remains having failed, we inspected with a glass the dim and distant track of an old-time avalanche that once swept down from some pine-grown summits behind the town and swept away the houses and buried the people; then we struck down the road that leads toward the Rhone, to see the famous *Ladders*. These perilous things are built against the perpendicular face of a cliff two or three hundred feet high. The peasants, of both sexes, were climbing up and down them, with heavy loads on their backs. I ordered Harris to make the ascent, so I could put the thrill and horror of it in my book, and he accomplished the feat successfully, through a sub-agent, for three francs, which I paid. It makes me shudder yet when I think of what I felt when I was clinging there between heaven and earth in the person of that proxy. At times the world swam around me, and I could hardly keep from letting go, so dizzying was the appalling danger. Many a person would have given up and descended, but I stuck to my task, and would not yield until I had accomplished it. I felt a just pride in my exploit, but I would not have repeated it for the wealth of the world. I shall break my neck yet with some such foolhardy performance, for warnings never seem to have any lasting effect upon me. When the people of the hotel found that I had been climbing those crazy Ladders, it made me an object of considerable attention.

Next morning, early, we drove to the Rhone valley and took the train for Visp. There we shouldered our knapsacks and things, and set out on foot, in a tremendous rain, up the winding gorge, toward Zermatt. Hour after hour we slopped along, by the roaring torrent, and under noble Lesser Alps which were clothed in rich velvety green all the way up and had little atomy Swiss homes perched upon grassy benches along their mist-dimmed heights.

The rain continued to pour and the torrent to

boom, and we continued to enjoy both. At the one spot where this torrent tossed its white mane highest, and thundered loudest, and lashed the big bowlders fiercest, the canton had done itself the honor to build the flimsiest wooden bridge that exists in the world. While we were walking over it, along with a party of horsemen, I noticed that even the larger raindrops made it shake. I called Harris's attention to it, and he noticed it, too. It seemed to me that if I owned an elephant that was a keepsake, and I thought a good deal of him, I would think twice before I would ride him over that bridge.

We climbed up to the village of St. Nicholas, about half past four in the afternoon, waded ankle deep through the fertilizer-juice, and stopped at a new and nice hotel close by the little church. We stripped and went to bed, and sent our clothes down to be baked. All the horde of soaked tourists did the same. That chaos of clothing got mixed in the kitchen, and there were consequences. I did not get back the same drawers I sent down, when our things came up at 6.15; I got a pair on a new plan. They were merely a pair of white ruffle-cuffed absurdities, hitched together at the top with a narrow band, and they did not come quite down to my knees. They were pretty enough, but they made me feel like two people, and disconnected at that. The man must have been an idiot that got himself up like that, to rough it in the Swiss mountains. The shirt they brought me was shorter than

the drawers, and hadn't any sleeves to it,— at least
it hadn't anything more than what Mr. Darwin
would call "rudimentary" sleeves; these had
"edging" around them, but the bosom was ridicu-
lously plain. The knit silk undershirt they brought
me was on a new plan, and was really a sensible thing;
it opened behind, and had pockets in it to put your
shoulder blades in; but they did not seem to fit
mine, and so I found it a sort of uncomfortable
garment. They gave my bob-tail coat to somebody
else, and sent me an ulster suitable for a giraffe. I
had to tie my collar on, because there was no button
behind on that foolish little shirt which I described
a while ago.

When I was dressed for dinner at 6.30, I was too
loose in some places and too tight in others, and
altogether I felt slovenly and ill conditioned. However, the people at the table d'hôte were no better
off than I was; they had everybody's clothes but
their own on. A long stranger recognized his ulster as
soon as he saw the tail of it following me in, but
nobody claimed my shirt or my drawers, though I
described them as well as I was able. I gave them
to the chambermaid that night when I went to bed,
and she probably found the owner, for my own
things were on a chair outside my door in the
morning.

There was a lovable English clergyman who did
not get to the table d'hôte at all. His breeches had
turned up missing, and without any equivalent. He

said he was not more particular than other people,
but he had noticed that a clergyman at dinner
without any breeches was almost sure to excite
remark.

## CHAPTER VII.

WE did not oversleep at St. Nicholas. The church bell began to ring at 4.30 in the morning, and from the length of time it continued to ring I judged that it takes the Swiss sinner a good while to get the invitation through his head. Most church bells in the world are of poor quality, and have a harsh and rasping sound which upsets the temper and produces much sin, but the St. Nicholas bell is a good deal the worst one that has been contrived yet, and is peculiarly maddening in its operation. Still, it may have its right and its excuse to exist, for the community is poor and not every citizen can afford a clock, perhaps; but there cannot be any excuse for our church bells at home, for there is no family in America without a clock, and consequently there is no fair pretext for the usual Sunday medley of dreadful sounds that issues from our steeples. There is much more profanity in America on Sunday than in all the other six days of the week put together, and it is of a more bitter and malignant character than the week-day profanity, too. It is produced by the cracked-pot clangor of the cheap church bells.

We build our churches almost without regard to cost; we rear an edifice which is an adornment to the town, and we gild it, and fresco it, and mortgage it, and do everything we can think of to perfect it, and then spoil it all by putting a bell on it which afflicts everybody who hears it, giving some the headache, others St. Vitus's dance, and the rest the blind staggers.

An American village at ten o'clock on a summer Sunday is the quietest and peacefulest and holiest thing in nature; but it is a pretty different thing half an hour later. Mr. Poe's poem of the "Bells" stands incomplete to this day; but it is well enough that it is so, for the public reciter or "reader" who goes around trying to imitate the sounds of the various sorts of bells with his voice would find himself "up a stump" when he got to the church bell — as Joseph Addison would say. The church is always trying to get other people to reform; it might not be a bad idea to reform itself a little, by way of example. It is still clinging to one or two things which were useful once, but which are not useful now, neither are they ornamental. One is the bell ringing to remind a clock-caked town that it is church time, and another is the reading from the pulpit of a tedious list of "notices" which everybody who is interested has already read in the newspaper. The clergyman even reads the hymn through,— a relic of an ancient time when hymn books were scarce and costly; but everybody has a hymn book, now, and so the public reading is no longer necessary. It is not merely unnecessary, it is generally painful; for the average clergyman could not fire into his congregation with a shotgun and hit a worse reader than himself, unless the weapon scattered shamefully. I am not meaning to be flippant and irreverent, I am only meaning to be truthful. The average clergyman, in all countries and of all denominations, is a very bad reader. One would think he would at least learn how to read the Lord's Prayer, by and by, but it is not so. He races through it as if he thought the quicker he got it in, the sooner it would be answered. A person who does not appreciate the exceeding value of pauses, and does not know how to measure their duration judiciously, cannot render the grand simplicity and dignity of a composition like that effectively.

We took a tolerably early breakfast, and tramped off toward Zermatt through the reeking lanes of the village, glad to get away from that bell. By and by we had a fine spectacle on our right. It was the wall-like butt end of a huge glacier, which looked down on us from an Alpine height which was well up in the blue sky. It was an astonishing amount of ice to be compacted together in one mass. We ciphered upon it and decided that it was not less than several hundred feet from the base of the wall of solid ice to the top of it,— Harris believed it was really twice that. We judged that if St. Paul's, St. Peter's, the

7**

Great Pyramid, the Strasburg Cathedral and the Capitol at Washington were clustered against that wall, a man sitting on its upper edge could not hang his hat on the top of any one of them without reaching down three or four hundred feet, — a thing which, of course, no man could do.

To me, that mighty glacier was very beautiful. I did not imagine that anybody could find fault with it; but I was mistaken. Harris had been snarling for several days. He was a rabid Protestant, and he was always saying:

"In the Protestant cantons you never see such poverty and dirt and squalor as you do in this Catholic one; you never see the lanes and alleys flowing with foulness; you never see such wretched little sties of houses; you never see an inverted tin turnip on top of a church for a dome; and as for a church bell, why, you never hear a church bell at all."

All this morning he had been finding fault, straight along. First it was with the mud. He said, "It ain't muddy in a Protestant canton when it rains." Then it was with the dogs: "They don't have those lop-eared dogs in a Protestant canton." Then it was with the roads: "They don't leave the roads to make themselves in a Protestant canton, the people make them,— and they make a road that *is* a road, too." Next it was the goats: "You never see a goat shedding tears in a Protestant canton — a goat, there, is one of the cheerfulest objects in nature." Next it was the chamois:

"You never see a Protestant chamois act like one of these,— they take a bite or two and go; but these fellows camp with you and stay." Then it was the guideboards: "In a Protestant canton you couldn't get lost if you wanted to, but you never see a guideboard in a Catholic canton." Next, "You never see any flower boxes in the windows, here, — never anything but now and then a cat, — a torpid one; but you take a Protestant canton: windows perfectly lovely with flowers,— and as for cats, there's just acres of them. These folks in this canton leave a road to make itself, and then fine you three francs if you 'trot' over it — as if a horse could trot over such a sarcasm of a road." Next about the goitre: "*They* talk about goitre! — I haven't seen a goitre in this whole canton that I couldn't put in a hat."

He had growled at everything, but I judged it would puzzle him to find anything the matter with this majestic glacier. I intimated as much; but he was ready, and said with surly discontent: "You ought to see them in the Protestant cantons."

This irritated me. But I concealed the feeling, and asked:

"What is the matter with this one?"

"Matter? Why, it ain't in any kind of condition. They never take any care of a glacier here. The moraine has been spilling gravel around it, and got it all dirty."

"Why, man, *they* can't help that."

" *They?* You're right. That is, they *won't*. They could if they wanted to. You never see a speck of dirt on a Protestant glacier. Look at the Rhone glacier. It is fifteen miles long, and seven hundred feet thick. If this was a Protestant glacier you wouldn't see it looking like this, I can tell you."

"That is nonsense. What would they do with it?"

"They would whitewash it. They always do."

I did not believe a word of this, but rather than have trouble I let it go; for it is a waste of breath to argue with a bigot. I even doubted if the Rhone glacier *was* in a Protestant canton; but I did not know, so I could not make anything by contradicting a man who would probably put me down at once with manufactured evidence.

About nine miles from St. Nicholas we crossed a bridge over the raging torrent of the Visp, and came to a long strip of flimsy fencing which was pretending to secure people from tumbling over a perpendicular wall forty feet high and into the river. Three children were approaching; one of them, a little girl, about eight years old, was running; when pretty close to us she stumbled and fell, and her feet shot under the rail of the fence and for a moment projected over the stream. It gave us a sharp shock, for we thought she was gone, sure, for the ground slanted steeply, and to save herself seemed a sheer impossibility; but she managed to scramble up, and ran by us laughing.

We went forward and examined the place and saw the long tracks which her feet had made in the dirt when they darted over the verge. If she had finished her trip she would have struck some big rocks in the edge of the water, and then the torrent would have snatched her down stream among the half-covered bowlders and she would have been pounded to pulp in two minutes. We had come exceedingly near witnessing her death.

And now Harris's contrary nature and inborn selfishness were strikingly manifested. He has no spirit of self-denial. He began straight off, and continued for an hour, to express his gratitude that the child was not destroyed. I never saw such a man. That was the kind of person he was; just so *he* was gratified, he never cared anything about anybody else. I had noticed that trait in him, over and over again. Often, of course, it was mere heedlessness, mere want of reflection. Doubtless this may have been the case in most instances, but it was not the less hard to bear on that account,— and after all, its bottom, its groundwork, was selfishness. There is no avoiding that conclusion. In the instance under consideration, I did think the indecency of running on in that way might occur to him; but no, the child was saved and he was glad, that was sufficient,— he cared not a straw for *my* feelings, or my loss of such a literary plum, snatched from my very mouth at the instant it was ready to drop into it. His selfishness was sufficient to place his own gratification in being spared suffering clear before all concern for me, his friend. Apparently, he did not once reflect upon the valuable details which would have fallen like a windfall to me: fishing the child out,— witnessing the surprise of the family and the stir the thing would have made among the peasants,— then a Swiss funeral,— then the roadside monument, to be paid for by us and have our names mentioned in it. And we should have gone into Baedeker and been immortal. I was silent. I was too much hurt to complain. If he could act so, and be so heedless and so frivolous at such a time, and actually seem to glory in it, after all I had done for him, I would have cut my hand off before I would let him see that I was wounded.

We were approaching Zermatt; consequently, we were approaching the renowned Matterhorn. A month before, this mountain had been only a name to us, but latterly we had been moving through a steadily thickening double row of pictures of it, done in oil, water, chromo, wood, steel, copper, crayon, and photography, and so it had at length become a shape to us,— and a very distinct, decided, and familiar one, too. We were expecting to recognize that mountain whenever or wherever we should run across it. We were not deceived. The monarch was far away when we first saw him, but there was no such thing as mistaking him. He has the rare peculiarity of standing by himself; he is peculiarly steep, too, and is also most oddly shaped. He towers into the sky like a colossal wedge, with the upper third of its blade bent a little to the left. The broad base of this monster wedge is planted upon a grand glacier-paved Alpine platform whose elevation is ten thousand feet above sea level; as the wedge itself is some five thousand feet high, it follows that its apex is about fifteen thousand feet above sea level. So the whole bulk of this stately piece of rock, this sky-cleaving monolith, is above the line of eternal snow. Yet while all its giant neighbors have the look of being built of solid snow, from their waists up, the Matterhorn stands black and naked and forbidding, the year round, or merely powdered or streaked with white in places, for its sides are so steep that the snow cannot stay there. Its strange form, its august isolation, and its majestic unkinship with its own kind, make it,— so to speak,— the Napoleon of the mountain world. "Grand, gloomy, and peculiar," is a phrase which fits it as aptly as it fitted the great captain.

Think of a monument a mile high, standing on a pedestal two miles high! This is what the Matterhorn is,— a monument. Its office, henceforth, for all time, will be to keep watch and ward over the secret resting-place of the young Lord Douglas, who, in 1865, was precipitated from the summit over a precipice 4,000 feet high, and never seen again. No man ever had such a monument as this before; the most imposing of the world's other monuments are but atoms compared to it; and they will perish, and their places will pass from memory, but this will remain.*

A walk from St. Nicholas to Zermatt is a wonderful experience.   Nature is built on a stupendous plan in that region.   One marches continually between walls that are piled into the skies, with their upper heights broken into a confusion of sublime shapes that gleam white and cold against the background of blue; and here and there one sees a big glacier displaying its grandeurs on the top of a precipice, or a graceful cascade leaping and flashing down the green declivities.   There is nothing tame, or cheap, or trivial,— it is all magnificent.   That short valley is a picture gallery of a notable kind, for it contains no mediocrities; from end to end the Creator has hung it with His masterpieces.

We made Zermatt at three in the afternoon, nine hours out from St. Nicholas.  Distance, by guide-book, 12 miles, by pedometer 72.  We were in the heart and home of the mountain-climbers, now, as all visible things testified.  The snow-peaks did not hold themselves aloof, in aristocratic reserve, they nestled close around, in a friendly, sociable way;

---

*The accident which cost Lord Douglas his life (see chapter 12) also cost the lives of three other men.  These three fell four-fifths of a mile, and their bodies were afterwards found, lying side by side, upon a glacier, whence they were borne to Zermatt and buried in the church-yard.  The remains of Lord Douglas have never been found.  The secret of his sepulture, like that of Moses, must remain a mystery always.

guides, with the ropes and axes and other implements of their fearful calling slung about their persons, roosted in a long line upon a stone wall in
front of the hotel, and waited for customers; sun-
burned climbers, in mountaineering costume, and
followed by their guides and porters, arrived from
time to time, from breakneck expeditions among
the peaks and glaciers of the High Alps; male and
female tourists, on mules, filed by, in a continuous
procession, hotelward-bound from wild adventures
which would grow in grandeur every time they
were described at the English or American fireside,
and at last outgrow the possible itself.

We were not dreaming; this was not a make-
believe home of the Alp-climber, created by our
heated imaginations; no, for here was Mr. Girdlestone himself, the famous Englishman who hunts his
way to the most formidable Alpine summits without
a guide. I was not equal to imagining a Girdlestone; it was all I could do to even realize him,
while looking straight at him at short range. I
would rather face whole Hyde Parks of artillery than
the ghastly forms of death which he has faced
among the peaks and precipices of the mountains.
There is probably no pleasure equal to the pleasure
of climbing a dangerous Alp; but it is a pleasure
which is confined strictly to people who can find
pleasure in it. I have not jumped to this conclusion; I have traveled to it per gravel train, so to
speak. I have thought the thing all out, and am

quite sure I am right. A born climber's appetite for climbing is hard to satisfy; when it comes upon him he is like a starving man with a feast before him; he may have other business on hand, but it must wait. Mr. Girdlestone had had his usual summer holiday in the Alps, and had spent it in his usual way, hunting for unique chances to break his neck; his vacation was over, and his luggage packed for England, but all of a sudden a hunger had come upon him to climb the tremendous Weisshorn once more, for he had heard of a new and utterly impossible route up it. His baggage was unpacked at once, and now he and a friend, laden with knapsacks, ice-axes, coils of rope, and canteens of milk, were just setting out. They would spend the night high up among the snows, somewhere, and get up at two in the morning and finish the enterprise. I had a strong desire to go with them, but forced it down,—a feat which Mr. Girdlestone, with all his fortitude, could not do.

Even ladies catch the climbing mania, and are unable to throw it off. A famous climber, of that sex, had attempted the Weisshorn a few days before our arrival, and she and her guides had lost their way in a snowstorm high up among the peaks and glaciers and been forced to wander around a good while before they could find a way down. When this lady reached the bottom, she had been on her feet twenty-three hours !

Our guides, hired on the Gemmi, were already at

Zermatt when we reached there. So there was
nothing to interfere with our getting up an adventure whenever we should choose the time and the
object. I resolved to devote my first evening in
Zermatt to studying up the subject of Alpine climbing, by way of preparation.

I read several books, and here are some of the
things I found out. One's shoes must be strong
and heavy, and have pointed hob-nails in them.
The alpenstock must be of the best wood, for if it
should break, loss of life might be the result. One
should carry an axe, to cut steps in the ice with, on
the great heights. There must be a ladder, for
there are steep bits of rock which can be surmounted
with this instrument,— or this utensil,— but could
not be surmounted without it; such an obstruction
has compelled the tourist to waste hours hunting
another route, when a ladder would have saved him
all trouble. One must have from 150 to 500 feet
of strong rope, to be used in lowering the party
down steep declivities which are too steep and
smooth to be traversed in any other way. One
must have a steel hook, on another rope, — a very
useful thing; for when one is ascending and comes
to a low bluff which is yet too high for the ladder,
he swings this rope aloft like a lasso, the hook
catches at the top of the bluff, and then the tourist
climbs the rope, hand over hand,— being always
particular to try and forget that if the hook gives
way he will never stop falling till he arrives in som

part of Switzerland where they are not expecting him. Another important thing — there must be a rope to tie the whole party together with, so that if one falls from a mountain or down a bottomless chasm in a glacier, the others may brace back on the rope and save him. One must have a silk veil, to protect his face from snow, sleet, hail and gale, and colored goggles to protect his eyes from that dangerous enemy, snow-blindness. Finally, there must be some porters, to carry provisions, wine and scientific instruments, and also blanket bags for the party to sleep in.

I closed my readings with a fearful adventure which Mr. Whymper once had on the Matterhorn when he was prowling around alone, 5,000 feet above the town of Breil. He was edging his way gingerly around the corner of a precipice where the upper edge of a sharp declivity of ice-glazed snow joined it. This declivity swept down a couple of hundred feet, into a gully which curved around and ended at a precipice 800 feet high, overlooking a glacier. His foot slipped, and he fell. He says:

" My knapsack brought my head down first, and I pitched into some rock about a dozen feet below; they caught something, and tumbled me off the edge, head over heels, into the gully; the baton was dashed from my hands, and I whirled downwards in a series of bounds, each longer than the last; now over ice, now into rocks, striking my head four or five times, each time with increased force. The last bound sent me spinning through the air in a leap of fifty or sixty feet, from one side of the gully to the other, and I struck the rocks, luckily, with the whole of my left side. They caught my clothes for a moment, and I fell back on to the snow with motion arrested. My head fortunately came the right side up, and a few frantic catches brought me to a halt, in the neck of the gully and on the verge of the precipice. Baton, hat, and veil skimmed by and disappeared, and the crash of the rocks — which I had started — as they fell on to the glacier, told how narrow had been the escape from utter destruction. As it was, I fell nearly 200 feet in seven or eight bounds. Ten feet more would have taken me in one gigantic leap of 800 feet on to the glacier below.

"The situation was sufficiently serious. The rocks could not be let go for a moment, and the blood was spurting out of more than twenty cuts. The most serious ones were in the head, and I vainly tried to close them with one hand, while holding on with the other. It was useless; the blood gushed out in blinding jets at each pulsation. At last, in a moment of inspiration, I kicked out a big lump of snow and stuck it as plaster on my head. The idea was a happy one, and the flow of blood diminished. Then, scrambling up, I got, not a moment too soon, to a place of safety, and fainted away. The sun was setting when consciousness returned, and it was pitch dark before the Great

Staircase was descended; but by a combination
of luck and care, the whole 4,700 feet of descent to
Breil was accomplished without a slip, or once missing the way."

His wounds kept him abed some days. Then he
got up and climbed that mountain again. That is
the way with a true Alp-climber; the more fun he
has, the more he wants.

# CHAPTER VIII.

AFTER I had finished my readings, I was no longer myself; I was tranced, uplifted, intoxicated, by the almost incredible perils and adventures I had been following my authors through, and the triumphs I had been sharing with them. I sat silent some time, then turned to Harris and said:

"My mind is made up."

Something in my tone struck him; and when he glanced at my eye and read what was written there, his face paled perceptibly. He hesitated a moment, then said:

"Speak."

I answered, with perfect calmness:

"I WILL ASCEND THE RIFFELBERG."

If I had shot my poor friend he could not have fallen from his chair more suddenly. If I had been his father he could not have pleaded harder to get me to give up my purpose. But I turned a deaf ear to all he said. When he perceived at last that nothing could alter my determination, he ceased to urge, and for a while the deep silence was broken only by his sobs. I sat in marble resolution, with my eyes fixed upon vacancy, for in spirit I was already wrestling with the perils of the mountains, and my friend sat gazing at me in adoring admiration through his tears. At last he threw himself upon me in a loving embrace and exclaimed in broken tones:

"Your Harris will never desert you. We will die together!"

I cheered the noble fellow with praises, and soon his fears were forgotten and he was eager for the adventure. He wanted to summon the guides at once and leave at two in the morning, as he supposed the custom was; but I explained that nobody was looking at that hour; and that the start in the dark was not usually made from the village but from the first night's resting place on the mountain side. I said we would leave the village at 3 or 4 P.M. on the morrow; meantime he could notify the guides, and also let the public know of the attempt which we proposed to make.

I went to bed, but not to sleep. No man can sleep when he is about to undertake one of these Alpine exploits. I tossed feverishly all night long, and was glad enough when I heard the clock strike half past eleven and knew it was time to get up for dinner. I rose, jaded and rusty, and went to the noon meal, where I found myself the center of interest and curiosity; for the news was already abroad. It is not easy to eat calmly when you are a lion, but it is very pleasant, nevertheless.

As usual, at Zermatt, when a great ascent is about to be undertaken, everybody, native and foreign, laid aside his own projects and took up a good position to observe the start. The expedition consisted of 198 persons, including the mules; or 205, including the cows. As follows:

| CHIEFS OF SERVICE. | | SUBORDINATES. |
|---|---|---|
| | Myself. | 1 Veterinary Surgeon. |
| | Mr. Harris. | 1 Butler. |
| 17 | Guides. | 12 Waiters. |
| 4 | Surgeons. | 1 Footman. |
| 1 | Geologist. | 1 Barber. |
| 1 | Botanist. | 1 Head Cook. |
| 3 | Chaplains. | 9 Assistants. |
| 2 | Draftsmen. | 4 Pastry Cooks. |
| 15 | Barkeepers. | 1 Confectionery Artist. |
| 1 | Latinist. | |

TRANSPORTATION, ETC.

| 27 | Porters. | 3 | Coarse Washers and Ironers |
|---|---|---|---|
| 44 | Mules. | 1 | Fine ditto. |
| 44 | Muleteers. | 7 | Cows. |
| | | 2 | Milkers. |

Total, 154 men, 51 animals. Grand Total, 205.

| RATIONS, ETC. | | APPARATUS. | |
|---|---|---|---|
| 16 | Cases Hams. | 25 | Spring Mattresses. |
| 2 | Barrels Flour. | 2 | Hair ditto. |
| 22 | Barrels Whisky. | | Bedding for same. |
| 1 | Barrel Sugar. | 2 | Mosquito Nets. |
| 1 | Keg Lemons. | 29 | Tents. |
| 2000 | Cigars. | | Scientific Instruments. |
| 1 | Barrel Pies. | 97 | Ice-axes. |
| 1 | Ton of Pemmican. | 5 | Cases Dynamite. |
| 143 | Pair Crutches. | 7 | Cans Nitro-glycerine. |
| 2 | Barrels Arnica. | 22 | 40-foot Ladders. |
| 1 | Bale of Lint. | 2 | Miles of Rope. |
| 27 | Kegs Paregoric. | 154 | Umbrellas. |

8**

It was full four o'clock in the afternoon before my cavalcade was entirely ready. At that hour it began to move. In point of numbers and spectacular effect, it was the most imposing expedition that had ever marched from Zermatt.

I commanded the chief guide to arrange the men and animals in single file, twelve feet apart, and lash them all together on a strong rope. He objected that the first two miles was a dead level, with plenty of room, and that the rope was never used except in very dangerous places. But I would not listen to that. My reading had taught me that many serious accidents had happened in the Alps simply from not having the people tied up soon enough; I was not going to add one to the list. The guide then obeyed my order.

When the procession stood at ease, roped together, and ready to move, I never saw a finer sight. It was 3,122 feet long—over half a mile; every man but Harris and me was on foot, and had on his green veil and his blue goggles, and his white rag around his hat, and his coil of rope over one shoulder and under the other, and his ice-axe in his belt, and carried his alpenstock in his left hand, his umbrella (closed) in his right, and his crutches slung at his back. The burdens of the pack mules and the horns of the cows were decked with the Edelweiss and the Alpine rose.

I and my agent were the only persons mounted. We were in the post of danger in the extreme rear, and tied securely to five guides apiece. Our armor-bearers carried our ice-axes, alpenstocks, and other implements for us. We were mounted upon very small donkeys, as a measure of safety; in time of peril we could straighten our legs and stand up, and let the donkey walk from under. Still, I cannot recommend this sort of animal,— at least for excursions of mere pleasure,— because his ears interrupt the view. I and my agent possessed the regulation mountaineering costumes, but concluded to leave them behind. Out of respect for the great numbers of tourists of both sexes who would be assembled in front of the hotels to see us pass, and also out of respect for the many tourists whom we expected to encounter on our expedition, we decided to make the ascent in evening dress.

At fifteen minutes past four I gave the command to move, and my subordinates passed it along the line. The great crowd in front of the Monte Rosa hotel parted in twain, with a cheer, as the procession approached; and as the head of it was filing by I gave the order, — " Unlimber — make ready — HOIST !" — and with one impulse up went my half mile of umbrellas. It was a beautiful sight, and a total surprise to the spectators. Nothing like that had ever been seen in the Alps before. The applause it brought forth was deeply gratifying to me, and I rode by with my plug hat in my hand to testify my appreciation of it. It was the only testimony I could offer, for I was too full to speak.

We watered the caravan at the cold stream which rushes down a trough near the end of the village, and soon afterward left the haunts of civilization behind us. About half past five o'clock we arrived at a bridge which spans the Visp, and after throwing over a detachment to see if it was safe, the caravan crossed without accident. The way now led, by a gentle ascent, carpeted with fresh green grass, to the church at Winkelmatten. Without stopping to examine this edifice, I executed a flank movement to the right and crossed the bridge over the Findelenbach, after first testing its strength. Here I deployed to the right again, and presently entered an inviting stretch of meadow land which was unoccupied save by a couple of deserted huts toward its furthest extremity. These meadows offered an excellent camping place. We pitched our tents, supped, established a proper guard, recorded the events of the day, and then went to bed.

We rose at two in the morning and dressed by candle-light. It was a dismal and chilly business. A few stars were shining, but the general heavens were overcast, and the great shaft of the Matterhorn was draped in a sable pall of clouds. The chief guide advised a delay; he said he feared it was going to rain. We waited until nine o'clock, and then got away in tolerably clear weather.

Our course led up some terrific steeps, densely wooded with larches and cedars, and traversed by paths which the rains had guttered and which were

CLIMBING THE RIFFELBERG

obstructed by loose stones. To add to the danger
and inconvenience, we were constantly meeting returning tourists on foot or horseback, and as constantly being crowded and battered by ascending
tourists who were in a hurry and wanted to get by.

Our troubles thickened. About the middle of
the afternoon the seventeen guides called a halt and
held a consultation. After consulting an hour they
said their first suspicion remained intact,— that is to
say, they believed they were lost. I asked if they
did not *know* it? No, they said, they *couldn't*
absolutely know whether they were lost or not, because none of them had ever been in that part of
the country before. They had a strong instinct that
they were lost, but they had no proofs,— except
that they did not know where they were. They had
met no tourists for some time, and they considered
that a suspicious sign.

Plainly we were in an ugly fix. The guides were
naturally unwilling to go alone and seek a way out
of the difficulty; so we all went together. For
better security we moved slow and cautiously, for
the forest was very dense. We did not move up
the mountain, but around it, hoping to strike across
the old trail. Toward nightfall, when we were about
tired out, we came up against a rock as big as a
cottage. This barrier took all the remaining spirit
out of the men, and a panic of fear and despair
ensued. They moaned and wept, and said they
should never see their homes and their dear ones

8**

again. Then they began to upraid me for bringing them upon this fatal expedition. Some even muttered threats against me.

Clearly it was no time to show weakness. So I made a speech in which I said that other Alp-climbers had been in as perilous a position as this, and yet by courage and perseverance had escaped. I promised to stand by them, I promised to rescue them. I closed by saying we had plenty of provisions to maintain us for quite a siege,— and did they suppose Zermatt would allow half a mile of men and mules to mysteriously disappear during any considerable time, right above their noses, and make no inquiries? No, Zermatt would send out searching-expeditions and we should be saved.

This speech had a great effect. The men pitched the tents with some little show of cheerfulness, and we were snugly under cover when the night shut down. I now reaped the reward of my wisdom in providing one article which is not mentioned in any book of Alpine adventure but this. I refer to the paregoric. But for that beneficent drug, not one of those men would have slept a moment during that fearful night. But for that gentle persuader they must have tossed, unsoothed, the night through; for the whisky was for me. Yes, they would have risen in the morning unfitted for their heavy task. As it was, everybody slept but my agent and me,— only we two and the barkeepers. I would not permit myself to sleep at such a time. I considered myself responsible for all those lives. I meant to be on hand and ready, in case of avalanches. I am aware now, that there were no avalanches up there, but I did not know it then.

We watched the weather all through that awful night, and kept an eye on the barometer, to be prepared for the least change. There was not the slightest change recorded by the instrument, during the whole time. Words cannot describe the comfort that that friendly, hopeful, steadfast thing was to me in that season of trouble. It was a defective barometer, and had no hand but the stationary brass pointer, but I did not know that until afterward. If I should be in such a situation again, I should not wish for any barometer but that one.

All hands rose at two in the morning and took breakfast, and as soon as it was light we roped ourselves together and went at that rock. For some time we tried the hook-rope and other means of scaling it, but without success — that is, without perfect success. The hook caught once, and Harris started up it hand over hand, but the hold broke and if there had not happened to be a chaplain sitting underneath at the time, Harris would certainly have been crippled. As it was, it was the chaplain. He took to his crutches, and I ordered the hook-rope to be laid aside. It was too dangerous an implement where so many people were standing around.

We were puzzled for a while; then somebody

E**

thought of the ladders. One of these was leaned against the rock, and the men went up it tied together in couples. Another ladder was sent up for use in descending. At the end of half an hour everybody was over, and that rock was conquered. We gave our first grand shout of triumph. But the joy was short-lived, for somebody asked how we were going to get the animals over.

This was a serious difficulty; in fact, it was an impossibility. The courage of the men began to waver immediately; once more we were threatened with a panic. But when the danger was most imminent, we were saved in a mysterious way. A mule which had attracted attention from the beginning by its disposition to experiment, tried to eat a five-pound can of nitroglycerine. This happened right alongside the rock. The explosion threw us all to the ground, and covered us with dirt and débris; it frightened us extremely, too, for the crash it made was deafening, and the violence of the shock made the ground tremble. However, we were grateful, for the rock was gone. Its place was occupied by a new cellar, about thirty feet across, by fifteen feet deep. The explosion was heard as far as Zermatt; and an hour and a half afterward, many citizens of that town were knocked down and quite seriously injured by descending portions of mule meat, frozen solid. This shows, better than any estimate in figures, how high the experimenter went.

We had nothing to do, now, but bridge the cellar and proceed on our way. With a cheer the men went at their work. I attended to the engineering, myself. I appointed a strong detail to cut down trees with ice-axes and trim them for piers to support the bridge. This was a slow business, for ice-axes are not good to cut wood with. I caused my piers to be firmly set up in ranks in the cellar, and upon them I laid six of my forty-foot ladders, side by side, and laid six more on top of them. Upon this bridge I caused a bed of boughs to be spread, and on top of the boughs a bed of earth six inches deep. I stretched ropes upon either side to serve as railings, and then my bridge was complete. A train of elephants could have crossed it in safety and comfort. By nightfall the caravan was on the other side and the ladders taken up.

Next morning we went on in good spirits for a while, though our way was slow and difficult, by reason of the steep and rocky nature of the ground and the thickness of the forest; but at last a dull despondency crept into the men's faces and it was apparent that not only they, but even the guides, were now convinced that we were lost. The fact that we still met no tourists was a circumstance that was but too significant. Another thing seemed to suggest that we were not only lost, but very badly lost; for there must surely be searching-parties on the road before this time, yet we had seen no sign of them.

Demoralization was spreading; something must be done, and done quickly, too. Fortunately, I am not unfertile in expedients. I contrived one now which commended itself to all, for it promised well. I took three-quarters of a mile of rope and fastened one end of it around the waist of a guide, and told him to go and find the road, while the caravan waited. I instructed him to guide himself back by the rope, in case of failure; in case of success, he was to give the rope a series of violent jerks, whereupon the Expedition would go to him at once. He departed, and in two minutes had disappeared among the trees. I payed out the rope myself, while everybody watched the crawling thing with eager eyes. The rope crept away quite slowly, at times, at other times with some briskness. Twice or thrice we seemed to get the signal, and a shout was just ready to break from the men's lips when they perceived it was a false alarm. But at last, when over half a mile of rope had slidden away it stopped gliding and stood absolutely still,— one minute,— two minutes,— three,— while we held our breath and watched.

Was the guide resting? Was he scanning the country from some high point? Was he inquiring of a chance mountaineer? Stop,— had he fainted from excess of fatigue and anxiety?

This thought gave us a shock. I was in the very act of detailing an Expedition to succor him, when the cord was assailed with a series of such frantic jerks that I could hardly keep hold of it. The huzza that went up, then, was good to hear. "Saved! saved!" was the word that rang out, all down the long rank of the caravan.

We rose up and started at once. We found the route to be good enough for a while, but it began to grow difficult, by and by, and this feature steadily increased. When we judged we had gone half a mile, we momently expected to see the guide; but no, he was not visible anywhere; neither was he waiting, for the rope was still moving, consequently he was doing the same. This argued that he had not found the road, yet, but was marching to it with some peasant. There was nothing for us to do but plod along,—and this we did. At the end of three hours we were still plodding. This was not only mysterious, but exasperating. And very fatiguing, too; for we had tried hard, along at first, to catch up with the guide, but had only fagged ourselves, in vain; for although he was traveling slowly he was yet able to go faster than the hampered caravan over such ground.

At three in the afternoon we were nearly dead with exhaustion,—and still the rope was slowly gliding out. The murmurs against the guide had been growing steadily, and at last they were become loud and savage. A mutiny ensued. The men refused to proceed. They declared that we had been traveling over and over the same ground all day, in a kind of circle. They demanded that our end of

the rope be made fast to a tree, so as to halt the
guide until we could overtake him and kill him.
This was not an unreasonable requirement, so I gave
the order.

As soon as the rope was tied, the Expedition
moved forward with that alacrity which the thirst
for vengeance usually inspires.   But after a tiresome
march of almost half a mile, we came to a hill
covered thick with a crumbly rubbish of stones, and
so steep that no man of us all was now in a condition to climb it.   Every attempt failed, and ended
in crippling somebody.   Within twenty minutes I
had five men on crutches.   Whenever a climber
tried to assist himself by the rope, it yielded and
let him tumble backwards.   The frequency of this
result suggested an idea to me.   I ordered the
caravan to 'bout face and form in marching order;
I then made the tow-rope fast to the rear mule, and
gave the command:

" Mark time — by the right flank — forward —
march!"

The procession began to move, to the impressive
strains of a battle-chant, and I said to myself,
" Now, if the rope don't break I judge *this* will
fetch that guide into the camp."   I watched the
rope gliding down the hill, and presently when I
was all fixed for triumph I was confronted by a
bitter disappointment; there was no guide tied to
the rope, it was only a very indignant old black
ram.   The fury of the baffled Expedition exceeded

all bounds. They even wanted to wreak their un-
reasoning vengeance on this innocent dumb brute.
But I stood between them and their prey, menaced
by a bristling wall of ice-axes and alpenstocks, and
proclaimed that there was but one road to this
murder, and it was directly over my corse. Even
as I spoke I saw that my doom was sealed, except a
miracle supervened to divert these madmen from
their fell purpose. I see that sickening wall of
weapons now; I see that advancing host as I saw it
then, I see the hate in those cruel eyes; I remember
how I drooped my head upon my breast, I feel
again the sudden earthquake shock in my rear, administered by the very ram I was sacrificing myself
to save; I hear once more the typhoon of laughter
that burst from the assaulting column as I clove it
from van to rear like a Sepoy shot from a Rodman
gun.

I was saved. Yes, I was saved, and by the
merciful instinct of ingratitude which nature had
planted in the breast of that treacherous beast. The
grace which eloquence had failed to work in those
men's hearts, had been wrought by a laugh. The
ram was set free and my life was spared.

We lived to find out that that guide had deserted
us as soon as he had placed a half mile between
himself and us. To avert suspicion, he had judged
it best that the line should continue to move; so he
caught th  m, and at the time that he was sitting
on it making the rope fast to it, we were imagining

that he was lying in a swoon, overcome by fatigue and distress. When he allowed the ram to get up it fell to plunging around, trying to rid itself of the rope, and this was the signal which we had risen up with glad shouts to obey. We had followed this ram round and round in a circle all day — a thing which was proven by the discovery that we had watered the Expedition seven times at one and the same spring in seven hours. As expert a woodman as I am, I had somehow failed to notice this until my attention was called to it by a hog. This hog was always wallowing there, and as he was the only hog we saw, his frequent repetition, together with his unvarying similarity to himself, finally caused me to reflect that he must be the same hog, and this led me to the deduction that this must be the same spring, also,— which indeed it was.

I made a note of this curious thing, as showing in a striking manner the relative difference between glacial action and the action of the hog. It is now a well-established fact, that glaciers move; I consider that my observations go to show, with equal conclusiveness, that a hog in a spring does not move. I shall be glad to receive the opinions of other observers upon this point.

To return, for an explanatory moment, to that guide, and then I shall be done with him. After leaving the ram tied to the rope, he had wandered at large a while, and then happened to run across a cow. Judging that a cow would naturally know more than a guide, he took her by the tail, and the result justified his judgment. She nibbled her leisurely way down hill till it was near milking time, then she struck for home and towed him into Zermatt.

# CHAPTER IX.

WE went into camp on that wild spot to which that ram had brought us. The men were greatly fatigued. Their conviction that we were lost was forgotten in the cheer of a good supper, and before the reaction had a chance to set in, I loaded them up with paregoric and put them to bed.

Next morning I was considering in my mind our desperate situation and trying to think of a remedy, when Harris came to me with a Baedeker map which showed conclusively that the mountain we were on was still in Switzerland,— yes, every part of it was in Switzerland. So we were not lost, after all. This was an immense relief; it lifted the weight of two such mountains from my breast. I immediately had the news disseminated and the map exhibited. The effect was wonderful. As soon as the men saw with their own eyes that they knew where they were, and that it was only the summit that was lost and not themselves, they cheered up instantly and said with one accord, let the summit take care of itself, they were not interested in its troubles.

Our distresses being at an end, I now determined to rest the men in camp and give the scientific depart- ment of the Expedition a chance. First, I made a barometric observation, to get our altitude, but I could not perceive that there was any result. I knew, by my scientific reading, that either ther- mometers or barometers ought to be boiled, to make them accurate; I did not know which it was, so I boiled both. There was still no result; so I ex- amined these instruments and discovered that they possessed radical blemishes: the barometer had no hand but the brass pointer and the ball of the thermometer was stuffed with tin foil. I might have boiled those things to rags, and never found out anything.

I hunted up another barometer; it was new and perfect. I boiled it half an hour in a pot of bean soup which the cooks were making. The result was unexpected: the instrument was not affected at all, but there was such a strong barometer taste to the soup that the head cook, who was a most conscien- tious person, changed its name in the bill of fare. The dish was so greatly liked by all, that I ordered the cook to have barometer soup every day. It was believed that the barometer might eventually be injured, but I did not care for that. I had demon- strated to my satisfaction that it could not tell how high a mountain was, therefore I had no real use for it. Changes of the weather I could take care of without it; I did not wish to know when the weather

was going to be good, what I wanted to know was
when it was going to be bad, and this I could find
out from Harris's corns.   Harris had had his corns
tested and regulated at the government observatory
in Heidelberg, and one could depend upon them
with confidence.   So I transferred the new barometer
to the cooking department, to be used for the official
mess.   It was found that even a pretty fair article of
soup could be made with the defective barometer;
so I allowed that one to be transferred to the subordinate messes.

I next boiled the thermometer, and got a most excellent result; the mercury went up to about 200°
Fahrenheit.   In the opinion of the other scientists of
the Expedition, this seemed to indicate that we
had attained the extraordinary altitude of 200,000
feet above sea level.   Science places the line of
eternal snow at about 10,000 feet above sea level.
There was no snow where we were, consequently it
was proven that the eternal snow line ceases somewhere above the 10,000-foot level and does not begin
any more.   This was an interesting fact, and one
which had not been observed by any observer before.   It was as valuable as interesting, too, since
it would open up the deserted summits of the highest
Alps to population and agriculture.   It was a proud
thing to be where we were, yet it caused us a pang
to reflect that but for that ram we might just as
well have been 200,000 feet higher.

The success of my last experiment induced me to

try an experiment with my photographic apparatus. I got it out, and boiled one of my cameras, but the thing was a failure: it made the wood swell up and burst, and I could not see that the lenses were any better than they were before.

I now concluded to boil a guide. It might improve him, it could not impair his usefulness. But I was not allowed to proceed. Guides have no feeling for science, and this one would not consent to be made uncomfortable in its interest.

In the midst of my scientific work, one of those needless accidents happened which are always occurring among the ignorant and thoughtless. A porter shot at a chamois and missed it and crippled the Latinist. This was not a serious matter to me, for a Latinist's duties are as well performed on crutches as otherwise,— but the fact remained that if the Latinist had not happened to be in the way a mule would have got that load. That would have been quite another matter, for when it comes down to a question of value there is a palpable difference between a Latinist and a mule. I could not depend on having a Latinist in the right place every time; so, to make things safe, I ordered that in the future the chamois must not be hunted within limits of the camp with any other weapon than the forefinger.

My nerves had hardly grown quiet after this affair when they got another shake-up,— one which utterly unmanned me for a moment: a rumor swept sud-

denly through the camp that one of the barkeepers
had fallen over a precipice!

However, it turned out that it was only a chaplain.
I had laid in an extra force of chaplains, purposely
to be prepared for emergencies like this, but by
some unaccountable oversight had come away rather
short-handed in the matter of barkeepers.

On the following morning we moved on, well re-
freshed and in good spirits. I remember this day
with peculiar pleasure, because it saw our road
restored to us. Yes, we found our road again, and
in quite an extraordinary way. We had plodded
along some two hours and a half, when we came up
against a solid mass of rock about twenty feet high.
I did not need to be instructed by a mule this time.
I was already beginning to know more than any mule
in the Expedition. I at once put in a blast of
dynamite, and lifted that rock out of the way. But
to my surprise and mortification, I found that there
had been a chalet on top of it.

I picked up such members of the family as fell in
my vicinity, and subordinates of my corps collected
the rest. None of these poor people were injured,
happily, but they were much annoyed. I explained
to the head chaleteer just how the thing happened,
and that I was only searching for the road, and
would certainly have given him timely notice if I had
known he was up there. I said I had meant no
harm, and hoped I had not lowered myself in his
estimation by raising him a few rods in the air. I

said many other judicious things, and finally when I offered to rebuild his chalet, and pay for the breakages, and throw in the cellar, he was mollified and satisfied. He hadn't any cellar at all, before; he would not have as good a view, now, as formerly, but what he had lost in view he had gained in cellar, by exact measurement. He said there wasn't another hole like that in the mountains,— and he would have been right if the late mule had not tried to eat up the nitroglycerine.

I put a hundred and sixteen men at work, and they rebuilt the chalet from its own débris in fifteen minutes. It was a good deal more picturesque than it was before, too. The man said we were now on the Feli-Stutz, above the Schwegmatt,— information which I was glad to get, since it gave us our position to a degree of particularity which we had not been accustomed to for a day or so. We also learned that we were standing at the foot of the Riffelberg proper, and that the initial chapter of our work was completed.

We had a fine view, from here, of the energetic Visp, as it makes its first plunge into the world from under a huge arch of solid ice, worn through the foot-wall of the great Gorner Glacier; and we could also see the Furggenbach, which is the outlet of the Furggen Glacier.

The mule road to the summit of the Riffelberg passed right in front of the chalet, a circumstance which we almost immediately noticed, because a pro-

9**

cession of tourists was filing along it pretty much all the time.* The chaleteer's business consisted in furnishing refreshments to tourists. My blast had interrupted this trade for a few minutes, by breaking all the bottles on the place; but I gave the man a lot of whisky to sell for Alpine champagne, and a lot of vinegar which would answer for Rhine wine, consequently trade was soon as brisk as ever.

Leaving the Expedition outside to rest, I quartered myself in the chalet, with Harris, purposing to correct my journals and scientific observations before continuing the ascent. I had hardly begun my work when a tall, slender, vigorous American youth of about twenty-three, who was on his way down the mountain, entered and came toward me with that breezy self-complacency which is the adolescent's idea of the well-bred ease of the man of the world. His hair was short and parted accurately in the middle, and he had all the look of an American person who would be likely to begin his signature with an initial, and spell his middle name out. He introduced himself, smiling a smirky smile borrowed from the courtiers of the stage, extended a fair-skinned talon, and while he gripped my hand in it he bent his body forward three times at the hips, as the stage-courtier does, and said in the airiest and most condescending and patronizing way,— I quote his exact language:

---

* "Pretty much" may not be elegant English, but it is high time it was. There is no elegant word or phrase which means just what it means. — M. T.

"Very glad to make your acquaintance, 'm sure; very glad indeed, assure you. I've read all your little efforts and greatly admired them, and when I heard you were here, I . . . ."

I indicated a chair, and he sat down. This grandee was the grandson of an American of considerable note in his day, and not wholly forgotten yet,— a man who came so near being a great man that he was quite generally accounted one while he lived.

I slowly paced the floor, pondering scientific problems, and heard this conversation:

*Grandson.* First visit to Europe?

*Harris.* Mine? Yes.

*G. S.* (With a soft reminiscent sigh suggestive of bygone joys that may be tasted in their freshness but once.) Ah, I know what it is to you. A first visit!— ah, the romance of it! I wish I could feel it again.

*H.* Yes, I find it exceeds all my dreams. It is enchantment. I go . . .

*G. S.* (With a dainty gesture of the hand signifying "Spare me your callow enthusiasms, good friend.") Yes, *I* know, I know; you go to cathedrals, and exclaim; and you drag through league-long picture-galleries and exclaim; and you stand here, and there, and yonder, upon historic ground, and continue to exclaim; and you are permeated with your first crude conceptions of Art, and are proud and happy. Ah, yes, proud and happy—

J**

that expresses it. Yes-yes, enjoy it — it is right,— it is an innocent revel.

*H.* And you? Don't you do these things now?

*G. S.* I! Oh, that is *very* good! My dear sir, when you are as old a traveler as I am, you will not ask such a question as that. *I* visit the regulation gallery, moon around the regulation cathedral, do the worn round of the regulation sights, *yet ?* — Excuse me!

*H.* Well, what *do* you do, then?

*G. S.* Do? I flit,— and flit,— for I am ever on the wing,— but I avoid the herd. To-day I am in Paris, to-morrow in Berlin, anon in Rome; but you would look for me in vain in the galleries of the Louvre or the common resorts of the gazers in those other capitals. If you would find me, you must look in the unvisited nooks and corners where others never think of going. One day you will find me making myself at home in some obscure peasant's cabin, another day you will find me in some forgotten castle worshiping some little gem of art which the careless eye has overlooked and which the unexperienced would despise; again you will find me a guest in the inner sanctuaries of palaces while the herd is content to get a hurried glimpse of the unused chambers by feeing a servant.

*H.* You are a *guest* in such places?

*G. S.* And a welcome one.

*H.* It is surprising. How does it come?

*G. S.* My grandfather's name is a passport to all

the courts in Europe. I have only to utter that name and every door is open to me. I flit from court to court at my own free will and pleasure, and am always welcome. I am as much at home in the palaces of Europe as you are among your relatives. I know every titled person in Europe, I think. I have my pockets full of invitations all the time. I am under promise now to go to Italy, where I am to be the guest of a succession of the noblest houses in the land. In Berlin my life is a continued round of gayety in the imperial palace. It is the same, wherever I go.

*H.* It must be very pleasant. But it must make Boston seem a little slow when you are at home.

*G. S.* Yes, of course it does. But I don't go home much. There's no life there — little to feed a man's higher nature. Boston's very narrow, you know. She doesn't know it, and you couldn't convince her of it — so I say nothing when I'm there: where's the use? Yes, Boston is very narrow, but she has such a good opinion of herself that she can't see it. A man who has traveled as much as I have, and seen as much of the world, sees it plain enough, but he can't cure it, you know, so the best way is to leave it and seek a sphere which is more in harmony with his tastes and culture. I run across there, once a year, perhaps, when I have nothing important on hand, but I'm very soon back again. I spend my time in Europe.

*H.* I see. You map out your plans and . . .

*G. S.* No, excuse me. I don't map out any plans. I simply follow the inclination of the day. I am limited by no ties, no requirements, I am not bound in any way. I am too old a traveler to hamper myself with deliberate purposes. I am simply a traveler — an inveterate traveler — a man of the world, in a word,— I can call myself by no other name. I do not say, " I am going here, or I am going there "— I say nothing at all, I only act. For instance, next week you may find me the guest of a grandee of Spain, or you may find me off for Venice, or flitting toward Dresden. I shall probably go to Egypt presently; friends will say to friends, " He is at the Nile cataracts "— and at that very moment they will be surprised to learn that I'm away off yonder in India somewhere. I am a constant surprise to people. They are always saying, " Yes, he was in Jerusalem when we heard of him last, but goodness knows where he is now."

Presently the Grandson rose to leave — discovered he had an appointment with some Emperor, perhaps. He did his graces over again: gripped me with one talon, at arm's length, pressed his hat against his stomach with the other, bent his body in the middle three times, murmuring:

" Pleasure, 'm sure; great pleasure, 'm sure. Wish you much success "

Then he removed his gracious presence. It is a great and solemn thing to have a grandfather.

I have not purposed to misrepresent this boy in

any way, for what little indignation he excited in me
soon passed and left nothing behind it but compassion. One cannot keep up a grudge against a
vacuum. I have tried to repeat the lad's very
words; if I have failed anywhere I have at least not
failed to reproduce the marrow and meaning of what
he said. He and the innocent chatterbox whom I
met on the Swiss lake are the most unique and interesting specimens of Young America I came across
during my foreign tramping. I have made honest
portraits of them, not caricatures. The Grandson of
twenty-three referred to himself five or six times as
an " old traveler," and as many as three times (with
a serene complacency which was maddening) as a
" man of the world." There was something very
delicious about his leaving Boston to her " narrow-
ness," unreproved and uninstructed.

I formed the caravan in marching order, presently,
and after riding down the line to see that it was
properly roped together, gave the command to proceed. In a little while the road carried us to open,
grassy land. We were above the troublesome
forest, now, and had an uninterrupted view, straight
before us, of our summit,— the summit of the
Riffelberg.

We followed the mule road, a zigzag course, now
to the right, now to the left, but always up, and
always crowded and incommoded by going and coming files of reckless tourists who were never, in a
single instance, tied together. I was obliged to

exert the utmost care and caution, for in many
places the road was not two yards wide, and often
the lower side of it sloped away in slanting precipices
eight and even nine feet deep. I had to encourage
the men constantly, to keep them from giving way
to their unmanly fears.

We might have made the summit before night, but
for a delay caused by the loss of an umbrella. I
was for allowing the umbrella to remain lost, but
the men murmured, and with reason, for in this exposed region we stood in peculiar need of protection
against avalanches; so I went into camp and detached a strong party to go after the missing article.

The difficulties of the next morning were severe,
but our courage was high, for our goal was near.
At noon we conquered the last impediment — we
stood at last upon the summit, and without the loss
of a single man except the mule that ate the
glycerine. Our great achievement was achieved —
the possibility of the impossible was demonstrated,
and Harris and I walked proudly into the great
dining-room of the Riffelberg Hotel and stood our
alpenstocks up in the corner.

Yes, I had made the grand ascent; but it was a
mistake to do it in evening dress. The plug hats
were battered, the swallow-tails were fluttering rags,
mud added no grace, the general effect was unpleasant and even disreputable.

There were about seventy-five tourists at the hotel,
— mainly ladies and little children, — and they gave

us an admiring welcome which paid us for all our privations and sufferings. The ascent had been made, and the names and dates now stand recorded on a stone monument there to prove it to all future tourists.

I boiled a thermometer and took an altitude, with a most curious result: *the summit was not as high as the point on the mountain-side where I had taken the first altitude.* Suspecting that I had made an important discovery, I prepared to verify it. There happened to be a still higher summit (called the Gorner Grat), above the hotel, and notwithstanding the fact that it overlooks a glacier from a dizzy height, and that the ascent is difficult and dangerous, I resolved to venture up there and boil a thermometer. So I sent a strong party, with some borrowed hoes, in charge of two chiefs of service, to dig a stairway in the soil all the way, and this I ascended, roped to the guides. This breezy height was the summit proper — so I accomplished even more than I had originally purposed to do. This foolhardy exploit is recorded on another stone monument.

I boiled my thermometer, and sure enough, this spot, which purported to be 2,000 feet higher than the locality of the hotel, turned out to be 9,000 feet *lower.* Thus the fact was clearly demonstrated, that, *above a certain point, the higher a point seems to be, the lower it actually is.* Our ascent itself was a great achievement, but this contribution to science was an inconceivably greater matter.

Cavilers object that water boils at a lower and lower temperature the higher and higher you go, and hence the apparent anomaly. I answer that I do not base my theory upon what the boiling water does, but upon what a boiled thermometer says. You can't go behind the thermometer.

I had a magnificent view of Monte Rosa, and apparently all the rest of the Alpine world, from that high place. All the circling horizon was piled high with a mighty tumult of snowy crests. One might have imagined he saw before him the tented camps of a beleaguering host of Brobdingnagians.

But lonely, conspicuous, and superb, rose that wonderful upright wedge, the Matterhorn. Its precipitous sides were powdered over with snow, and the upper half hidden in thick clouds which now and then dissolved to cobweb films and gave brief glimpses of the imposing tower as through a veil. A little later the Matterhorn took to himself the semblance of a volcano; he was stripped naked to his apex — around this circled vast wreaths of white cloud which strung slowly out and streamed away slantwise toward the sun, a twenty-mile stretch of rolling and tumbling vapor, and looking just as if it

NOTE — I had the very unusual luck to catch one little momentary glimpse of the Matterhorn wholly unencumbered by clouds. I leveled my photographic apparatus at it without the loss of an instant, and should have got an elegant picture if my donkey had not interfered. It was my purpose to draw this photograph all by myself for my book, but was obliged to put the mountain part of it into the hands of the professional artist because I found I could not do landscape well.

were pouring out of a crater. Later again, one of the mountain's sides was clean and clear, and another side densely clothed from base to summit in thick smoke-like cloud which feathered off and blew around the shaft's sharp edge like the smoke around the corners of a burning building. The Matterhorn is always experimenting, and always gets up fine effects, too. In the sunset, when all the lower world is palled in gloom, it points toward heaven out of the pervading blackness like a finger of fire. In the sunrise — well, they say it is very fine in the sunrise.

Authorities agree that there is no such tremendous "layout" of snowy Alpine magnitude, grandeur, and sublimity to be seen from any other accessible point as the tourist may see from the summit of the Riffelberg. Therefore, let the tourist rope himself up and go there; for I have shown that with nerve, caution, and judgment, the thing can be done.

I wish to add one remark, here, — in parentheses, so to speak, — suggested by the word "snowy," which I have just used. We have all seen hills and mountains and levels with snow on them, and so we think we know all the aspects and effects produced by snow. But indeed we do not until we have seen the Alps. Possibly mass and distance add something — at any rate, something *is* added. Among other noticeable things, there is a dazzling, intense whiteness about the distant Alpine snow, when the sun is on it, which one recognizes as peculiar, and not

familiar to the eye.   The snow which one is accustomed to has a tint to it,— painters usually give it a
bluish cast,— but there is no perceptible tint to the
distant Alpine snow when it is trying to look its
whitest.   As to the unimaginable splendor of it when
the sun is blazing down on it,— well, it simply *is*
unimaginable.

# CHAPTER X.

A GUIDE-BOOK is a queer thing. The reader has just seen what a man who undertakes the great ascent from Zermatt to the Riffelberg hotel must experience. Yet Baedeker makes these strange statements concerning this matter:

1. Distance,— 3 hours.
2. The road cannot be mistaken.
3. Guide unnecessary.
4. Distance from Riffelberg Hotel to the Gorner Grat, one hour and a half.
5. Ascent simple and easy. Guide unnecessary.
6. Elevation of Zermatt above sea level, 5,315 feet.
7. Elevation of Riffelberg Hotel above sea level, 8,429 feet.
8. Elevation of the Gorner Grat above sea level, 10,289 feet.

I have pretty effectually throttled these errors by sending him the following demonstrated facts:

1. Distance from Zermatt to Riffelberg hotel, 7 days.
2. The road *can* be mistaken. If I am the first that did it, I want the credit of it, too.

3. Guides *are* necessary, for none but a native can read those finger-boards.

4. The estimate of the elevation of the several localities above sea level is pretty correct — for Baedeker. He only misses it about a hundred and eighty or ninety thousand feet.

I found my arnica invaluable. My men were suffering excruciatingly, from the friction of sitting down so much. During two or three days, not one of them was able to do more than lie down or walk about; yet so effective was the arnica, that on the fourth all were able to sit up. I consider that, more than to anything else, I owe the success of our great undertaking to arnica and paregoric.

My men being restored to health and strength, my main perplexity, now, was how to get them down the mountain again. I was not willing to expose the brave fellows to the perils, fatigues, and hardships of that fearful route again if it could be helped. First I thought of balloons; but, of course, I had to give that idea up, for balloons were not procurable. I thought of several other expedients, but upon consideration discarded them, for cause. But at last I hit it. I was aware that the movement of glaciers is an established fact, for I had read it in Baedeker; so I resolved to take passage for Zermatt on the great Gorner Glacier.

Very good. The next thing was, how to get down to the glacier comfortably, — for the mule-road to it was long, and winding, and wearisome.

I set my mind at work, and soon thought out a plan.
One looks straight down upon tne vast frozen river
called the Gorner Glacier, from the Gorner Grat, a
sheer precipice 1,200 feet high.   We had 154 umbrellas,— and what is an umbrella but a parachute?

I mentioned this noble idea to Harris, with enthusiasm, and was about to order the Expedition to
form on the Gorner Grat, with their umbrellas, and
prepare for flight by platoons, each platoon in command of a guide, when Harris stopped me and
urged me not to be too hasty.   He asked me if this
method of descending the Alps had ever been tried
before.   I said no, I had not heard of an instance.
Then, in his opinion, it was a matter of considerable
gravity; in his opinion it would not be well to send
the whole command over the cliff at once; a better
way would be to send down a single individual, first,
and see how he fared.

I saw the wisdom of this idea instantly.   I said as
much, and thanked my agent cordially, and told
him to take his umbrella and try the thing right
away, and wave his hat when he got down, if he
struck in a soft place, and then I would ship the rest
right along.

Harris was greatly touched with this mark of confidence, and said so, in a voice that had a perceptible tremble in it; but at the same time he said he
did not feel himself worthy of sc conspicuous a
favor; that it might cause jealousy in the command,
for there were plenty who would not hesitate to say

he had used underhanded means to get the appointment, whereas his conscience would bear him witness that he had not sought it at all, nor even, in
his secret heart, desired it.

I said these words did him extreme credit, but
that he must not throw away the imperishable distinction of being the first man to descend an Alp
per parachute, simply to save the feelings of some
envious underlings.  No, I said, he *must* accept the
appointment,— it was no longer an invitation, it was
a command.

He thanked me with effusion, and said that putting the thing in this form removed every objection.
He retired, and soon returned with his umbrella, his
eyes flaming with gratitude and his cheeks pallid
with joy.  Just then the head guide passed along.
Harris' expression changed to one of infinite tender-
ness, and he said:

"That man did me a cruel injury four days ago,
and I said in my heart he should live to perceive
and confess that the only noble revenge a man can
take upon his enemy is to return good for evil.  I
resign in his favor.  Appoint him."

I threw my arms around the generous fellow and
said:

"Harris, you are the noblest soul that lives.  You
shall not regret this sublime act, neither shall the
world fail to know of it.  You shall have opportunities far transcending this one, too, if I live,—
remember that."

I called the head guide to me and appointed him on the spot. But the thing aroused no enthusiasm in him. He did not take to the idea at all. He said:

"Tie myself to an umbrella and jump over the Gorner Grat! Excuse me, there are a great many pleasanter roads to the devil than that."

Upon a discussion of the subject with him, it appeared that he considered the project distinctly and decidedly dangerous. I was not convinced, yet I was not willing to try the experiment in any risky way — that is, in a way that might cripple the strength and efficiency of the Expedition. I was about at my wits' end when it occurred to me to try it on the Latinist.

He was called in. But he declined, on the plea of inexperience, diffidence in public, lack of curiosity, and I don't know what all. Another man declined on account of a cold in the head; thought he ought to avoid exposure. Another could not jump well — never *could* jump well — did not believe he could jump so far without long and patient practice. Another was afraid it was going to rain, and his umbrella had a hole in it. Everybody had an excuse. The result was what the reader has by this time guessed: the most magnificent idea that was ever conceived had to be abandoned, from sheer lack of a person with enterprise enough to carry it out. Yes, I actually had to give that thing up,— whilst doubtless I should live to see somebody use it and take all the credit from me.

10

Well, I had to go overland — there was no other way. I marched the Expedition down the steep and tedious mule-path and took up as good a position as I could upon the middle of the glacier — because Baedeker said the middle part travels the fastest. As a measure of economy, however, I put some of the heavier baggage on the shoreward parts, to go as slow freight.

I waited and waited, but the glacier did not move. Night was coming on, the darkness began to gather — still we did not budge. It occurred to me then, that there might be a time-table in Baedeker; it would be well to find out the hours of starting. I called for the book — it could not be found. Bradshaw would certainly contain a time-table; but no Bradshaw could be found.

Very well, I must make the best of the situation. So I pitched the tents, picketed the animals, milked the cows, had supper, paregoricked the men, established the watch, and went to bed — with orders to call me as soon as we came in sight of Zermatt.

I awoke about half-past ten next morning, and looked around. We hadn't budged a peg! At first I could not understand it; then it occurred to me that the old thing must be aground. So I cut down some trees and rigged a spar on the starboard and another on the port side, and fooled away upwards of three hours trying to spar her off. But it was no use. She was half a mile wide and fifteen or twenty miles long, and there was no telling just whereabouts she *was* aground. The men began to show uneasiness, too, and presently they came flying to me with ashy faces, saying she had sprung a leak.

Nothing but my cool behavior at this critical time saved us from another panic. I ordered them to show me the place. They led me to a spot where a huge bowlder lay in a deep pool of clear and brilliant water. It did look like a pretty bad leak, but I kept that to myself. I made a pump and set the men to work to pump out the glacier. We made a success of it. I perceived, then, that it was not a leak at all. This bowlder had descended from a precipice and stopped on the ice in the middle of the glacier, and the sun had warmed it up, every day, and consequently it had melted its way deeper and deeper into the ice, until at last it reposed, as we had found it, in a deep pool of the clearest and coldest water.

Presently Baedeker was found again, and I hunted eagerly for the time-table. There was none. The book simply said the glacier was moving all the time. This was satisfactory, so I shut up the book and chose a good position to view the scenery as we passed along. I stood there some time enjoying the trip, but at last it occurred to me that we did not seem to be gaining any on the scenery. I said to myself, "This confounded old thing's aground again, sure,"— and opened Baedeker to see if I could run across any remedy for these annoying interruptions. I soon found a sentence which threw

J**

a dazzling light upon the matter. It said, "The Gorner Glacier travels at an average rate of a little less than an inch a day." I have seldom felt so outraged. I have seldom had my confidence so wantonly betrayed. I made a small calculation: 1 inch a day, say 30 feet a year; estimated distance to Zermatt, 3 1-18 miles. Time required to go by glacier, *a little over five hundred years!* I said to myself, "I can *walk* it quicker — and before I will patronize such a fraud as this, I will do it."

When I revealed to Harris the fact that the passenger-part of this glacier, — the central part, — the lightning-express part, so to speak, — was not due in Zermatt till the summer of 2378, and that the baggage, coming along the slow edge, would not arrive until some generations later, he burst out with:

"That is European management, all over! An inch a day — think of that! Five hundred years to go a trifle over three miles! But I am not a bit surprised. It's a Catholic glacier. You can tell by the look of it. And the management."

I said, no, I believed nothing but the extreme end of it was in a Catholic canton.

"Well, then, it's a government glacier," said Harris. "It's all the same. Over here the government runs everything, — so everything's slow; slow, and ill-managed. But with us, everything's done by private enterprise — and then there ain't much lolling around, you can depend on it. I wish Tom Scott could get his hands on this torpid old slab once,— you'd see it take a different gait from this."

I said I was sure he would increase the speed, if there was trade enough to justify it.

"He'd *make* trade," said Harris. "That's the difference between governments and individuals. Governments don't care, individuals do. Tom Scott would take all the trade; in two years Gorner stock would go to 200, and inside of two more you would see all the other glaciers under the hammer for taxes." After a reflective pause, Harris added, "A little less than an inch a day; a little less than an *inch*, mind you. Well, I'm losing my reverence for glaciers."

I was feeling much the same way myself. I have traveled by canal-boat, ox-wagon, raft, and by the Ephesus and Smyrna railway; but when it comes down to good solid honest slow motion, I bet my money on the glacier. As a means of passenger transportation, I consider the glacier a failure; but as a vehicle for slow freight, I think she fills the bill. In the matter of putting the fine shades on that line of business, I judge she could teach the Germans something.

I ordered the men to break camp and prepare for the land journey to Zermatt. At this moment a most interesting find was made; a dark object, bedded in the glacial ice, was cut out with the ice-axes, and it proved to be a piece of the undressed skin of some animal,— a hair trunk, perhaps; but a close inspection disabled the hair trunk theory, and further discussion and examination exploded it entirely,— that is, in the opinion of all the scientists except the one who had advanced it. This one clung to his theory with the affectionate fidelity characteristic of originators of scientific theories, and afterward won many of the first scientists of the age to his view, by a very able pamphlet which he wrote, entitled, "Evidences going to show that the hair trunk, in a wild state, belonged to the early glacial period, and roamed the wastes of chaos in company with the cave bear, primeval man, and the other Oölitics of the Old Silurian family."

Each of our scientists had a theory of his own, and put forward an animal of his own as a candidate for the skin. I sided with the geologist of the Expedition in the belief that this patch of skin had once helped to cover a Siberian elephant, in some old forgotten age — but we divided there, the geologist believing that this discovery proved that Siberia had formerly been located where Switzerland is now, whereas I held the opinion that it merely proved that the primeval Swiss was not the dull savage he is represented to have been, but was a being of high intellectual development, who liked to go to the menagerie.

We arrived that evening, after many hardships and adventures, in some fields close to the great ice-arch where the mad Visp boils and surges out from under the foot of the great Gorner Glacier, and here we camped, our perils over and our magnificent undertaking successfully completed. We marched into Zermatt the next day, and were received with the most lavish honors and applause. A document, signed and sealed by all the authorities, was given to me which established and endorsed the fact that I had made the ascent of the Riffelberg. This I wear around my neck, and it will be buried with me when I am no more.

# CHAPTER XI.

I AM not so ignorant about glacial movement, now, as I was when I took passage on the Gorner Glacier. I have " read up " since. I am aware that these vast bodies of ice do not travel at the same rate of speed; whilst the Gorner Glacier makes less than an inch a day, the Unter-Aar Glacier makes as much as eight; and still other glaciers are said to go twelve, sixteen, and even twenty inches a day. One writer says that the slowest glacier travels twenty-five feet a year, and the fastest 400.

What is a glacier? It is easy to say it looks like a frozen river which occupies the bed of a winding gorge or gully between mountains. But that gives no notion of its vastness. For it is sometimes 600 feet thick, and we are not accustomed to rivers 600 feet deep; no, our rivers are six feet, twenty feet, and sometimes fifty feet deep; we are not quite able to grasp so large a fact as an ice-river 600 feet deep.

The glacier's surface is not smooth and level, but has deep swales and swelling elevations, and sometimes has the look of a tossing sea whose turbulent billows were frozen hard in the instant of their most

violent motion; the glacier's surface is not a flawless
mass, but is a river with cracks or crevasses, some
narrow, some gaping wide. Many a man, the victim
of a slip or a misstep, has plunged down one of
these and met his death. Men have been fished out
of them alive, but it was when they did not go to a
great depth; the cold of the great depths would
quickly stupefy a man, whether he was hurt or un-
hurt. These cracks do not go straight down; one
can seldom see more than twenty to forty feet down
them; consequently men who have disappeared in
them have been sought for, in the hope that they
had stopped within helping distance, whereas their
case, in most instances, had really been hopeless
from the beginning.

In 1864 a party of tourists was descending Mont
Blanc, and while picking their way over one of the
mighty glaciers of that lofty region, roped together,
as was proper, a young porter disengaged himself
from the line and started across an ice-bridge which
spanned a crevasse. It broke under him with a
crash, and he disappeared. The others could not
see how deep he had gone, so it might be worth
while to try and rescue him. A brave young guide
named Michel Payot volunteered.

Two ropes were made fast to his leather belt and
he bore the end of a third one in his hand to tie to
the victim in case he found him. He was lowered
into the crevasse, he descended deeper and deeper
between the clear blue walls of solid ice, he ap-

proached a bend in the crack and disappeared under it. Down, and still down, he went, into this profound grave; when he had reached a depth of eighty feet he passed under another bend in the crack, and thence descended eighty feet lower, as between perpendicular precipices. Arrived at this stage of 160 feet below the surface of the glacier, he peered through the twilight dimness and perceived that the chasm took another turn and stretched away at a steep slant to unknown deeps, for its course was lost in darkness. What a place that was to be in — especially if that leather belt should break! The compression of the belt threatened to suffocate the intrepid fellow; he called to his friends to draw him up, but could not make them hear. They still lowered him, deeper and deeper. Then he jerked his third cord as vigorously as he could; his friends understood, and dragged him out of those icy jaws of death.

Then they attached a bottle to a cord and sent it down 200 feet, but it found no bottom. It came up covered with congelations — evidence enough that even if the poor porter reached the bottom with unbroken bones, a swift death from cold was sure, anyway.

A glacier is a stupendous, ever progressing, resistless plow. It pushes ahead of it masses of bowlders which are packed together, and they stretch across the gorge, right in front of it, like a long grave or a long, sharp roof. This is called a moraine. It also shoves out a moraine along each side of its course.

Imposing as the modern glaciers are, they are not so huge as were some that once existed. For instance, Mr. Whymper says:

" At some very remote period the Valley of Aosta was occupied by a vast glacier, which flowed down its entire length from Mont Blanc to the plain of Piedmont, remained stationary, or nearly so, at its mouth for many centuries, and deposited there enormous masses of débris. The length of this glacier exceeded *eighty miles*, and it drained a basin twenty-five to thirty-five miles across, bounded by the highest mountains in the Alps. The great peaks rose several thousand feet above the glaciers, and then, as now, shattered by sun and frost, poured down their showers of rocks and stones, in witness of which there are the immense piles of angular fragments that constitute the moraines of Ivrea.

" The moraines around Ivrea are of extraordinary dimensions. That which was on the left bank of the glacier is about *thirteen miles* long, and in some places rises to a height of *two thousand one hundred and thirty feet* above the floor of the valley! The terminal moraines (those which are pushed in front of the glaciers) cover something like twenty square miles of country. At the mouth of the Valley of Aosta, the thickness of the glacier must have been at least *two thousand* feet, and its width, at that part, *five miles and a quarter.*"

It is not easy to get at a comprehension of a mass of ice like that. If one could cleave off the butt end of such a glacier — an oblong block two or three miles wide by five and a quarter long and 2,000 feet thick — he could completely hide the city of New York under it, and Trinity steeple would only stick up into it relatively as far as a shingle nail would stick up into the bottom of a Saratoga trunk.

"The bowlders from Mont Blanc, upon the plain below Ivrea, assure us that the glacier which transported them existed for a prodigious length of time. Their present distance from the cliffs from which they were derived is about 420,000 feet, and if we assume that they traveled at the rate of 400 feet per annum, their journey must have occupied them no less than 1055 years! In all probability they did not travel so fast."

Glaciers are sometimes hurried out of their characteristic snail-pace. A marvelous spectacle is presented then. Mr. Whymper refers to a case which occurred in Iceland in 1721:

"It seems that in the neighborhood of the mountain Kotlugja, large bodies of water formed underneath, or within the glaciers (either on account of the interior heat of the earth, or from other causes), and at length acquired irresistible power, tore the glaciers from their mooring on the land, and swept them over every obstacle into the sea. Prodigious masses of ice were thus borne for a distance of about ten miles over land in the space of a few hours; and their bulk was so enormous that they covered the sea for seven miles from the shore, and remained aground in 600 feet of water! The denudation of the land was upon a grand scale. All superficial accumulations were swept away, and the bed-rock was exposed. It was described, in graphic language, how all irregularities and depressions were obliterated, and a smooth surface of several miles area laid bare, and that this area had the appearance of having been *planed by a plane*."

The account translated from the Icelandic says that the mountain-like ruins of this majestic glacier so covered the sea that as far as the eye could reach no open water was discoverable, even from the highest peaks. A monster wall or barrier of ice was built across a considerable stretch of land, too, by this strange irruption:

" One can form some idea of the altitude of this barrier of ice when it is mentioned that from Hofdabrekka farm, which lies high up on a fjeld, one could not see Hjorleifshofdi opposite, which is a fell 640 feet in height; but in order to do so had to clamber up a mountain slope east of Hofdabrekka 1,200 feet high."

These things will help the reader to understand why it is that a man who keeps company with glaciers comes to feel tolerably insignificant by and by. The Alps and the glaciers together are able to take every bit of conceit out of a man and reduce his self-importance to zero if he will only remain within the

influence of their sublime presence long enough to
give it a fair and reasonable chance to do its work.

The Alpine glaciers move — that is granted, now,
by everybody. But there was a time when people
scoffed at the idea; they said you might as well expect leagues of solid rock to crawl along the ground
as expect solid leagues of ice to do it. But proof
after proof was furnished, and finally the world had
to believe.

The wise men not only said the glacier moved,
but they timed its movement. They ciphered out a
glacier's gait, and then said confidently that it would
travel just so far in so many years. There is record
of a striking and curious example of the accuracy
which may be attained in these reckonings.

In 1820 the ascent of Mont Blanc was attempted
by a Russian and two Englishmen, with seven
guides. They had reached a prodigious altitude,
and were approaching the summit, when an avalanche
swept several of the party down a sharp slope of
two hundred feet and hurled five of them (all
guides) into one of the crevasses of a glacier. The
life of one of the five was saved by a long barometer
which was strapped to his back — it bridged the
crevasse and suspended him until help came. The
alpenstock or baton of another saved its owner in a
similar way. Three men were lost — Pierre Balmat,
Pierre Carrier, and Auguste Tairraz. They had
been hurled down into the fathomless great deeps of
the crevasse.

Dr. Forbes, the English geologist, had made frequent visits to the Mont Blanc region, and had given much attention to the disputed question of the movement of glaciers. During one of these visits he completed his estimates of the rate of movement of the glacier which had swallowed up the three guides, and uttered the prediction that the glacier would deliver up its dead at the foot of the mountain thirty-five years from the time of the accident, or possibly forty.

A dull, slow journey — a movement imperceptible to any eye — but it was proceeding, nevertheless, and without cessation. It was a journey which a rolling stone would make in a few seconds — the lofty point of departure was visible from the village below in the valley.

The prediction cut curiously close to the truth; forty-one years after the catastrophe, the remains were cast forth at the foot of the glacier.

I find an interesting account of the matter in the "Histoire du Mont Blanc," by Stephen d'Arve. I will condense this account, as follows:

On the 12th of August, 1861, at the hour of the close of mass, a guide arrived out of breath at the mairie of Chamonix, and bearing on his shoulders a very lugubrious burden. It was a sack filled with human remains which he had gathered from the orifice of a crevasse in the Glacier des Bossons. He conjectured that these were remains of the victims of the catastrophe of 1820, and a minute inquest, imme-

diately instituted by the local authorities, soon
demonstrated the correctness of his supposition.
The contents of the sack were spread upon a long
table, and officially inventoried, as follows:

Portions of three human skulls. Several tufts of
black and blonde hair. A human jaw, furnished
with fine white teeth. A forearm and hand, all the
fingers of the latter intact. The flesh was white and
fresh, and both the arm and hand preserved a degree
of flexibility in the articulations.

The ring-finger had suffered a slight abrasion, and
the stain of the blood was still visible and unchanged
after forty-one years. A left foot, the flesh white
and fresh.

Along with these fragments were portions of
waistcoats, hats, hob-nailed shoes, and other clothing;
a wing of a pigeon, with black feathers; a fragment
of an alpenstock; a tin lantern; and lastly, a boiled
leg of mutton, the only flesh among all the remains
that exhaled an unpleasant odor. The guide said
that the mutton had no odor when he took it from
the glacier; an hour's exposure to the sun had
already begun the work of decomposition upon it.

Persons were called for, to identify these poor
pathetic relics, and a touching scene ensued. Two
men were still living who had witnessed the grim
catastrophe of nearly half a century before,— Marie
Couttet (saved by his baton) and Julien Davouassoux
(saved by the barometer). These aged men entered
and approached the table. Davouassoux, more

than eighty years old, contemplated the mournful remains mutely and with a vacant eye, for his intelligence and his memory were torpid with age; but Couttet's faculties were still perfect at seventy-two, and he exhibited strong emotion. He said:

"Pierre Balmat was fair; he wore a straw hat. This bit of skull, with the tuft of blond hair, was his; this is his hat. Pierre Carrier was very dark; this skull was his, and this felt hat. This is Balmat's hand, I remember it so well!" and the old man bent down and kissed it reverently, then closed his fingers upon it in an affectionate grasp, crying out, "I could never have dared to believe that before quitting this world it would be granted me to press once more the hand of one of those brave comrades, the hand of my good friend Balmat."

There is something weirdly pathetic about the picture of that white-haired veteran greeting with his loving handshake this friend who had been dead forty years. When these hands had met last, they were alike in the softness and freshness of youth; now, one was brown and wrinkled and horny with age, while the other was still as young and fair and blemishless as if those forty years had come and gone in a single moment, leaving no mark of their passage. Time had gone on, in the one case; it had stood still in the other. A man who has not seen a friend for a generation, keeps him in mind always as he saw him last, and is somehow surprised, and is also shocked, to see the aging change

the years have wrought when he sees him again.
Marie Couttet's experience, in finding his friend's
hand unaltered from the image of it which he had
carried in his memory for forty years, is an experience which stands alone in the history of man,
perhaps.

Couttet identified other relics:

"This hat belonged to Auguste Tairraz. He
carried the cage of pigeons which we proposed to
set free upon the summit. Here is the wing of one
of those pigeons. And here is the fragment of my
broken baton; it was by grace of that baton that
my life was saved. Who could have told me that I
should one day have the satisfaction to look again
upon this bit of wood that supported me above the
grave that swallowed up my unfortunate companions!"

No portions of the body of Tairraz had been
found. A diligent search was made, but without
result. However, another search was instituted a
year later, and this had better success. Many fragments of clothing which had belonged to the lost
guides were discovered; also, part of a lantern, and
a green veil with blood-stains on it. But the interesting feature was this:

One of the searchers came suddenly upon a
sleeved arm projecting from a crevice in the ice-
wall, with the hand outstretched as if offering greeting! "The nails of this white hand were still rosy,
and the pose of the extended fingers seemed to

express an eloquent welcome to the long-lost light
of day."

The hand and arm were alone; there was no
trunk. After being removed from the ice the flesh-
tints quickly faded out and the rosy nails took on
the alabaster hue of death. This was the third *right*
hand found; therefore, all three of the lost men
were accounted for, beyond cavil or question.

Dr. Hamel was the Russian gentleman of the
party which made the ascent at the time of the
famous disaster. He left Chamonix as soon as he
conveniently could after the descent; and as he had
shown a chilly indifference about the calamity, and
offered neither sympathy nor assistance to the
widows and orphans, he carried with him the cordial
execrations of the whole community. Four months
before the first remains were found, a Chamonix
guide named Balmat,— a relative of one of the lost
men,— was in London, and one day encountered a
hale old gentleman in the British Museum, who said:

"I overheard your name. Are you from Chamonix, Monsieur Balmat?"

"Yes, sir."

"Haven't they found the bodies of my three
guides, yet? I am Dr. Hamel."

"Alas, no, monsieur."

"Well, you'll find them, sooner or later."

"Yes, it is the opinion of Dr. Forbes and Mr.
Tyndall, that the glacier will sooner or later restore
to us the remains of the unfortunate victims."

K**

" Without a doubt, without a doubt.   And it will
be a great thing for Chamonix, in the matter of
attracting tourists.   You can get up a museum with
those remains that will draw !''

This savage idea has not improved the odor of
Dr. Hamel's name in Chamonix by any means.
But after all, the man was sound on human nature.
His idea was conveyed to the public officials of
Chamonix, and they gravely discussed it around the
official council-table.   They were only prevented
from carrying it into execution by the determined
opposition of the friends and descendants of the
lost guides, who insisted on giving the remains
Christian burial, and succeeded in their purpose.

A close watch had to be kept upon all the poor
remnants and fragments, to prevent embezzlement.
A few accessory odds and ends were sold.   Rags
and scraps of the coarse clothing were parted with
at a rate equal to about twenty dollars a yard; a
piece of a lantern and one or two other trifles
brought nearly their weight in gold; and an Englishman offered a pound sterling for a single breeches-
button.

THE MATTERHORN

# CHAPTER XII.

ONE of the most memorable of all the Alpine catastrophes was that of July, 1865, on the Matterhorn,—already slightly referred to, a few pages back. The details of it are scarcely known in America. To the vast majority of readers they are not known at all. Mr. Whymper's account is the only authentic one. I will import the chief portion of it into this book, partly because of its intrinsic interest, and partly because it gives such a vivid idea of what the perilous pastime of Alp-climbing is. This was Mr. Whymper's *ninth* attempt during a series of years, to vanquish that steep and stubborn pillar of rock; it succeeded, the other eight were failures. No man had ever accomplished the ascent before, though the attempts had been numerous.

## MR. WHYMPER'S NARRATIVE

We started from Zermatt on the 13th of July, at half-past five, on a brilliant and perfectly cloudless morning. We were eight in number — Croz (guide), old Peter Taugwalder (guide) and his two sons; Lord F. Douglas, Mr. Hadow, Rev. Mr. Hudson, and I.  To ensure steady motion, one tourist and one native walked together.  The youngest Taugwalder fell to my share.  The wine-bags also fell to my lot to carry, and throughout the day, after each drink, I replenished them secretly with water, so that at the next halt they were found fuller than before!  This was considered a good omen, and little short of miraculous.

On the first day we did not intend to ascend to any great height, and we mounted, accordingly, very leisurely.  Before twelve o'clock we had found a good position for the tent, at a height of 11,000 feet.  We passed the remaining hours of daylight — some basking in the sunshine, some sketching, some collecting; Hudson made tea, I coffee, and at length we retired, each one to his blanket-bag.

We assembled together before dawn on the 14th and started directly it was light enough to move. One of the young Taugwalders returned to Zermatt. In a few minutes we turned the rib which had intercepted the view of the Eastern face from our tent platform.  The whole of this great slope was now revealed, rising for 3,000 feet like a huge natural staircase.  Some parts were more, and others were less easy, but we were not once brought to a halt by any serious impediment, for when an obstruction was met in front it could always be turned to the right or to the left.  For the greater part of the way there was no occasion, indeed, for the rope, and sometimes Hudson led, sometimes myself.

At 6.20 we had attained a height of 12,800 feet, and halted for half an hour; we then continued the ascent without a break until 9.55, when we stopped for fifty minutes, at a height of 14,000 feet.

We had now arrived at the foot of that part which, seen from the Riffelberg, seems perpendicular or overhanging. We could no longer continue on the eastern side. For a little distance we ascended by snow upon the *arête* — that is, the ridge — then turned over to the right, or northern side. The work became difficult, and required caution. In some places there was little to hold; the general slope of the mountain was *less* than 40 degrees, and snow had accumulated in, and had filled up, the interstices of the rock-face, leaving only occasional fragments projecting here and there. These were at times covered with a thin film of ice. It was a place which any fair mountaineer might pass in safety. We bore away nearly horizontally for about 400 feet, then ascended directly toward the summit for about sixty feet, then doubled back to the ridge which descends toward Zermatt. A long stride round a rather awkward corner brought us to snow once more. The last doubt vanished! The Matterhorn was ours! Nothing but 200 feet of easy snow remained to be surmounted.

The higher we rose, the more intense became the excitement. The slope eased off, at length we could be detached, and Croz and I, dashing away, ran a

neck-and-neck race, which ended in a dead heat.
At 1.40 P. M., the world was at our feet, and the
Matterhorn was conquered!

The others arrived. Croz now took the tent-pole,
and planted it in the highest snow. "Yes," we
said, "there is the flag-staff, but where is the
flag?" "Here it is," he answered, pulling off his
blouse and fixing it to the stick. It made a poor
flag, and there was no wind to float it out, yet it
was seen all around. They saw it at Zermatt — at
the Riffel — in the Val Tournanche. . . .

We remained on the summit for one hour—

"One crowded hour of glorious life."

It passed away too quickly, and we began to
prepare for the descent.

Hudson and I consulted as to the best and safest
arrangement of the party. We agreed that it was
best for Croz to go first, and Hadow second; Hudson, who was almost equal to a guide in sureness of
foot, wished to be third; Lord Douglas was placed
next, and old Peter, the strongest of the remainder,
after him. I suggested to Hudson that we should
attach a rope to the rocks on our arrival at the
difficult bit, and hold it as we descended, as an
additional protection. He approved the idea, but it
was not definitely decided that it should be done.
The party was being arranged in the above order
whilst I was sketching the summit, and they had
finished, and were waiting for me to be tied in line,
when some one remembered that our names had not

been left in a bottle. They requested me to write them down, and moved off while it was being done.

A few minutes afterward I tied myself to young Peter, ran down after the others, and caught them just as they were commencing the descent of the difficult part. Great care was being taken. Only one man was moving at a time; when he was firmly planted the next advanced, and so on. They had not, however, attached the additional rope to rocks, and nothing was said about it. The suggestion was not made for my own sake, and I am not sure that it even occurred to me again. For some little dis-tance we two followed the others, detached from them, and should have continued so had not Lord Douglas asked me, about 3 P.M., to tie on to old Peter, as he feared, he said, that Taugwalder would not be able to hold his ground if a slip occurred.

A few minutes later, a sharp-eyed lad ran into the Monte Rosa Hotel, at Zermatt, saying that he had seen an avalanche fall from the summit of the Mat-terhorn on to the Matterhorn glacier. The boy was reproved for telling idle stories; he was right, never-theless, and this was what he saw.

Michel Croz had laid aside his axe, and in order to give Mr. Hadow greater security, was absolutely taking hold of his legs, and putting his feet, one by one, into their proper positions. As far as I know, no one was actually descending. I cannot speak with certainty, because the two leading men were partially hidden from my sight by an intervening

mass of rock, but it is my belief, from the movements of their shoulders, that Croz, having done as
I have said, was in the act of turning round to go
down a step or two himself; at this moment Mr.
Hadow slipped, fell against him, and knocked him
over. I heard one startled exclamation from Croz,
then saw him and Mr. Hadow flying downwards; in
another moment Hudson was dragged from his
steps, and Lord Douglas immediately after him.
All this was the work of a moment. Immediately
we heard Croz's exclamation, old Peter and I
planted ourselves as firmly as the rocks would permit; the rope was taut between us, and the jerk
came on us both as on one man. We held; but
the rope broke midway between Taugwalder and
Lord Francis Douglas. For a few seconds we saw
our unfortunate companions sliding downwards on
their backs, and spreading out their hands, endeavor-
ing to save themselves. They passed from our
sight uninjured, disappeared one by one, and fell
from precipice to precipice on to the Matterhorn
glacier below, a distance of nearly 4,000 feet in
height. From the moment the rope broke it was
impossible to help them. So perished our comrades!

. . . . . .

For more than two hours afterwards I thought
almost every moment that the next would be my
last; for the Taugwalders, utterly unnerved, were
not only incapable of giving assistance, but were in
such a state that a slip might have been expected

from them at any moment. After a time we were able to do that which should have been done at first, and fixed rope to firm rocks, in addition to being tied together. These ropes were cut from time to time, and were left behind. Even with their assurance the men were afraid to proceed, and several times old Peter turned, with ashy face and faltering limbs, and said, with terrible emphasis, "*I cannot!*"

About 6 P. M., we arrived at the snow upon the ridge descending towards Zermatt, and all peril was over. We frequently looked, but in vain, for traces of our unfortunate companions; we bent over the ridge and cried to them, but no sound returned. Convinced at last that they were neither within sight nor hearing, we ceased from our useless efforts; and, too cast down for speech, silently gathered up our things, and the little effects of those who were lost, and then completed the descent.

———

Such is Mr. Whymper's graphic and thrilling narrative. Zermatt gossip darkly hints that the elder Taugwalder cut the rope, when the accident occurred, in order to preserve himself from being dragged into the abyss; but Mr. Whymper says that the ends of the rope showed no evidence of cutting, but only of breaking. He adds that if Taugwalder had had the disposition to cut the rope, he would not have had time to do it, the accident was so sudden and unexpected.

Lord Douglas' body has never been found. It

probably lodged upon some inaccessible shelf in the face of the mighty precipice. Lord Douglas was a youth of nineteen. The three other victims fell nearly 4,000 feet, and their bodies lay together upon the glacier when found by Mr. Whymper and the other searchers the next morning. Their graves are beside the little church in Zermatt.

# CHAPTER XIII.

SWITZERLAND is simply a large, humpy, solid rock, with a thin skin of grass stretched over it. Consequently, they do not dig graves, they blast them out with powder and fuse. They cannot afford to have large graveyards, the grass skin is too circumscribed and too valuable. It is all required for the support of the living.

The graveyard in Zermatt occupies only about one-eighth of an acre. The graves are sunk in the living rock, and are very permanent; but occupation of them is only temporary; the occupant can only stay till his grave is needed by a later subject, he is removed, then, for they do not bury one body on top of another. As I understand it, a family owns a grave, just as it owns a house. A man dies and leaves his house to his son,— and at the same time, this dead father succeeds to his own father's grave. He moves out of the house and into the grave, and his predecessor moves out of the grave and into the cellar of the chapel. I saw a black box lying in the churchyard, with skull and cross-bones painted on

12**                                    (173)

it, and was told that this was used in transferring remains to the cellar.

In that cellar the bones and skulls of several hundreds of former citizens were compactly corded up. They made a pile 18 feet long, 7 feet high, and 8 feet wide. I was told that in some of the receptacles of this kind in the Swiss villages, the skulls were all marked, and if a man wished to find the skulls of his ancestors for several generations back, he could do it by these marks, preserved in the family records.

An English gentleman who had lived some years in this region, said it was the cradle of compulsory education. But he said that the English idea that compulsory education would reduce bastardy and intemperance was an error — it has not that effect. He said there was more seduction in the Protestant than in the Catholic cantons, because the confessional protected the girls. I wonder why it doesn't protect married women in France and Spain?

This gentleman said that among the poorer peasants in the Valais, it was common for the brothers in a family to cast lots to determine which of them should have the coveted privilege of marrying. Then the lucky one got married, and his brethren — doomed bachelors, — heroically banded themselves together to help support the new family.

We left Zermatt in a wagon — and in a rainstorm, too, — for St. Nicholas about ten o'clock one morning. Again we passed between those grass-clad, prodigious cliffs, specked with wee dwellings peeping over at us from velvety green walls ten and twelve hundred feet high. It did not seem possible that the imaginary chamois even could climb those precipices. Lovers on opposite cliffs probably kiss through a spy-glass, and correspond with a rifle.

In Switzerland the farmer's plow is a wide shovel, which scrapes up and turns over the thin earthy skin of his native rock — and there the man of the plow is a hero. Now here, by our St. Nicholas road, was a grave, and it had a tragic story. A plowman was skinning his farm one morning,— not the steepest part of it, but still a steep part — that is, he was not skinning the front of his farm, but the roof of it, near the eaves,— when he absent-mindedly let go of the plow-handles to moisten his hands, in the usual way; he lost his balance and fell out of his farm backwards; poor fellow, he never touched anything till he struck bottom, 1,500 feet below.* We throw a halo of heroism around the life of the soldier and the sailor, because of the deadly dangers they are facing all the time. But we are not used to looking upon farming as a heroic occupation. This is because we have not lived in Switzerland.

From St. Nicholas we struck out for Visp,— or Vispach — on foot. The rain-storms had been at work during several days, and had done a deal of damage in Switzerland and Savoy. We came to

---

* This was on a Sunday.— M. T.

one place where a stream had changed its course and plunged down the mountain in a new place, sweeping everything before it. Two poor but precious farms by the roadside were ruined. One was washed clear away, and the bed-rock exposed; the other was buried out of sight under a tumbled chaos of rocks, gravel, mud, and rubbish. The resistless might of water was well exemplified. Some saplings which had stood in the way were bent to the ground, stripped clean of their bark, and buried under rocky débris. The road had been swept away, too.

In another place, where the road was high up on the mountain's face, and its outside edge protected by flimsy masonry, we frequently came across spots where this masonry had caved off and left dangerous gaps for mules to get over; and with still more frequency we found the masonry slightly crumbled, and marked by mule-hoofs, thus showing that there had been danger of an accident to somebody. When at last we came to a badly ruptured bit of masonry, with hoof-prints evidencing a desperate struggle to regain the lost foothold, I looked quite hopefully over the dizzy precipice. But there was nobody down there.

They take exceedingly good care of their rivers in Switzerland and other portions of Europe. They wall up both banks with slanting solid stone masonry —so that from end to end of these rivers the banks look like the wharves at St. Louis and other towns on the Mississippi river.

It was during this walk from St. Nicholas, in the shadow of the majestic Alps, that we came across some little children amusing themselves in what seemed, at first, a most odd and original way — but it wasn't; it was in simply a natural and character-istic way. They were roped together with a string, they had mimic alpenstocks and ice-axes, and were climbing a meek and lowly manure pile with a most blood-curdling amount of care and caution. The "guide" at the head of the line cut imaginary steps, in a laborious and painstaking way, and not a monkey budged till the step above him was vacated. If we had waited we should have witnessed an imaginary accident, no doubt; and we should have heard the intrepid band hurrah when they made the summit and looked around upon the "magnificent view," and seen them throw themselves down in exhausted attitudes for a rest in that commanding situation.

In Nevada I used to see the children play at silver mining. Of course, the great thing was an accident in a mine, and there were two "star" parts; that of the man who fell down the mimic shaft, and that of the daring hero who was lowered into the depths to bring him up. I knew one small chap who always insisted on playing *both* of these parts,— and he carried his point. He would tumble into the shaft and die, and then come to the surface and go back after his own remains.

It is the smartest boy that gets the hero-part
12**

everywhere; he is head guide in Switzerland, head
miner in Nevada, head bull-fighter in Spain, etc.;
but I knew a preacher's son, seven years old, who
once selected a part for himself compared to which
those just mentioned are tame and unimpressive.
Jimmy's father stopped him from driving imaginary
horse-cars one Sunday — stopped him from playing
captain of an imaginary steamboat next Sunday —
stopped him from leading an imaginary army to
battle the following Sunday — and so on. Finally
the little fellow said:

" I've tried everything, and they won't any of
them do. What *can* I play?"

" I hardly know, Jimmy; but you *must* play
only things that are suitable to the Sabbath day."

Next Sunday the preacher stepped softly to a
back-room door to see if the children were rightly
employed. He peeped in. A chair occupied the
middle of the room, and on the back of it hung
Jimmy's cap; one of the little sisters took the cap
down, nibbled at it, then passed it to another small
sister and said, " Eat of this fruit, for it is good."
The Reverend took in the situation — alas, they were
playing the Expulsion from Eden! Yet he found
one little crumb of comfort. He said to himself,
" For once Jimmy has yielded the chief rôle — I
have been wronging him, I did not believe there was
so much modesty in him; I should have expected
him to be either Adam or Eve." This crumb of
comfort lasted but a very little while; he glanced

around and discovered Jimmy standing in an imposing attitude in a corner, with a dark and deadly
frown on his face. What that meant was very plain
— *he was personating the Deity!* Think of the
guileless sublimity of that idea.

We reached Vispach at 8 P.M., only about seven
hours out from St. Nicholas. So we must have
made fully a mile and a half an hour, and it was all
down hill, too, and very muddy at that. We stayed
all night at the Hôtel du Soleil; I remember it because the landlady, the portier, the waitress, and the
chambermaid were not separate persons, but were
all contained in one neat and chipper suit of spotless
muslin, and she was the prettiest young creature I
saw in all that region. She was the landlord's
daughter. And I remember that the only native
match to her I saw in all Europe was the young
daughter of the landlord of a village inn in the Black
Forest. Why don't more people in Europe marry
and keep hotel?

Next morning we left with a family of English
friends and went by train to Brevet, and thence by
boat across the lake to Ouchy (Lausanne).

Ouchy is memorable to me, not on account of its
beautiful situation and lovely surroundings,— although these would make it stick long in one's
memory,— but as the place where I caught the
London *Times* dropping into humor. It was not
aware of it, though. It did not do it on purpose.
An English friend called my attention to this lapse,

and cut out the reprehensible paragraph for me. Think of encountering a grin like this on the face of that grim journal:

ERRATUM.— We are requested by Reuter's Telegram Company to correct an erroneous announcement made in their Brisbane telegram of the 2d inst., published in our impression of the 5th inst., stating that "Lady Kennedy had given birth to twins, the eldest being a son." The Company explain that the message they received contained the words "Governor of Queensland, *twins first son*." Being, however, subsequently informed that Sir Arthur Kennedy was unmarried and that there must be some mistake, a telegraphic repetition was at once demanded. It has been received to-day (11th inst.) and shows that the words really telegraphed by Reuter's agent were "Governor Queensland *turns first sod*," alluding to the Maryborough-Gympic Railway in course of construction. The words in italics were mutilated by the telegraph in transmission from Australia, and reaching the company in the form mentioned above gave rise to the mistake.

I had always had a deep and reverent compassion for the sufferings of the " prisoner of Chillon," whose story Byron has told in such moving verse; so I took the steamer and made pilgrimage to the dungeons of the Castle of Chillon, to see the place where poor Bonnivard endured his dreary captivity 300 years ago. I am glad I did that, for it took away some of the pain I was feeling on the prisoner's account. His dungeon was a nice, cool, roomy place, and I cannot see why he should have been so dissatisfied with it. If he had been imprisoned in a St. Nicholas private dwelling, where the fertilizer prevails, and the goat sleeps with the guest, and the chickens roost on him, and the cow comes in and bothers him when he wants to muse, it would have been another matter altogether; but he surely could

not have had a very cheerless time of it in that
pretty dungeon. It has romantic window-slits that
let in generous bars of light, and it has tall, noble
columns, carved apparently from the living rock;
and what is more, they are written all over with
thousands of names; some of them,— like Byron's
and Victor Hugo's — of the first celebrity. Why
didn't he amuse himself reading these names?
Then there are the couriers and tourists — swarms
of them every day — what was to hinder him from
having a good time with them? I think Bonnivard's
sufferings have been overrated.

Next, we took the train and went to Martigny, on
the way to Mont Blanc. Next morning we started,
about eight o'clock, on foot. We had plenty of
company, in the way of wagon-loads and mule-loads
of tourists — and dust. This scattering procession
of travelers was perhaps a mile long. The road was
up hill — interminably up hill,— and tolerably steep.
The weather was blistering hot, and the man or
woman who had to sit on a creeping mule, or in a
crawling wagon, and broil in the beating sun, was
an object to be pitied. We could dodge among the
bushes, and have the relief of shade, but those
people could not. They paid for a conveyance, and
to get their money's worth they rode.

We went by the way of the Tête Noir, and after
we reached high ground there was no lack of fine
scenery. In one place the road was tunneled
through a shoulder of the mountain; from there

one looked down into a gorge with a rushing torrent
in it, and on every hand was a charming view of
rocky buttresses and wooded heights. There was a
liberal allowance of pretty waterfalls, too, on the
Tête Noir route.

About half an hour before we reached the village
of Argentière a vast dome of snow with the sun
blazing on it drifted into view and framed itself in a
strong V-shaped gateway of the mountains, and we
recognized Mont Blanc, the "monarch of the Alps."
With every step, after that, this stately dome rose
higher and higher into the blue sky, and at last
seemed to occupy the zenith.

Some of Mont Blanc's neighbors — bare, light-
brown, steeple-like rocks, — were very peculiarly
shaped. Some were whittled to a sharp point, and
slightly bent at the upper end, like a lady's finger;
one monster sugar-loaf resembled a bishop's hat; it
was too steep to hold snow on its sides, but had
some in the division.

While we were still on very high ground, and
before the descent toward Argentière began, we
looked up toward a neighboring mountain-top, and
saw exquisite prismatic colors playing about some
white clouds which were so delicate as to almost
resemble gossamer webs. The faint pinks and
greens were peculiarly beautiful; none of the colors
were deep, they were the lightest shades. They
were bewitchingly commingled. We sat down to
study and enjoy this singular spectacle. The tints

remained during several minutes — flitting, changing, melting into each other; paling almost away for a moment, then re-flushing,— a shifting, restless, unstable succession of soft opaline gleams, shimmering over that airy film of white cloud, and turning it into a fabric dainty enough to clothe an angel with.

By and by we perceived what those super-delicate colors, and their continuous play and movement, reminded us of; it is what one sees in a soap-bubble that is drifting along, catching changes of tint from the objects it passes. A soap-bubble is the most beautiful thing, and the most exquisite, in nature; that lovely phantom fabric in the sky was suggestive of a soap-bubble split open, and spread out in the sun. I wonder how much it would take to buy a soap-bubble, if there was only one in the world? One could buy a hatful of Koh-i-Noors with the same money, no doubt.

We made the tramp from Martigny to Argentière in eight hours. We beat all the mules and wagons; we didn't usually do that. We hired a sort of open baggage-wagon for the trip down the valley to Chamonix, and then devoted an hour to dining. This gave the driver time to get drunk. He had a friend with him, and this friend also had had time to get drunk.

When we drove off, the driver said all the tourists had arrived and gone by while we were at dinner: but," said he, impressively, " be not disturbed

by that — remain tranquil — give yourselves no uneasiness — their dust rises far before us, you shall
see it fade and disappear far behind us — rest you
tranquil, leave all to me — I am the king of drivers.
Behold!"

Down came his whip, and away we clattered. I
never had such a shaking up in my life. The recent
flooding rains had washed the road clear away in
places, but we never stopped, we never slowed
down for anything. We tore right along, over
rocks, rubbish, gullies, open fields — sometimes
with one or two wheels on the ground, but generally
with none. Every now and then that calm, good-
natured madman would bend a majestic look over
his shoulder at us and say, "Ah, you perceive? It
is as I have said — I am the king of drivers."
Every time we just missed going to destruction, he
would say, with tranquil happiness, "Enjoy it,
gentlemen, it is very rare, it is very unusual — it is
given to few to ride with the king of drivers — and
observe, it is as I have said, *I* am he."

He spoke in French, and punctuated with hic-
coughs. His friend was French, too, but spoke in
German — using the same system of punctuation,
however. The friend called himself the "Captain
of Mont Blanc," and wanted us to make the ascent
with him. He said he had made more ascents than
any other man, — forty-seven, — and his brother had
made thirty-seven. His brother was the best guide
in the world, except himself — but he, yes, observe

him well,— he was the " Captain of Mont Blanc "—
that title belonged to none other.

The " king " was as good as his word — he overtook that long procession of tourists and went by it
like a hurricane.  The result was that we got choicer
rooms at the hotel in Chamonix than we should have
done if his majesty had been a slower artist — or
rather, if he hadn't most providentially got drunk
before he left Argentière.

# CHAPTER XIV.

EVERYBODY was out of doors; everybody was in the principal street of the village,— not on the sidewalks, but all over the street; everybody was lounging, loafing, chatting, waiting, alert, expectant, interested,— for it was train-time. That is to say, it was diligence-time,— the half dozen big diligences would soon be arriving from Geneva, and the village was interested, in many ways, in knowing how many people were coming and what sort of folk they might be. It was altogether the livest looking street we had seen in any village on the continent.

The hotel was by the side of a booming torrent, whose music was loud and strong; we could not see this torrent, for it was dark, now, but one could locate it without a light. There was a large enclosed yard in front of the hotel, and this was filled with groups of villagers waiting to see the diligences arrive, or to hire themselves to excursionists for the morrow. A telescope stood in the yard, with its huge barrel canted up toward the lustrous evening star. The long porch of the hotel was populous with tourists, who sat in shawls and wraps under the

vast overshadowing bulk of Mont Blanc, and gos-
siped or meditated.

Never did a mountain seem so close; its big sides
seemed at one's very elbow, and its majestic dome,
and the lofty cluster of slender minarets that were its
neighbors, seemed to be almost over one's head.    It
was night in the streets, and the lamps were sparkling
everywhere; the broad bases and shoulders of the
mountains were in a deep gloom, but their summits
swam in a strange rich glow which was really daylight, and yet had a mellow something about it which
was very different from the hard white glare of the
kind of daylight I was used to.    Its radiance was
strong and clear, but at the same time it was singularly soft, and spiritual, and benignant.    No, it was
not our harsh, aggressive, realistic daylight; it
seemed properer to an enchanted land — or to
heaven.

I had seen moonlight and daylight together before,
but I had not seen daylight and black night elbow to
elbow before.    At least I had not seen the daylight
resting upon an object sufficiently close at hand, before, to make the contrast startling and at war with
nature.

The daylight passed away.    Presently the moon
rose up behind some of those sky-piercing fingers or
pinnacles of bare rock of which I have spoken —
they were a little to the left of the crest of Mont
Blanc, and right over our heads, — but she couldn't
manage to climb high enough toward heaven to get

entirely above them. She would show the glittering
arch of her upper third, occasionally, and scrape it
along behind the comb-like row; sometimes a pinnacle stood straight up, like a statuette of ebony,
against that glittering white shield, then seemed to
glide out of it by its own volition and power, and
become a dim specter, while the next pinnacle
glided into its place and blotted the spotless disk
with the black exclamation point of its presence.
The top of one pinnacle took the shapely, clean-cut
form of a rabbit's head, in the inkiest silhouette,
while it rested against the moon. The unillumined
peaks and minarets, hovering vague and phantom-
like above us while the others were painfully white
and strong with snow and moonlight, made a
peculiar effect.

But when the moon, having passed the line of
pinnacles, was hidden behind the stupendous white
swell of Mont Blanc, the masterpiece of the evening
was flung on the canvas. A rich greenish radiance
sprang into the sky from behind the mountain, and
in this some airy shreds and ribbons of vapor floated
about, and being flushed with that strange tint, went
waving to and fro like pale green flames. After a
while, radiating bars,— vast broadening fan-shaped
shadows,— grew up and stretched away to the zenith
from behind the mountain. It was a spectacle to
take one's breath, for the wonder of it, and the
sublimity.

Indeed, those mighty bars of alternate light and

shadow streaming up from behind that dark and prodigious form and occupying the half of the dull and
opaque heavens, was the most imposing and impressive marvel I had ever looked upon.    There is no
simile for it, for nothing is like it.    If a child had
asked me what it was, I should have said, " Humble
yourself, in this presence, it is the glory flowing from
the hidden head of the Creator."    One falls shorter
of the truth than that, sometimes, in trying to explain mysteries to the little people.    I could have
found out the cause of this awe-compelling miracle
by inquiring, for it is not infrequent at Mont Blanc,
—but I did not wish to know.    We have not the
reverent feeling for the rainbow that a savage has,
because we know how it is made.    We have lost as
much as we gained by prying into that matter.

We took a walk down street, a block or two, and
at a place where four streets met and the principal
shops were clustered, found the groups of men in
the roadway thicker than ever — for this was the
Exchange of Chamonix.    These men were in the
costumes of guides and porters, and were there to
be hired.

The office of that great personage, the Guide-in-
Chief of the Chamonix Guild of Guides, was near
by.    This guild is a close corporation, and is gov-
erned by strict laws.    There are many excursion
routes, some dangerous and some not, some that can
be made safely without a guide, and some that cannot.    The bureau determines these things.    Where
13**

it decides that a guide is necessary, you are forbidden to go without one. Neither are you allowed to be a victim of extortion: the law states what you are to pay. The guides serve in rotation; you cannot select the man who is to take your life into his hands, you must take the worst in the lot, if it is his turn. A guide's fee ranges all the way up from a half dollar (for some trifling excursion of a few rods) to twenty dollars, according to the distance traversed and the nature of the ground. A guide's fee for taking a person to the summit of Mont Blanc and back, is twenty dollars — and he earns it. The time employed is usually three days, and there is enough early rising in it to make a man far more "healthy and wealthy and wise" than any one man has any right to be. The porter's fee for the same trip is ten dollars. Several fools,— no, I mean several tourists,— usually go together, and divide up the expense, and thus make it light; for if only one f— tourist, I mean — went, he would have to have several guides and porters, and that would make the matter costly.

We went into the Chief's office. There were maps of mountains on the walls; also one or two lithographs of celebrated guides, and a portrait of the scientist De Saussure.

In glass cases were some labeled fragments of boots and batons, and other suggestive relics and remembrancers of casualties on Mont Blanc. In a book was a record of all the ascents which have ever been made, beginning with Nos. 1 and 2,—being those of Jacques Balmat and De Saussure, in 1787, and ending with No. 685, which wasn't cold yet. In fact No. 685 was standing by the official table waiting to receive the precious official diploma which should prove to his German household and to his descendants that he had once been indiscreet enough to climb to the top of Mont Blanc. He looked very happy when he got his document; in fact, he spoke up and said he *was* happy.

I tried to buy a diploma for an invalid friend at home who had never traveled, and whose desire all his life has been to ascend Mont Blanc, but the Guide-in-Chief rather insolently refused to sell me one. I was very much offended. I said I did not propose to be discriminated against on account of my nationality; that he had just sold a diploma to this German gentleman, and my money was as good as his; I would see to it that he couldn't keep shop for Germans and deny his produce to Americans; I would have his license taken away from him at the dropping of a handkerchief; if France refused to break him, I would make an international matter of it and bring on a war; the soil should be drenched with blood; and not only that, but I would set up an opposition shop and sell diplomas at half price.

For two cents I would have done these things, too; but nobody offered me the two cents. I tried to move that German's feelings, but it could not be done; he would not give me his diploma, neither would he sell it to me. I *told* him my friend was sick and could not come himself, but he said he did not care a verdammtes pfennig, he wanted his diploma for himself — did I suppose he was going to risk his neck for that thing and then give it to a sick stranger? Indeed he wouldn't, so he wouldn't. I resolved, then, that I would do all I could to injure Mont Blanc.

In the record book was a list of all the fatal accidents which had happened on the mountain. It began with the one in 1820 when the Russian Dr. Hamel's three guides were lost in a crevasse of the glacier, and it recorded the delivery of the remains in the valley by the slow-moving glacier 41 years later. The latest catastrophe bore date 1877.

We stepped out and roved about the village a while. In front of the little church was a monument to the memory of the bold guide Jacques Balmat, the first man who ever stood upon the summit of Mont Blanc. He made that wild trip solitary and alone. He accomplished the ascent a number of times afterward. A stretch of nearly half a century lay between his first ascent and his last one. At the ripe old age of 72 he was climbing around a corner of a lofty precipice of the Pic du Midi — nobody with him — when he slipped and fell. So he died in the harness.

He had grown very avaricious in his old age, and used to go off stealthily to hunt for non-existent and impossible gold among those perilous peaks and

precipices.   He was on a quest of that kind when he
lost his life.   There was a statue to him, and another
to De Saussure, in the hall of our hotel, and a metal
plate on the door of a room up stairs bore an inscription to the effect that that room had been occupied
by Albert Smith.   Balmat and De Saussure discovered Mont Blanc — so to speak — but it was Smith
who made it a paying property.   His articles in
Blackwood and his lectures on Mont Blanc in
London advertised it and made people as anxious to
see it as if it owed them money.

As we strolled along the road we looked up and
saw a red signal light glowing in the darkness of the
mountain side.   It seemed but a trifling way up,—
perhaps a hundred yards, a climb of ten minutes.
It was a lucky piece of sagacity in us that we concluded to stop a man whom we met and get a light
for our pipes from him instead of continuing the
climb to that lantern to get a light, as had been our
purpose.   The man said that that lantern was on
the Grands Mulets, some 6,500 feet above the valley!
I know by our Riffelberg experience, that it would
have taken us a good part of a week to go up there.
I would sooner not smoke at all, than take all that
trouble for a light.

Even in the daytime the foreshortening effect of
this mountain's close proximity creates curious decep-
tions.   For instance, one sees with the naked eye a
cabin up there beside the glacier, and a little above
and beyond he sees the spot where that red light was

13.**

located; he thinks he could throw a stone from the one place to the other. But he couldn't, for the difference between the two altitudes is more than 3,000 feet. It looks impossible, from below, that this can be true, but it is true, nevertheless.

While strolling about, we kept the run of the moon all the time, and we still kept an eye on her after we got back to the hotel portico. I had a theory that the gravitation of refraction, being subsidiary to atmospheric compensation, the refrangibility of the earth's surface would emphasize this effect in regions where great mountain ranges occur, and possibly so even-handedly impact the odic and idyllic forces together, the one upon the other, as to prevent the moon from rising higher than 12,200 feet above sea level. This daring theory had been received with frantic scorn by some of my fellow-scientists, and with an eager silence by others. Among the former I may mention Prof. H———y; and among the latter Prof. T———l. Such is professional jealousy; a scientist will never show any kindness for a theory which he did not start himself. There is no feeling of brotherhood among these people. Indeed, they always resent it when I call them brother. To show how far their ungenerosity can carry them, I will state that I offered to let Prof. H———y publish my great theory as his own discovery; I even begged him to do it; I even proposed to print it myself as his theory. Instead of thanking me. he said that if I tried to fasten that theory on him he would sue me for slander. I was going to offer it to Mr. Darwin, whom I understood to be a man without prejudices, but it occurred to me that perhaps he would not be interested in it since it did not concern heraldry.

But I am glad, now, that I was forced to father my intrepid theory myself, for, on the night of which I am writing, it was triumphantly justified and established. Mont Blanc is nearly 16,000 feet high; he hid the moon utterly; near him is a peak which is 12,216 feet high; the moon slid along behind the pinnacles, and when she approached that one I watched her with intense interest, for my reputation as a scientist must stand or fall by its decision. I cannot describe the emotions which surged like tidal waves through my breast when I saw the moon glide behind that lofty needle and pass it by without exposing more than two feet four inches of her upper rim above it! I was secure, then. I knew she could rise no higher, and I was right. She sailed behind all the peaks and never succeeded in hoisting her disk above a single one of them.

While the moon was behind one of those sharp fingers, its shadow was flung athwart the vacant heavens — a long, slanting, clean-cut, dark ray — with a streaming and energetic suggestion of *force* about it, such as the ascending jet of water from a powerful fire engine affords. It was curious to see a good strong shadow of an earthly object cast upon so intangible a field as the atmosphere.

M*₂

We went to bed, at last, and went quickly to
sleep, but I woke up, after about three hours, with
throbbing temples, and a head which was physically
sore, outside and in. I was dazed, dreamy,
wretched, seedy, unrefreshed. I recognized the
occasion of all this: it was that torrent. In the
mountain villages of Switzerland, and along the
roads, one has always the roar of the torrent in his
ears. He imagines it is music, and he thinks poetic
things about it; he lies in his comfortable bed and
is lulled to sleep by it. But by and by he begins to
notice that his head is very sore — he cannot account
for it; in solitudes where the profoundest silence
reigns, he notices a sullen, distant, continuous roar
in his ears, which is like what he would experience
if he had sea shells pressed against them — he cannot
account for it; he is drowsy and absent-minded;
there is no tenacity to his mind, he cannot keep
hold of a thought and follow it out; if he sits down
to write, his vocabulary is empty, no suitable words
will come, he forgets what he started to do, and
remains there, pen in hand, head tilted up, eyes
closed, listening painfully to the muffled roar of a
distant train in his ears; in his soundest sleep the
strain continues, he goes on listening, always listening
intently, anxiously, and wakes at last, harassed, irritable, unrefreshed. He cannot manage to account
for these things. Day after day he feels as if he had
spent his nights in a sleeping car. It actually takes
him weeks to find out that it is those persecuting

torrents that have been making all the mischief. It is time for him to get out of Switzerland, then, for as soon as he has discovered the cause, the misery is magnified several fold. The roar of the torrent is maddening, then, for his imagination is assisting; the physical pain it inflicts is exquisite. When he finds he is approaching one of those streams, his dread is so lively that he is disposed to fly the track and avoid the implacable foe.

Eight or nine months after the distress of the torrents had departed from me, the roar and thunder of the streets of Paris brought it all back again. I moved to the sixth story of the hotel to hunt for peace. About midnight the noises dulled away, and I was sinking to sleep, when I heard a new and curious sound; I listened: evidently some joyous lunatic was softly dancing a "double shuffle" in the room over my head. I had to wait for him to get through, of course. Five long, long minutes he smoothly shuffled away — a pause followed, then something fell with a heavy thump on the floor. I said to myself "There — he is pulling off his boots — thank heavens he is done." Another slight pause — he went to shuffling again! I said to myself, "Is he trying to see what he can do with only one boot on?" Presently came another pause and another thump on the floor. I said "Good, he has pulled off his other boot — *now* he is done." But he wasn't. The next moment he was shuffling again. I said, "Confound him, he is at it in his slippers!"

After a little came that same old pause, and right
after it that thump on the floor once more. I said,
"Hang him, he had on *two* pair of boots!" For an
hour that magician went on shuffling and pulling off
boots till he had shed as many as twenty-five pair, and
I was hovering on the verge of lunacy. I got my
gun and stole up there. The fellow was in the midst
of an acre of sprawling boots, and he had a boot in
his hand, shuffling it — no I mean *polishing* it. The
mystery was explained. He hadn't been dancing.
He was the "Boots" of the hotel, and was attending to business.

# CHAPTER XV.

AFTER breakfast, that next morning in Chamonix, we went out in the yard and watched the gangs of excursionizing tourists arriving and departing with their mules and guides and porters; then we took a look through the telescope at the snowy hump of Mont Blanc. It was brilliant with sunshine, and the vast smooth bulge seemed hardly five hundred yards away. With the naked eye we could dimly make out the house at the Pierre Pointue, which is located by the side of the great glacier, and is more than 3,000 feet above the level of the valley; but with the telescope we could see all its details. While I looked, a woman rode by the house on a mule, and I saw her with sharp distinctness; I could have described her dress. I saw her nod to the people of the house, and rein up her mule, and put her hand up to shield her eyes from the sun. I was not used to telescopes; in fact, I had never looked through a good one before; it seemed incredible to me that this woman could be so far away. I was satisfied that I could see all these details with my naked eye; but when I tried it, that mule and those vivid people

(199)

had wholly vanished, and the house itself was become small and vague. I tried the telescope again,
and again everything was vivid. The strong black
shadows of the mule and the woman were flung
against the side of the house, and I saw the mule's
silhouette wave its ears.

The telescopulist,— or the telescopulariat,— I do
not know which is right,— said a party were making
a grand ascent, and would come in sight on the remote upper heights, presently; so we waited to observe this performance.

Presently I had a superb idea. I wanted to stand
with a party on the summit of Mont Blanc, merely
to be able to say I had done it, and I believed the
telescope could set me within seven feet of the
uppermost man. The telescoper assured me that it
could. I then asked him how much I owed him for
as far as I had got? He said, one franc. I asked
him how much it would cost me to make the entire
ascent? Three francs. I at once determined to
make the entire ascent. But first I inquired if there
was any danger? He said no,— not by telescope;
said he had taken a great many parties to the summit, and never lost a man. I asked what he would
charge to let my agent go with me, together with
such guides and porters as might be necessary? He
said he would let Harris go for two francs; and that
unless we were unusually timid, he should consider
guides and porters unnecessary; it was not customary
to take them, when going by telescope, for they were

rather an incumbrance than a help. He said that the party now on the mountain were approaching the most difficult part, and if we hurried we should overtake them within ten minutes, and could then join them and have the benefit of their guides and porters without their knowledge, and without expense to us.

I then said we would start immediately. I believe I said it calmly, though I was conscious of a shudder and of a paling cheek, in view of the nature of the exploit I was so unreflectingly engaging in. But the old dare-devil spirit was upon me, and I said that as I had committed myself I would not back down; I would ascend Mont Blanc if it cost me my life. I told the man to slant his machine in the proper direction and let us be off.

Harris was afraid and did not want to go, but I heartened him up and said I would hold his hand all the way; so he gave his consent, though he trembled a little at first. I took a last pathetic look upon the pleasant summer scene about me, then boldly put my eye to the glass and prepared to mount among the grim glaciers and the everlasting snows.

We took our way carefully and cautiously across the great Glacier des Bossons, over yawning and terrific crevasses and amongst imposing crags and buttresses of ice which were fringed with icicles of gigantic proportions. The desert of ice that stretched far and wide about us was wild and

desolate beyond description, and the perils which
beset us were so great that at times I was minded to
turn back. But I pulled my pluck together and
pushed on.

We passed the glacier safely and began to mount
the steeps beyond, with great celerity. When we
were seven minutes out from the starting point, we
reached an altitude where the scene took a new
aspect; an apparently limitless continent of gleaming snow was tilted heavenward before our faces.
As my eye followed that awful acclivity far away up
into the remote skies, it seemed to me that all I had
ever seen before of sublimity and magnitude was
small and insignificant compared to this.

We rested a moment, and then began to mount
with speed. Within three minutes we caught sight
of the party ahead of us, and stopped to observe
them. They were toiling up a long, slanting ridge
of snow — twelve persons, roped together some
fifteen feet apart, marching in single file, and strongly
marked against the clear blue sky. One was a
woman. We could see them lift their feet and put
them down; we saw them swing their alpenstocks
forward in unison, like so many pendulums, and
then bear their weight upon them; we saw the lady
wave her handkerchief. They dragged themselves
upward in a worn and weary way, for they had been
climbing steadily from the Grands Mulets, on the
Glacier des Bossons, since three in the morning, and
it was eleven, now. We saw them sink down in the

snow and rest, and drink something from a bottle.
After a while they moved on, and as they approached
the final short dash of the home-stretch we closed up
on them and joined them.

Presently we all stood together on the summit!
What a view was spread out below! Away off under
the northwestern horizon rolled the silent billows of
the Farnese Oberland, their snowy crests glinting
softly in the subdued lights of distance; in the north
rose the giant form of the Wobblehorn, draped from
peak to shoulder in sable thunder-clouds; beyond
him, to the right, stretched the grand processional
summits of the Cisalpine Cordillera, drowned in a
sensuous haze; to the east loomed the colossal
masses of the Yodelhorn, the Fuddlehorn, and the
Dinnerhorn, their cloudless summits flashing white
and cold in the sun; beyond them shimmered the
faint far line of the Ghauts of Jubbelpore and the
Aiguilles des Alleghenies; in the south towered the
smoking peak of Popocatapetl and the unapproachable altitudes of the peerless Scrabblehorn; in the
west-southwest the stately range of the Himalayas
lay dreaming in a purple gloom; and thence all
around the curving horizon the eye roved over a
troubled sea of sun-kissed Alps, and noted, here and
there, the noble proportions and soaring domes of
the Bottlehorn, and the Saddlehorn, and the Shovel-
horn, and the Powderhorn, all bathed in the glory of
noon and mottled with softly-gliding blots, the
shadows flung from drifting clouds.

Overcome by the scene, we all raised a triumphant, tremendous shout, in unison. A startled man at my elbow said:

" Confound you, what do you yell like that for, right here in the street? "

That brought me down to Chamonix, like a flirt. I gave that man some spiritual advice and disposed of him, and then paid the telescope man his full fee, and said that we were charmed with the trip and would remain down, and not re-ascend and require him to fetch us down by telescope. This pleased him very much, for of course we could have stepped back to the summit and put him to the trouble of bringing us home if we had wanted to.

I judged we could get diplomas, now, anyhow; so we went after them, but the Chief Guide put us off, with one pretext or another, during all the time we staid in Chamonix, and we ended by never getting them at all. So much for his prejudice against people's nationality. However, we worried him enough to make him remember us and our ascent for some time. He even said, once, that he wished there was a lunatic asylum in Chamonix. This shows that he really had fears that we were going to drive him mad. It was what we intended to do, but lack of time defeated it.

I cannot venture to advise the reader one way or the other, as to ascending Mont Blanc. I say only this: if he is at all timid, the enjoyments of the trip will hardly make up for the hardships and sufferings he will have to endure. But if he has good nerve, youth, health, and a bold, firm will, and could leave his family comfortably provided for in case the worst happened, he would find the ascent a wonderful experience, and the view from the top a vision to dream about, and tell about, and recall with exultation all the days of his life.

While I do not advise such a person to attempt the ascent, I do not advise him against it. But if he elects to attempt it, let him be warily careful of two things: choose a calm, clear day; and do not pay the telescope man in advance. There are dark stories of his getting advance payers on the summit and then leaving them there to rot.

A frightful tragedy was once witnessed through the Chamonix telescopes. Think of questions and answers like these, on an inquest:

*Coroner.* You saw deceased lose his life?

*Witness.* I did.

*C.* Where was he, at the time?

*W.* Close to the summit of Mont Blanc.

*C.* Where were you?

*W.* In the main street of Chamonix.

*C.* What was the distance between you?

*W. A little over five miles,* as the bird flies.

This accident occurred in 1866, a year and a month after the disaster on the Matterhorn. Three adventurous English gentlemen,* of great experience in mountain climbing, made up their minds to ascend

---

* Sir George Young and his brothers James and Albert.

14**

Mont Blanc without guides or porters. All en-
deavors to dissuade them from their project failed.
Powerful telescopes are numerous in Chamonix.
These huge brass tubes, mounted on their scaffold-
ings and pointing skyward from every choice vantage-
ground, have the formidable look of artillery, and
give the town the general aspect of getting ready to
repel a charge of angels. The reader may easily
believe that the telescopes had plenty of custom on
that August morning in 1866, for everybody knew
of the dangerous undertaking which was on foot,
and all had fears that misfortune would result. All
the morning the tubes remained directed toward the
mountain heights, each with its anxious group
around it; but the white deserts were vacant.

At last, toward eleven o'clock, the people who
were looking through the telescopes cried out
"There they are!"— and sure enough, far up, on
the loftiest terraces of the Grand Plateau, the three
pygmies appeared, climbing with remarkable vigor
and spirit. They disappeared in the "Corridor,"
and were lost to sight during an hour. Then they
reappeared, and were presently seen standing together
upon the extreme summit of Mont Blanc. So far,
all was well. They remained a few minutes on that
highest point of land in Europe, a target for all the
telescopes, and were then seen to begin the descent.
Suddenly all three vanished. An instant after, they
appeared again, *two thousand feet below!*

Evidently, they had tripped and been shot down

an almost perpendicular slope of ice to a point where it joined the border of the upper glacier. Naturally, the distant witnesses supposed they were now looking upon three corpses; so they could hardly believe their eyes when they presently saw two of the men rise to their feet and bend over the third. During two hours and a half they watched the two busying themselves over the extended form of their brother, who seemed entirely inert. Chamonix's affairs stood still; everybody was in the street, all interest was centered upon what was going on upon that lofty and isolated stage five miles away. Finally the two,—one of them walking with great difficulty,—were seen to begin the descent, abandoning the third, who was no doubt lifeless. Their movements were followed, step by step, until they reached the "Corridor" and disappeared behind its ridge. Before they had had time to traverse the "Corridor" and reappear, twilight was come, and the power of the telescope was at an end.

The survivors had a most perilous journey before them in the gathering darkness, for they must get down to the Grands Mulets before they would find a safe stopping place — a long and tedious descent, and perilous enough even in good daylight. The oldest guides expressed the opinion that they could not succeed; that all the chances were that they would lose their lives.

Yet those brave men did succeed. They reached the Grands Mulets in safety. Even the fearful shock

which their nerves had sustained was not sufficient
to overcome their coolness and courage. It would
appear from the official account that they were
threading their way down through those dangers
from the closing in of twilight until 2 o'clock in the
morning, or later, because the rescuing party from
Chamonix reached the Grands Mulets about 3 in the
morning and moved thence toward the scene of the
disaster under the leadership of Sir George Young,
" who had only just arrived."

After having been on his feet twenty-four hours,
in the exhausting work of mountain climbing, Sir
George began the re-ascent at the head of the relief
party of six guides, to recover the corpse of his
brother. This was considered a new imprudence,
as the number was too few for the service required.
Another relief party presently arrived at the cabin
on the Grands Mulets and quartered themselves
there to await events. Ten hours after Sir George's
departure toward the summit, this new relief were still
scanning the snowy altitudes above them from their
own high perch among the ice deserts 10,000 feet
above the level of the sea, but the whole forenoon
had passed without a glimpse of any living thing
appearing up there.

This was alarming. Half a dozen of their number
set out, then early in the afternoon, to seek and succor
Sir George and his guides. The persons remaining
at the cabin saw these disappear, and then ensued
another distressing wait. Four hours passed, with-

out tidings. Then at 5 o'clock another relief, con-
sisting of three guides, set forward from the cabin.
They carried food and cordials for the refreshment
of their predecessors; they took lanterns with them,
too; night was coming on, and to make matters
worse, a fine, cold rain had begun to fall.

At the same hour that these three began their
dangerous ascent, the official Guide-in-Chief of the
Mont Blanc region undertook the dangerous descent
to Chamonix, all alone, to get reinforcements.
However, a couple of hours later, at 7 P. M., the
anxious solicitude came to an end, and happily. A
bugle note was heard, and a cluster of black specks
was distinguishable against the snows of the upper
heights. The watchers counted these specks eagerly
— 14, — nobody was missing. An hour and a half
later they were all safe under the roof of the cabin.
They had brought the corpse with them. Sir
George Young tarried there but a few minutes, and
then began the long and troublesome descent from
the cabin to Chamonix. He probably reached there
about 2 or 3 o'clock in the morning, after having
been afoot among the rocks and glaciers during two
days and two nights. His endurance was equal to
his daring.

The cause of the unaccountable delay of Sir George
and the relief parties among the heights where the
disaster had happened was a thick fog — or, partly
that and partly the slow and difficult work of convey-
ing the dead body down the perilous steeps.

14**

The corpse, upon being viewed at the inquest, showed no bruises, and it was some time before the surgeons discovered that the neck was broken. One of the surviving brothers had sustained some unimportant injuries, but the other had suffered no hurt at all. How these men could fall 2,000 feet, almost perpendicularly, and live afterward, is a most strange and unaccountable thing.

A great many women have made the ascent of Mont Blanc. An English girl, Miss Stratton, conceived the daring idea, two or three years ago, of attempting the ascent in the middle of winter. She tried it — and she succeeded. Moreover, she froze two of her fingers on the way up, she fell in love with her guide on the summit, and she married him when she got to the bottom again. There is nothing in romance, in the way of a striking " situation," which can beat this love scene in mid-heaven on an isolated ice-crest with the thermometer at zero and an Arctic gale blowing.

The first woman who ascended Mont Blanc was a girl aged 22 — Mlle. Maria Paradis — 1809. Nobody was with her but her sweetheart, and he was not a guide. The sex then took a rest for about 30 years, when a Mlle. d'Angeville made the ascent — 1838. In Chamonix I picked up a rude old lithograph of that day which pictured her " in the act."

However, I value it less as a work of art than as a fashion plate. Miss d'Angeville put on a pair of men's pantaloons to climb in, which was wise; but she cramped their utility by adding her petticoat, which was idiotic.

One of the mournfulest calamities which men's disposition to climb dangerous mountains has resulted in, happened on Mont Blanc in September, 1870. M. D'Arve tells the story briefly in his "Histoire du Mont Blanc." In the next chapter I will copy its chief features.

# CHAPTER XVI.

## A CATASTROPHE WHICH COST ELEVEN LIVES

ON the 5th of September, 1870, a caravan of eleven persons departed from Chamonix to make the ascent of Mont Blanc. Three of the party were tourists: Messrs. Randall and Bean, Americans, and Mr. George Corkindale, a Scotch gentleman; there were three guides and five porters. The cabin on the Grands Mulets was reached that day; the ascent was resumed early the next morning, September 6. The day was fine and clear, and the movements of the party were observed through the telescopes of Chamonix; at two o'clock in the afternoon they were seen to reach the summit. A few minutes later they were seen making the first steps of the descent; then a cloud closed around them and hid them from view.

Eight hours passed, the cloud still remained, night came, no one had returned to the Grands Mulets. Sylvain Couttet, keeper of the cabin there, suspected a misfortune, and sent down to the valley for help. A detachment of guides went up, but by the time they had made the tedious trip and reached the cabin, a raging storm had set in. They had to wait; nothing could be attempted in such a tempest.

The wild storm lasted *more than a week*, without ceasing; but on the 17th, Couttet, with several guides, left the cabin and succeeded in making the ascent. In the snowy wastes near the summit they came upon five bodies, lying upon their sides in a reposeful attitude which suggested that possibly they had fallen asleep there, while exhausted with fatigue and hunger and benumbed with cold, and never knew when death stole upon them. Couttet moved a few steps further and discovered five more bodies. The eleventh corpse,— that of a porter,— was not found, although diligent search was made for it.

In the pocket of Mr. Bean, one of the Americans, was found a note-book in which had been penciled some sentences which admit us, in flesh and spirit, as it were, to the presence of these men during their last hours of life, and to the grisly horrors which their fading vision looked upon and their failing consciousness took cognizance of:

*Tuesday, Sept. 6.*  I have made the ascent of Mont Blanc, with ten persons — eight guides, and Mr. Corkindale and Mr. Randall. We reached the summit at half past 2. Immediately after quitting it, we were enveloped in clouds of snow. We passed the night in a grotto hollowed in the snow, which afforded but poor shelter, and I was ill all night.

*Sept. 7 — Morning.*  The cold is excessive. The snow falls heavily and without interruption. The guides take no rest.

*Evening.*  My Dear Hessie, we have been two days on Mont Blanc, in the midst of a terrible hurricane of snow, we have lost our way, and are in a hole scooped in the snow, at an altitude of 15,000 feet. I have no longer any hope of descending.

They had wandered around, and around, in that blinding snow storm, hopelessly lost, in a space only a hundred yards square; and when cold and fatigue vanquished them at last, they scooped their cave and lay down there to die by inches, *unaware that five steps more would have brought them into the true path.* They were so near to life and safety as that, and did not suspect it. The thought of this gives the sharpest pang that the tragic story conveys.

The author of the " Histoire du Mont Blanc " introduces the closing sentences of Mr. Bean's pathetic record thus:

" Here the characters are large and unsteady; the hand which traces them is become chilled and torpid; but the spirit survives, and the faith and resignation of the dying man are expressed with a sublime simplicity."

Perhaps this note-book will be found and sent to you. We have nothing to eat, my feet are already frozen, and I am exhausted; I have strength to write only a few words more. I have left means for C.'s education; I know you will employ them wisely. I die with faith in God, and with loving thoughts of you. Farewell to all. We shall meet again, in Heaven. . . . I think of you always.

It is the way of the Alps to deliver death to their victims with a merciful swiftness, but here the rule failed. These men suffered the bitterest death that has been recorded in the history of those mountains, freighted as that history is with grisly tragedies.

# CHAPTER XVII.

MR. HARRIS and I took some guides and porters
and ascended to the Hôtel des Pyramides,
which is perched on the high moraine which borders
the Glacier des Bossons. The road led sharply up
hill, all the way, through grass and flowers and
woods, and was a pleasant walk, barring the fatigue
of the climb.

From the hotel we could view the huge glacier at
very close range. After a rest we followed down a
path which had been made in the steep inner
frontage of the moraine, and stepped upon the
glacier itself. One of the shows of the place was a
tunnel-like cavern, which had been hewn in the
glacier. The proprietor of this tunnel took candles
and conducted us into it. It was three or four feet
wide and about six feet high. Its walls of pure and
solid ice emitted a soft and rich blue light that produced a lovely effect, and suggested enchanted
caves, and that sort of thing. When we had proceeded some yards and were entering darkness, we
turned about and had a dainty sunlit picture of
distant woods and heights framed in the strong arch

(215)

of the tunnel and seen through the tender blue radi
ance of the tunnel's atmosphere.

The cavern was nearly a hundred yards long, and
when we reached its inner limit the proprietor
stepped into a branch tunnel with his candles and
left us buried in the bowels of the glacier, and in
pitch darkness. We judged his purpose was murder
and robbery; so we got out our matches and prepared to sell our lives as dearly as possible by setting
the glacier on fire if the worst came to the worst —
but we soon perceived that this man had changed
his mind; he began to sing, in a deep, melodious
voice, and woke some curious and pleasing echoes.
By and by he came back and pretended that that
was what he had gone behind there for. We believed as much of that as we wanted to.

Thus our lives had been once more in imminent
peril, but by the exercise of the swift sagacity and
cool courage which had saved us so often, we had
added another escape to the long list. The tourist
should visit that ice-cavern, by all means, for it is
well worth the trouble; but I would advise him to
go only with a strong and well-armed force. I do
not consider artillery necessary, yet it would not be
unadvisable to take it along, if convenient. The
journey, going and coming, is about three miles and
a half, three of which are on level ground. We
made it in less than a day, but I would counsel the
unpracticed, — if not pressed for time, — to allow
themselves two. Nothing is gained in the Alps by

over-exertion; nothing is gained by crowding two days' work into one for the poor sake of being able to boast of the exploit afterward. It will be found much better, in the long run, to do the thing in two days, and then subtract one of them from the narrative. This saves fatigue, and does not injure the narrative. All the more thoughtful among the Alpine tourists do this.

We now called upon the Guide-in-Chief, and asked for a squadron of guides and porters for the ascent of the Montanvert. This idiot glared at us, and said:

"You don't need guides and porters to go to the Montanvert."

"What do we need, then?"

"Such as *you* ? — an ambulance!"

I was so stung by this brutal remark that I took my custom elsewhere.

Betimes, next morning, we had reached an altitude of 5,000 feet above the level of the sea. Here we camped and breakfasted. There was a cabin there — the spot is called the *Caillet* — and a spring of ice-cold water. On the door of the cabin was a sign, in French, to the effect that "One may here see a living chamois for fifty centimes." We did not invest; what we wanted was to see a dead one.

A little after noon we ended the ascent and arrived at the new hotel on the Montanvert, and had a view of six miles, right up the great glacier, the famous Mer de Glace. At this point it is like a sea whose deep swales and long, rolling swells have been caught in mid-movement and frozen solid; but further up it is broken up into wildly-tossing billows of ice.

We descended a ticklish path in the steep side of the moraine, and invaded the glacier. There were tourists of both sexes scattered far and wide over it, everywhere, and it had the festive look of a skating rink.

The Empress Josephine came this far, once. She ascended the Montanvert in 1810 — but not alone; a small army of men preceded her to clear the path — and carpet it, perhaps,— and she followed, under the protection of *sixty-eight* guides.

Her successor visited Chamonix later, but in far different style. It was seven weeks after the first fall of the Empire, and poor Marie Louise, ex-Empress, was a fugitive. She came at night, and in a storm, with only two attendants, and stood before a peasant's hut, tired, bedraggled, soaked with rain, "the red print of her lost crown still girdling her brow," and implored admittance — and was refused! A few days before, the adulations and applauses of a nation were sounding in her ears, and now she was come to this!

We crossed the Mer de Glace in safety, but we had misgivings. The crevasses in the ice yawned deep and blue and mysterious, and it made one nervous to traverse them. The huge round waves of ice were slippery and difficult to climb, and the chances of tripping and sliding down them and darting into a crevasse were too many to be comfortable.

In the bottom of a deep swale between two of the biggest of the ice-waves, we found a fraud who pretended to be cutting steps to insure the safety of tourists. He was " soldiering " when we came upon him, but he hopped up and chipped out a couple of steps about big enough for a cat, and charged us a franc or two for it. Then he sat down again, to doze till the next party should come along. He had collected blackmail from two or three hundred people already, that day, but had not chipped out ice enough to impair the glacier perceptibly. I have heard of a good many soft sinecures, but it seems to me that keeping toll-bridge on a glacier is the softest one I have encountered yet.

That was a blazing hot day, and it brought a persistent and persecuting thirst with it. What an unspeakable luxury it was to slake that thirst with the pure and limpid ice-water of the glacier! Down the sides of every great rib of ice poured limpid rills in gutters carved by their own attrition; better still, wherever a rock had lain, there was now a bowl-shaped hole, with smooth white sides and bottom of ice, and this bowl was brimming with water of such absolute clearness that the careless observer would not see it at all, but would think the bowl was empty. These fountains had such an alluring look that I often stretched myself out when I was not

thirsty and dipped my face in and drank till my
teeth ached. Everywhere among the Swiss mountains we had at hand the blessing — not to be found
in Europe *except* in the mountains — of water capable of quenching thirst. Everywhere in the Swiss
highlands brilliant little rills of exquisitely cold water
went dancing along by the roadsides, and my com-
rade and I were always drinking and always deliver-
ing our deep gratitude.

But in Europe everywhere except in the mountains, the water is flat and insipid beyond the power
of words to describe. It is served lukewarm; but
no matter, ice could not help it; it is incurably flat,
incurably insipid. It is only good to wash with; I
wonder it doesn't occur to the average inhabitant to
try it for that. In Europe the people say con-
temptuously, "Nobody drinks water here." Indeed, they have a sound and sufficient reason. In
many places they even have what may be called
prohibitory reasons. In Paris and Munich, for instance, they say, "Don't drink the water, it is
simply poison."

Either America is healthier than Europe, notwithstanding her "deadly" indulgence in ice-water, or
she does not keep the run of her death rate as
sharply as Europe does. I think we do keep up the
death statistics accurately; and if we do, our cities
are healthier than the cities of Europe. Every
month the German government tabulates the death
rate of the world and publishes it. I scrap-booked

these reports during several months, and it was curious to see how regular and persistently each city repeated its same death rate month after month. The tables might as well have been stereotyped, they varied so little. These tables were based upon weekly reports showing the average of deaths in each 1,000 of population for a year. Munich was always present with her 33 deaths in each 1,000 of her population (yearly average), Chicago was as constant with her 15 or 17, Dublin with her 48 — and so on.

Only a few American cities appear in these tables, but they are scattered so widely over the country that they furnish a good general average of *city* health in the United States; and I think it will be granted that our towns and villages are healthier than our cities.

Here is the average of the only American cities reported in the German tables:

Chicago, deaths in 1,000 of population annually, 16; Philadelphia, 18; St. Louis, 18; San Francisco, 19; New York (the Dublin of America), 23.

See how the figures jump up, as soon as one arrives at the transatlantic list:

Paris, 27; Glasgow, 27; London, 28; Vienna, 28; Augsburg, 28; Braunschweig, 28; Königsberg, 29; Cologne, 29; Dresden, 29; Hamburg 29; Berlin, 30; Bombay, 30; Warsaw, 31; Breslau, 31; Odessa, 32; Munich, 33; Strasburg, 33; Pesth, 35; Cassel, 35; Lisbon, 36; Liverpool, 36·

Prague, 37; Madras, 37; Bucharest, 39; St. Peters-
burg, 40; Trieste, 40; Alexandria (Egypt), 43;
Dublin, 48; Calcutta, 55.

Edinburgh is as healthy as New York — 23; but
there is no *city* in the entire list which is healthier,
except Frankfort-on-the-Main — 20. But Frankfort
is not as healthy as Chicago, San Francisco, St.
Louis, or Philadelphia.

Perhaps a strict average of the world might de-
velop the fact that where 1 in 1,000 of America's
population dies, 2 in 1,000 of the other populations
of the earth succumb.

I do not like to make insinuations, but I do think
the above statistics darkly suggest that these people
over here drink this detestable water "on the sly."

We climbed the moraine on the opposite side of
the glacier, and then crept along its sharp ridge a
hundred yards or so, in pretty constant danger of a
tumble to the glacier below. The fall would have
been only 100 feet, but it would have closed me out
as effectually as 1,000, therefore I respected the
distance accordingly, and was glad when the trip
was done. A moraine is an ugly thing to assault
head-first. At a distance it looks like an endless
grave of fine sand, accurately shaped and nicely
smoothed; but close by, it is found to be made
mainly of rough bowlders of all sizes, from that of
a man's head to that of a cottage.

By and by we came to the *Mauvais Pas*, or the
Villainous Road, to translate it feelingly. It was a

breakneck path around the face of a precipice forty or fifty feet high, and nothing to hang on to but some iron railings. I got along, slowly, safely, and uncomfortably, and finally reached the middle. My hopes began to rise a little, but they were quickly blighted; for there I met a hog—a long-nosed, bristly fellow, that held up his snout and worked his nostrils at me inquiringly. A hog on a pleasure excursion in Switzerland — think of it. It is striking and unusual; a body might write a poem about it. He could not retreat, if he had been disposed to do it. It would have been foolish to stand upon our dignity in a place where there was hardly room to stand upon our feet, so we did nothing of the sort. There were twenty or thirty ladies and gentlemen behind us; we all turned about and went back, and the hog followed behind. The creature did not seem set up by what he had done; he had probably done it before.

We reached the restaurant on the height called the Chapeau at four in the afternoon. It was a memento-factory, and the stock was large, cheap, and varied. I bought the usual paper-cutter to remember the place by, and had Mont Blanc, the Mauvais Pas, and the rest of the region branded on my alpenstock; then we descended to the valley and walked home without being tied together. This was not dangerous, for the valley was five miles wide, and quite level.

We reached the hotel before nine o'clock. Next

morning we left for Geneva on top of the diligence,
under shelter of a gay awning. If I remember
rightly, there were more than twenty people up
there. It was so high that the ascent was made by
ladder. The huge vehicle was full everywhere, inside and out. Five other diligences left at the same
time, all full. We had engaged our seats two days
beforehand, to make sure, and paid the regulation
price, five dollars each; but the rest of the company
were wiser; they had trusted Baedeker, and waited;
consequently some of them got their seats for one
or two dollars. Baedeker knows all about hotels,
railway and diligence companies, and speaks his
mind freely. He is a trustworthy friend of the
traveler.

We never saw Mont Blanc at his best until we
were many miles away; then he lifted his majestic
proportions high into the heavens, all white and cold
and solemn, and made the rest of the world seem
little and plebeian, and cheap and trivial.

As he passed out of sight at last, an old Englishman settled himself in his seat and said:

"Well, I am satisfied, I have seen the principal
features of Swiss scenery — Mont Blanc and the
goitre — now for home!"

# CHAPTER XVIII.

WE spent a few pleasant restful days at Geneva, that delightful city where accurate time-pieces are made for all the rest of the world, but whose own clocks never give the correct time of day by any accident.

Geneva is filled with pretty little shops, and the shops are filled with the most enticing gimcrackery, but if one enters one of these places he is at once pounced upon, and followed up, and so persecuted to buy this, that, and the other thing, that he is very grateful to get out again, and is not at all apt to repeat his experiment. The shopkeepers of the smaller sort, in Geneva, are as troublesome and persistent as are the salesmen of that monster hive in Paris, the Grands Magasins du Louvre — an establishment where ill-mannered pestering, pursuing, and insistence have been reduced to a science.

In Geneva, prices in the smaller shops are very elastic — that is another bad feature. I was looking in at a window at a very pretty string of beads, suitable for a child. I was only admiring them; I had no use for them; I hardly ever wear beads.

15 **

The shopwoman came out and offered them to me for thirty-five francs. I said it was cheap, but I did not need them.

" Ah, but monsieur, they are so beautiful!"

I confessed it, but said they were not suitable for one of my age and simplicity of character. She darted in and brought them out and tried to force them into my hands, saying:

" Ah, but only see how lovely they are! Surely monsieur will take them; monsieur shall have them for thirty francs. There, I have said it — it is a loss, but one must live."

I dropped my hands, and tried to move her to respect my unprotected situation. But no, she dangled the beads in the sun before my face, exclaiming, " Ah, monsieur *cannot* resist them!" She hung them on my coat button, folded her hands resignedly, and said: " Gone, — and for thirty francs, the lovely things — it is incredible! — but the good God will sanctify the sacrifice to me."

I removed them gently, returned them, and walked away, shaking my head and smiling a smile of silly embarrassment while the passers-by halted to observe. The woman leaned out of her door, shook the beads, and screamed after me:

" Monsieur shall have them for twenty-eight!"

I shook my head.

" Twenty-seven! It is a cruel loss, it is ruin — but take them, only take them."

I still retreated, still wagging my head.

"Mon Dieu, they shall even go for twenty-six! There, I have said it. Come!"

I wagged another negative. A nurse and a little English girl had been near me, and were following me, now. The shopwoman ran to the nurse, thrust the beads into her hands, and said:

"Monsieur shall have them for twenty-five! Take them to the hotel — he shall send me the money to-morrow — next day — when he likes." Then to the child: "When thy father sends me the money, come thou also, my angel, and thou shalt have something oh so pretty!"

I was thus providentially saved. The nurse refused the beads squarely and firmly, and that ended the matter.

The "sights" of Geneva are not numerous. I made one attempt to hunt up the houses once inhabited by those two disagreeable people, Rousseau and Calvin, but had no success. Then I concluded to go home. I found it was easier to propose to do that than to do it; for that town is a bewildering place. I got lost in a tangle of narrow and crooked streets, and stayed lost for an hour or two. Finally I found a street which looked somewhat familiar, and said to myself, "Now I am at home, I judge." But I was wrong; this was "*Hell* street." Presently I found another place which had a familiar look, and said to myself, "Now I am at home, sure." It was another error. This was "*Purgatory* street." After a little I said, "*Now* I've got the right place,

O**

anyway.......no, this is '*Paradise* street'; I'm
further from home than I was in the beginning."
Those were queer names — Calvin was the author of
them, likely. "Hell" and "Purgatory" fitted
those two streets like a glove, but the "Paradise"
appeared to be sarcastic.

I came out on the lake front, at last, and then I
knew where I was. I was walking along before the
glittering jewelry shops when I saw a curious performance. A lady passed by, and a trim dandy
lounged across the walk in such an apparently care-
fully-timed way as to bring himself exactly in front
of her when she got to him; he made no offer to
step out of the way; he did not apologize; he did
not even notice her. She had to stop still and let
him lounge by. I wondered if he had done that
piece of brutality purposely. He strolled to a chair
and seated himself at a small table; two or three
other males were sitting at similar tables sipping
sweetened water. I waited; presently a youth came
by, and this fellow got up and served him the same
trick. Still, it did not seem possible that any one
could do such a thing deliberately. To satisfy my
curiosity I went around the block, and sure enough,
as I approached, at a good round speed, he got up
and lounged lazily across my path, fouling my
course exactly at the right moment to receive all my
weight. This proved that his previous performances
had not been accidental, but intentional.

I saw that dandy's curious game played after-

wards, in Paris, but not for amusement; not with a
motive of any sort, indeed, but simply from a selfish
indifference to other people's comfort and rights.
One does not see it as frequently in Paris as he
might expect to, for there the law says, in effect,
"it is the business of the weak to get out of the
way of the strong." We fine a cabman if he runs
over a citizen; Paris fines the citizen for being run
over. At least so everybody says — but I saw
something which caused me to doubt; I saw a
horseman run over an old woman one day,— the
police arrested him and took him away. That
looked as if they meant to punish him.

It will not do for me to find merit in American
manners — for are they not the standing butt for the
jests of critical and polished Europe? Still, I must
venture to claim one little matter of superiority in
our manners; a lady may traverse our streets all
day, going and coming as she chooses, and she will
never be molested by any man; but if a lady, un-
attended, walks abroad in the streets of London,
even at noonday, she will be pretty likely to be ac-
costed and insulted — and not by drunken sailors,
but by men who carry the look and wear the dress
of gentlemen. It is maintained that these people
are not gentlemen, but are a lower sort, disguised as
gentlemen. The case of Colonel Valentine Baker
obstructs that argument, for a man cannot become
an officer in the British army except he hold the
rank of gentleman. This person, finding himse'*

alone in a railway compartment with an unprotected girl,— but it is an atrocious story, and doubtless the reader remembers it well enough. London must have been more or less accustomed to Bakers, and the ways of Bakers, else London would have been offended, and excited. Baker was " imprisoned "— in a parlor; and he could not have been more visited, or more overwhelmed with attentions, if he had committed six murders and then — while the gallows was preparing —" got religion "— after the manner of the holy Charles Peace, of saintly memory. Arkansaw — it seems a little indelicate to be trumpeting forth our own superiorities, and comparisons are always odious, but still — Arkansaw would certainly have hanged Baker. I do not say she would have tried him first, but she would have hanged him, anyway.

Even the most degraded woman can walk our streets unmolested, her sex and her weakness being her sufficient protection. She will encounter less polish than she would in the old world, but she will run across enough humanity to make up for it.

The music of a donkey awoke us early in the morning, and we rose up and made ready for a pretty formidable walk — to Italy; but the road was so level that we took the train. We lost a good deal of time by this, but it was no matter, we were not in a hurry. We were four hours going to Chambèry. The Swiss trains go upwards of three miles an hour, in places, but they are quite safe.

That aged French town of Chambèry was as quaint and crooked as Heilbronn. A drowsy reposeful quiet reigned in the back streets which made strolling through them very pleasant, barring the almost unbearable heat of the sun. In one of these streets, which was eight feet wide, gracefully curved, and built up with small antiquated houses, I saw three fat hogs lying asleep, and a boy (also asleep) taking care of them. From queer old-fashioned windows along the curve projected boxes of bright flowers, and over the edge of one of these boxes hung the head and shoulders of a cat — asleep. The five sleeping creatures were the only living things visible in that street. There was not a sound; absolute stillness prevailed. It was Sunday; one is not used to such dreamy Sundays on the Continent. In our part of the town it was different that night. A regiment of brown and battered soldiers had arrived home from Algiers, and I judged they got thirsty on the way. They sang and drank till dawn, in the pleasant open air.

We left for Turin at ten the next morning by a railway which was profusely decorated with tunnels. We forgot to take a lantern along, consequently we missed all the scenery. Our compartment was full. A ponderous tow-headed Swiss woman, who put on many fine-lady airs, but was evidently more used to washing linen than wearing it, sat in a corner seat and put her legs across into the opposite one, propping them intermediately with her up-ended valise.

In the seat thus pirated, sat two Americans, greatly
incommoded by that woman's majestic coffin-clad
feet. One of them begged her, politely, to remove
them. She opened her wide eyes and gave him a
stare, but answered nothing. By and by he preferred his request again, with great respectfulness.
She said, in good English, and in a deeply offended
tone, that she had paid her passage and was not
going to be bullied out of her "rights" by ill-bred
foreigners, even if she *was* alone and unprotected.

"But I have rights, also, madam. My ticket
entitles me to a seat, but you are occupying half
of it."

"I will not talk with you, sir. What right have
you to speak to me? I do not know you. One
would know you came from a land where there are
no gentlemen. No *gentleman* would treat a lady as
you have treated me."

"I come from a region where a lady would hardly
give me the same provocation."

"You have insulted me, sir! You have intimated
that I am not a lady — and I hope I am *not* one,
after the pattern of your country."

"I beg that you will give yourself no alarm on
that head, madam; but at the same time I must
insist — always respectfully — that you let me have
my seat."

Here the fragile laundress burst into tears and
sobs.

"I never was so insulted before! Never, never!

It is shameful, it is brutal, it is base, to bully and abuse an unprotected lady who has lost the use of her limbs and cannot put her feet to the floor without agony!"

"Good heavens, madam, why didn't you say that at first! I offer a thousand pardons. And I offer them most sincerely. I did not know — I *could* not know — that anything was the matter. You are most welcome to the seat, and would have been from the first if I had only known. I am truly sorry it all happened, I do assure you."

But he couldn't get a word of forgiveness out of her. She simply sobbed and snuffled in a subdued but wholly unappeasable way for two long hours, meantime crowding the man more than ever with her undertaker-furniture and paying no sort of attention to his frequent and humble little efforts to do something for her comfort. Then the train halted at the Italian line and she hopped up and marched out of the car with as firm a leg as any washerwoman of all her tribe! And how sick I was, to see how she had fooled me.

Turin is a very fine city. In the matter of roominess it transcends anything that was ever dreamed of before, I fancy. It sits in the midst of a vast dead-level, and one is obliged to imagine that land may be had for the asking, and no taxes to pay, so lavishly do they use it. The streets are extravagantly wide, the paved squares are prodigious, the houses are huge and handsome, and compacted into uniform blocks that stretch away as straight as an arrow, into the distance. The sidewalks are about as wide as ordinary European *streets*, and are covered over with a double arcade supported on great stone piers or columns. One walks from one end to the other of these spacious streets, under shelter all the time, and all his course is lined with the prettiest of shops and the most inviting dining-houses.

There is a wide and lengthy court, glittering with the most wickedly-enticing shops, which is roofed with glass, high aloft overhead, and paved with soft-toned marbles laid in graceful figures; and at night when this place is brilliant with gas and populous with a sauntering and chatting and laughing multitude of pleasure-seekers, it is a spectacle worth seeing.

Everything is on a large scale; the public buildings, for instance — and they are architecturally imposing, too, as well as large. The big squares have big bronze monuments in them. At the hotel they gave us rooms that were alarming, for size, and a parlor to match. It was well the weather required no fire in the parlor, for I think one might as well have tried to warm a park. The place would have a warm look, though, in any weather, for the window curtains were of red silk damask, and the walls were covered with the same fire-hued goods — so, also, were the four sofas and the brigade of chairs. The furniture, the ornaments, the chandeliers, the carpets, were all new and bright and costly. We did not need a parlor, at all, but they said it belonged to the two bedrooms and we might use it if we chose. Since it was to cost nothing, we were not averse from using it, of course.

Turin must surely read a good deal, for it has more bookstores to the square rod than any other town I know of. And it has its own share of military folk. The Italian officers' uniforms are very much the most beautiful I have ever seen; and, as a general thing, the men in them were as handsome as the clothes. They were not large men, but they had fine forms, fine features, rich olive complexions, and lustrous black eyes.

For several weeks I had been culling all the information I could about Italy, from tourists. The tourists were all agreed upon one thing — one must expect to be cheated at every turn by the Italians. I took an evening walk in Turin, and presently came across a little Punch and Judy show in one of the great squares. Twelve or fifteen people constituted the audience. This miniature theater was not much bigger than a man's coffin stood on end; the upper part was open and displayed a tinseled parlor — a good-sized handkerchief would have answered for a drop-curtain; the footlights consisted of a couple of candle-ends an inch long; various manikins the size of dolls appeared on the stage and made long speeches at each other, gesticulating a good deal, and they generally had a fight before they got through. They were worked by strings from above, and the illusion was not perfect, for one saw not only the strings but the brawny hand that manipulated them — and the actors and actresses all talked in the same voice, too. The audience stood in front of the theater, and seemed to enjoy the performance heartily.

When the play was done, a youth in his shirt-sleeves started around with a small copper saucer to make a collection. I did not know how much to put in, but thought I would be guided by my predecessors. Unluckily, I only had two of these, and they did not help me much because they did not put in anything. I had no Italian money, so I put in a small Swiss coin worth about ten cents. The youth finished his collection-trip and emptied the result on the stage; he had some very animated talk with the concealed manager, then he came working his way through the little crowd — seeking me, I thought. I had a mind to slip away, but concluded I wouldn't; I would stand my ground, and confront the villainy, whatever it was. The youth stood before me and held up that Swiss coin, sure enough, and said something. I did not understand him, but I judged he was requiring Italian money of me. The crowd gathered close, to listen. I was irritated, and said,— in English, of course:

"I know it's Swiss, but you'll take that or none. I haven't any other."

He tried to put the coin in my hand, and spoke again. I drew my hand away, and said:

" *No*, sir. I know all about you people. You can't play any of your fraudful tricks on me. If there is a discount on that coin, I am sorry, but I am not going to make it good. I noticed that some of the audience didn't pay you anything at all. You let them go, without a word, but you come after me because you think I'm a stranger and will put up with an extortion rather than have a scene. But you are mistaken this time — you'll take that Swiss money or none."

The youth stood there with the coin in his fingers, nonplussed and bewildered; of course he had not understood a word. An English-speaking Italian spoke up, now, and said:

"You are misunderstanding the boy. He does not mean any harm. He did not suppose you gave him so much money purposely, so he hurried back to return you the coin lest you might get away before you discovered your mistake. Take it, and give him a penny — that will make everything smooth again."

I probably blushed, then, for there was occasion. Through the interpreter I begged the boy's pardon, but I nobly refused to take back the ten cents. I said I was accustomed to squandering large sums in that way — it was the kind of person I was. Then I retired to make a note to the effect that in Italy persons connected with the drama do not cheat.

The episode with the showman reminds me of a dark chapter in my history. I once robbed an aged

16**

and blind beggar-woman of four dollars — in a church. It happened in this way. When I was out with the Innocents Abroad, the ship stopped in the Russian port of Odessa, and I went ashore, with others, to view the town. I got separated from the rest, and wandered about alone, until late in the afternoon, when I entered a Greek church to see what it was like. When I was ready to leave, I observed two wrinkled old women standing stiffly upright against the inner wall, near the door, with their brown palms open to receive alms. I contributed to the nearer one, and passed out. I had gone fifty yards, perhaps, when it occurred to me that I must remain ashore all night, as I had heard that the ship's business would carry her away at four o'clock and keep her away until morning. It was a little after four now. I had come ashore with only two pieces of money, both about the same size, but differing largely in value — one was a French gold piece worth four dollars, the other a Turkish coin worth two cents and a half. With a sudden and horrified misgiving, I put my hand in my pocket, now, and, sure enough, I fetched out that Turkish penny!

Here was a situation. A hotel would require pay in advance — I must walk the street all night, and perhaps be arrested as a suspicious character. There was but one way out of the difficulty — I flew back to the church, and softly entered. There stood the old woman yet, and in the palm of the

nearest one still lay my gold piece. I was grateful.
I crept close, feeling unspeakably mean; I got my
Turkish penny ready, and was extending a trembling
hand to make the nefarious exchange, when I heard
a cough behind me. I jumped back as if I had
been accused, and stook quaking while a worshiper
entered and passed up the aisle.

I was there a year trying to steal that money;
that is, it seemed a year, though, of course, it must
have been much less. The worshipers went and
came; there were hardly ever three in the church at
once, but there was always one or more. Every
time I tried to commit my crime somebody came in
or somebody started out, and I was prevented; but
at last my opportunity came; for one moment there
was nobody in the church but the two beggar-women
and me. I whipped the gold piece out of the poor
old pauper's palm and dropped my Turkish penny
in its place. Poor old thing, she murmured her
thanks — they smote me to the heart. Then I sped
away in a guilty hurry, and even when I was a mile
from the church I was still glancing back, every
moment, to see if I was being pursued.

That experience has been of priceless value and
benefit to me; for I resolved then, that as long as I
lived I would never again rob a blind beggar-woman
in a church; and I have always kept my word.
The most permanent lessons in morals are those
which come, not of booky teaching, but of experience.

# CHAPTER XIX.

IN Milan we spent most of our time in the vast and beautiful Arcade or Gallery, or whatever it is called. Blocks of tall new buildings of the most sumptuous sort, rich with decoration and graced with statues, the streets between these blocks roofed over with glass at a great height, the pavements all of smooth and variegated marble, arranged in tasteful patterns — little tables all over these marble streets, people sitting at them, eating, drinking, or smoking — crowds of other people strolling by — such is the Arcade. I should like to live in it all the time. The windows of the sumptuous restaurants stand open, and one breakfasts there and enjoys the passing show.

We wandered all over the town, enjoying whatever was going on in the streets. We took one omnibus ride, and as I did not speak Italian and could not ask the price, I held out some copper coins to the conductor, and he took two. Then he went and got his tariff card and showed me that he had taken only the right sum. So I made a note — Italian omnibus conductors do not cheat.

Near the Cathedral I saw another instance of probity. An old man was peddling dolls and toy fans. Two small American children bought fans, and one gave the old man a franc and three copper coins, and both started away; but they were called back, and the franc and one of the coppers were restored to them. Hence it is plain that in Italy, parties connected with the drama and with the omnibus and toy interests do not cheat.

The stocks of goods in the shop were not extensive, generally. In the vestibule of what seemed to be a clothing store, we saw eight or ten wooden dummies grouped together, clothed in woolen business suits and each marked with its price. One suit was marked 45 francs — nine dollars. Harris stepped in and said he wanted a suit like that. Nothing easier: the old merchant dragged in the dummy, brushed him off with a broom, stripped him, and shipped the clothes to the hotel. He said he did not keep two suits of the same kind in stock, but manufactured a second when it was needed to re-clothe the dummy.

In another quarter we found six Italians engaged in a violent quarrel. They danced fiercely about, gesticulating with their heads, their arms, their legs, their whole bodies; they would rush forward occasionally in a sudden access of passion and shake their fists in each other's very faces. We lost half an hour there, waiting to help cord up the dead, but they finally embraced each other affectionately, and

16 **

the trouble was all over. The episode was interesting, but we could not have afforded all that time to
it if we had known nothing was going to come of it
but a reconciliation. Note made — in Italy, people
who quarrel cheat the spectator.

We had another disappointment afterward. We
approached a deeply interested crowd, and in the
midst of it found a fellow wildly chattering and
gesticulating over a box on the ground which was
covered with a piece of old blanket. Every little
while he would bend down and take hold of the edge
of the blanket with the extreme tips of his fingers,
as if to show there was no deception — chattering
away all the while,— but always, just as I was expecting to see a wonderful feat of legerdemain, he
would let go the blanket and rise to explain further.
However, at last he uncovered the box and got out
a spoon with a liquid in it, and held it fair and
frankly around, for people to see that it was all
right and he was taking no advantage — his chatter
became more excited than ever. I supposed he was
going to set fire to the liquid and swallow it, so I
was greatly wrought up and interested. I got a cent
ready in one hand and a florin in the other, intending to give him the former if he survived and the
latter if he killed himself — for his loss would be my
gain in a literary way, and I was willing to pay a fair
price for the item — but this impostor ended his in-
tensely moving performance by simply adding some
powder to the liquid and polishing the spoon!

Then he held it aloft, and he could not have shown
a wilder exultation if he had achieved an immortal
miracle. The crowd applauded in a gratified way,
and it seemed to me that history speaks the truth
when it says these children of the south are easily
entertained.

We spent an impressive hour in the noble cathedral, where long shafts of tinted light were cleaving
through the solemn dimness from the lofty windows
and falling on a pillar here, a picture there, and a
kneeling worshiper yonder. The organ was mutter-
ing, censers were swinging, candles were glinting on
the distant altar and robed priests were filing silently
past them; the scene was one to sweep all frivolous
thoughts away and steep the soul in a holy calm.
A trim young American lady paused a yard or two
from me, fixed her eyes on the mellow sparks fleck-
ing the far-off altar, bent her head reverently a
moment, then straightened up, kicked her train into
the air with her heel, caught it deftly in her hand,
and marched briskly out.

We visited the picture galleries and the other regulation " sights " of Milan — not because I wanted to
write about them again, but to see if I had learned
anything in twelve years. I afterwards visited the
great galleries of Rome and Florence for the same
purpose. I found I had learned one thing. When
I wrote about the Old Masters before, I said the
copies were better than the originals. That was a
mistake of large dimensions. The Old Masters were

P**

still unpleasing to me, but they were truly divine contrasted with the copies. The copy is to the original as the pallid, smart, inane new waxwork group is to the vigorous, earnest, dignified group of living men and women whom it professes to duplicate. There is a mellow richness, a subdued color, in the old pictures, which is to the eye what muffled and mellowed sound is to the ear. That is the merit which is most loudly praised in the old picture, and is the one which the copy most conspicuously lacks, and which the copyist must not hope to compass. It was generally conceded by the artists with whom I talked, that that subdued splendor, that mellow richness, is imparted to the picture by *age*. Then why should we worship the Old Master for it, who didn't impart it, instead of worshiping Old Time, who did? Perhaps the picture was a clanging bell, until Time muffled it and sweetened it.

In conversation with an artist in Venice, I asked: "What is it that people see in the Old Masters? I have been in the Doge's palace and I saw several acres of very bad drawing, very bad perspective, and very incorrect proportions. Paul Veronese's dogs do not resemble dogs; all the horses look like bladders on legs; one man had a *right* leg on the left side of his body; in the large picture where the Emperor (Barbarossa?) is prostrate before the Pope, there are three men in the foreground who are over thirty feet high, if one may judge by the size of a kneeling little boy in the center of the foreground;

and according to the same scale, the Pope is 7 feet
high and the Doge is a shriveled dwarf of 4 feet.''

The artist said:

"Yes, the Old Masters often drew badly; they
did not care much for truth and exactness in minor
details; but after all, in spite of bad drawing, bad
perspective, bad proportions, and a choice of subjects which no longer appeal to people as strongly
as they did three hundred years ago, there is a *something* about their pictures which is divine — a something which is above and beyond the art of any
epoch since — a something which would be the
despair of artists but that they never hope or expect
to attain it, and therefore do not worry about it.''

That is what he said — and he said what he believed; and not only believed, but felt.

Reasoning, — especially reasoning without tech-
nical knowledge,— must be put aside, in cases of
this kind.   It cannot assist the inquirer.   It will lead
him, in the most logical progression, to what, in the
eyes of artists, would be a most illogical conclusion.
Thus: bad drawing, bad proportion, bad perspective, indifference to truthful detail, color which
gets its merit from time, and not from the artist —
these things constitute the Old Master; conclusion,
the Old Master was a bad painter, the Old Master
was not an Old Master at all, but an Old Apprentice.
Your friend the artist will grant your premises, but
deny your conclusion; he will maintain that notwithstanding this formidable list of confessed defects,

there is still a something that is divine and unapproachable about the Old Master, and that there is
no arguing the fact away by any system of reasoning whatever.

I can believe that. There are women who have
an indefinable charm in their faces which makes them
beautiful to their intimates; but a cold stranger who
tried to reason the matter out and find this beauty
would fail. He would say of one of these women:
This chin is too short, this nose is too long, this fore-
head is too high, this hair is too red, this complexion
is too pallid, the perspective of the entire composition is incorrect; conclusion, the woman is not
beautiful. But her nearest friend might say, and
say truly, "Your premises are right, your logic is
faultless, but your conclusion is wrong, nevertheless;
she is an Old Master — she is beautiful, but only to
such as know her; it is a beauty which cannot be
formulated, but it is there, just the same."

I found more pleasure in contemplating the Old
Masters this time than I did when I was in Europe
in former years, but still it was a calm pleasure;
there was nothing overheated about it. When I was
in Venice before, I think I found no picture which
stirred me much, but this time there were two which
enticed me to the Doge's palace day after day, and
kept me there hours at a time. One of these was
Tintoretto's three-acre picture in the Great Council
Chamber. When I saw it twelve years ago I was
not strongly attracted to it — the guide told me it

was an insurrection in heaven—but this was an
error.

The movement of this great work is very fine.
There are ten thousand figures, and they are all
doing something. There is a wonderful "go" to the
whole composition. Some of the figures are diving
headlong downward, with clasped hands, others are
swimming through the cloud-shoals,—some on their
faces, some on their backs — great processions of
bishops, martyrs, and angels are pouring swiftly
centerwards from various
outlying directions—everywhere is enthusiastic joy,
there is rushing movement
everywhere. There are fifteen or twenty figures scattered here and there, with
books, but they cannot keep
their attention on their reading — they offer the books
to others, but no one wishes
to read, now. The Lion of
St. Mark is there with his
book; St. Mark is there
with his pen uplifted; he
and the Lion are looking
each other earnestly in the

THE LION OF ST. MARK

face, disputing about the way to spell a word—the
Lion looks up in rapt admiration while St. Mark
spells. This is wonderfully interpreted by the

artist. It is the master stroke of this incomparable painting.

I visited the place daily, and never grew tired of looking at that grand picture. As I have intimated, the movement is almost unimaginably vigorous; the figures are singing, hosannahing, and many are blowing trumpets. So vividly is noise suggested, that spectators who become absorbed in the picture almost always fall to shouting comments in each other's ears, making ear trumpets of their curved hands, fearing they may not otherwise be heard. One often sees a tourist, with the eloquent tears pouring down his cheeks, funnel his hands at his wife's ear, and hears him roar through them, "OH, TO BE THERE AND AT REST!"

None but the supremely great in art can produce effects like these with the silent brush.

Twelve years ago I could not have appreciated this picture. One year ago I could not have appreciated it. My study of Art in Heidelberg has been a noble education to me. All that I am to-day in Art, I owe to that.

The other great work which fascinated me was Bassano's immortal Hair Trunk. This is in the Chamber of the Council of Ten. It is in one of the three forty-foot pictures which decorate the walls of the room. The composition of this picture is beyond praise. The Hair Trunk is not hurled at the stranger's head,— so to speak — as the chief feature of an immortal work so often is; no, it is carefully guarded from prominence, it is subordinated, it is restrained, it is most deftly and cleverly held in reserve, it is most cautiously and ingeniously led up to, by the master, and consequently when the spectator reaches it at last, he is taken unawares, he is unprepared, and it bursts upon him with a stupefying surprise.

One is lost in wonder at all the thought and care which this elaborate planning must have cost. A general glance at the picture could never suggest that there was a hair trunk in it; the Hair Trunk is not mentioned in the title even,— which is, " Pope Alexander III and the Doge Ziani, the Conqueror of the Emperor Frederick Barbarossa; " you see, the title is actually utilized to help divert attention from the Trunk; thus, as I say, nothing suggests the presence of the Trunk, by any hint, yet everything studiedly leads up to it, step by step. Let us examine into this, and observe the exquisitely artful artlessness of the plan.

At the extreme left end of the picture are a couple of women, one of them with a child looking over her shoulder at a wounded man sitting with bandaged head on the ground. These people seem needless, but no, they are there for a purpose; one cannot look at them without seeing the gorgeous procession of grandees, bishops, halberdiers, and banner-bearers which is passing along behind them; one cannot see the procession without feeling a curiosity to follow it and learn whither it is going; it leads him to the Pope, in the center of the picture, who is talking with the bonnetless Doge —talking tranquilly, too, although within 12 feet of them a man is beating a drum, and not far from the drummer two persons are blowing horns, and many horsemen are plunging and rioting about— indeed, 22 feet of this great work is all a deep and happy holiday serenity and Sunday-school procession, and then we come suddenly upon 11½ feet of turmoil and racket and insubordination. This latter state of things is not an accident, it has its purpose. But for it, one would linger upon the Pope and the Doge, thinking them to be the motive and supreme feature of the picture; whereas one is drawn along, almost unconsciously, to see what the trouble is about. Now at the very *end* of this riot, within 4 feet of the end of the picture, and full 36 feet from the beginning of it, the Hair Trunk bursts with an electrifying suddenness upon the spectator, in all its matchless perfection, and the great master's triumph is sweeping and complete. From that moment no other thing in those forty feet of canvas has any charm; one sees the Hair Trunk, and the Hair Trunk only — and to see it is to worship it. Bassano even placed objects in the immediate vicinity of the Supreme Feature whose pretended purpose was to divert attention from it yet a little longer and thus delay and augment the surprise; for instance, to the right of it he has placed a stooping man with a cap so red that it is sure to hold the eye for a moment — to the left of it, some 6 feet away, he has placed a red-coated man on an inflated horse, and that coat plucks your eye to that locality the next moment — then, between the Trunk and the red horseman he has intruded a man, naked to his waist, who is carrying a fancy flour-sack on the middle of his back instead of on his shoulder — this admirable feat interests you, of course — keeps you at bay a little longer, like a sock or a jacket thrown to the pursuing wolf — but at last, in spite of all distractions and detentions, the eye of even the most dull and heedless spectator is sure to fall upon the World's Masterpiece, and in that moment he totters to his chair or leans upon his guide for support.

Descriptions of such a work as this must necessarily be imperfect, yet they are of value. The top of the Trunk is arched; the arch is a perfect half circle, in the Roman style of architecture, for in the then rapid decadence of Greek art, the rising influence of Rome was already beginning to be felt in the art of the Republic. The Trunk is bound or bordered with leather all around where the lid joins the main body. Many critics consider this leather too cold in tone; but I consider this its highest merit, since it was evidently made so to emphasize by contrast the im-passioned fervor of the hasp. The high lights in this part of the work are cleverly managed, the *motif* is admirably subordinated to the ground tints, and the *technique* is very fine. The brass nail-heads are in the purest style of the early Renaissance. The

strokes, here, are very firm and bold — every nail-
head is a portrait. The handle on the end of the
Trunk has evidently been retouched — I think, with
a piece of chalk — but one can still see the inspiration of the Old Master in the tranquil, almost too
tranquil, hang of it. The hair of this Trunk is *real*
hair — so to speak — white in patches, brown in
patches. The details are finely worked out; the
repose proper to hair in a recumbent and inactive
attitude is charmingly expressed. There is a feeling
about this part of the work which lifts it to the highest altitudes of art; the sense of sordid realism van-
ishes away — one recognizes that there is *soul* here.

View this Trunk as you will, it is a gem, it is a
marvel, it is a miracle. Some of the effects are very
daring, approaching even to the boldest flights of the
rococo, the sirocco, and the Byzantine schools —
yet the master's hand never falters — it moves on,
calm, majestic, confident, — and, with that art which
conceals art, it finally casts over the *tout ensemble*,
by mysterious methods of its own, a subtle something which refines, subdues, etherealizes the arid
components and endues them with the deep charm
and gracious witchery of poesy.

Among the art treasures of Europe there are pictures which approach the Hair Trunk — there are
two which may be said to equal it, possibly — but
there is none that surpasses it. So perfect is the
Hair Trunk that it moves even persons who or-
dinarily have no feeling for art. When an Erie bag-

gagemaster saw it two years ago, he could hardly keep from checking it; and once when a customs inspector was brought into its presence, he gazed upon it in silent rapture for some moments, then slowly and unconsciously placed one hand behind him with the palm uppermost, and got out his chalk with the other. These facts speak for themselves.

17**

# CHAPTER XX.

ONE lingers about the Cathedral a good deal, in Venice. There is a strong fascination about it — partly because it is so old, and partly because it is so ugly. Too many of the world's famous buildings fail of one chief virtue — harmony; they are made up of a methodless mixture of the ugly and the beautiful; this is bad; it is confusing, it is unrestful. One has a sense of uneasiness, of distress, without knowing why. But one is calm before St. Mark, one is calm within it, one would be calm on top of it, calm in the cellar; for its details are masterfully ugly, no misplaced and impertinent beauties are intruded anywhere; and the consequent result is a grand harmonious whole, of soothing, entrancing, tranquilizing, soul-satisfying ugliness. One's admiration of a perfect thing always grows, never declines; and this is the surest evidence to him that it *is* perfect. St. Mark is perfect. To me it soon grew to be so nobly, so augustly ugly, that it was difficult to stay away from it, even for a little while. Every time its squat domes disappeared from my view, I had a despondent feeling; when-

ever they reappeared, I felt an honest rapture — I
have not known any happier hours than those I
daily spent in front of Florian's, looking across the
Great Square at it. Propped on its long row of low
thick-legged columns, its back knobbed with domes,
it seemed like a vast warty bug taking a meditative
walk.

St. Mark is not the oldest building in the world,
of course, but it seems the oldest, and looks the
oldest — especially inside. When the ancient mo-
saics in its walls become damaged, they are repaired
but not altered; the grotesque old pattern is preserved. Antiquity has a charm of its own, and to
smarten it up would only damage it. One day I
was sitting on a red marble bench in the vestibule
looking up at an ancient piece of apprentice-work,
in mosaic, illustrative of the command to "multiply
and replenish the earth." The Cathedral itself had
seemed very old; but this picture was illustrating a
period in history which made the building seem
young by comparison. But I presently found an
antique which was older than either the battered
Cathedral or the date assigned to that piece of history; it was a spiral-shaped fossil as large as the
crown of a hat; it was embedded in the marble
bench, and had been sat upon by tourists until it
was worn smooth. Contrasted with the inconceiv-
able antiquity of this modest fossil, those other
things were flippantly modern — jejune — mere matters of day-before-yesterday. The sense of the old-

ness of the Cathedral vanished away under the influence of this truly venerable presence.

St. Mark's is monumental; it is an imperishable remembrancer of the profound and simple piety of the Middle Ages. Whoever could ravish a column from a pagan temple, did it and contributed his swag to this Christian one. So this fane is upheld by several hundred acquisitions procured in that peculiar way. In our day it would be immoral to go on the highway to get bricks for a church, but it was no sin in the old times. St. Mark's was itself the victim of a curious robbery once. The thing is set down in the history of Venice, but it might be smuggled into the Arabian Nights and not seem out of place there:

Nearly four hundred and fifty years ago, a Candian named Stammato, in the suite of a prince of the house of Este, was allowed to view the riches of St. Mark. His sinful eye was dazzled and he hid himself behind an altar, with an evil purpose in his heart, but a priest discovered him and turned him out. Afterward he got in again — by false keys, this time. He went there, night after night, and worked hard and patiently, all alone, overcoming difficulty after difficulty with his toil, and at last succeeded in removing a great block of the marble paneling which walled the lower part of the treasury; this block he fixed so that he could take it out and put it in at will. After that, for weeks, he spent all his midnights in his magnificent mine, inspecting it in security, gloating over its marvels at his leisure, and always slipping back to his obscure lodgings before dawn, with a duke's ransom under his cloak. He did not need to grab, haphazard, and run — there was no hurry. He could make deliberate and well-considered selections; he could consult his æsthetic tastes. One comprehends how undisturbed he was, and how safe from any danger of interruption, when it is stated that he even carried off a unicorn's horn — a mere curiosity — which would not pass through the egress entire, but had to be sawn in two — a bit of work which cost him hours of tedious labor. He continued to store up his treasures at home until his occupation lost the charm of novelty and became monotonous; then he ceased from it, contented. Well he might be; for his collection, raised to modern values, represented nearly $50,000,000!

He could have gone home much the richest citizen of his country, and it might have been years before the plunder was missed; but he was human — he could not enjoy his delight alone, he must have somebody to talk about it with. So he exacted a solemn oath from a Candian noble named Crioni, then led him to his lodgings and nearly took his breath away with a sight of his glittering hoard. He detected a look in his friend's face which excited his suspicion, and was about to slip a stiletto into him when Crioni saved himself by explaining that that look was only an expression of supreme and happy astonishment. Stammato made Crioni a present of one of the state's principal jewels — a huge carbuncle, which afterward figured in the Ducal cap of state — and the pair parted. Crioni went at once to the palace, denounced the criminal, and handed over the carbuncle as evidence. Stammato was arrested, tried, and condemned, with the old-time Venetian promptness. He was hanged between the two great columns in the Piazza — with a gilded rope, out of compliment to his love of gold, perhaps. He got no good of his booty at all — it was *all* recovered.

In Venice we had a luxury which very seldom fell to our lot on the Continent — a home dinner with a private family. If one could always stop with private families, when traveling, Europe would have a charm which it now lacks. As it is, one must live in the hotels, of course, and that is a sorrowful business. A man accustomed to American food and American domestic cookery would not starve to death suddenly in Europe; but I think he would gradually waste away, and eventually die.

He would have to do without his accustomed morning meal. That is too formidable a change altogether; he would necessarily suffer from it. He could get the shadow, the sham, the base counterfeit of that meal; but that would do him no good, and money could not buy the reality.

To particularize: the average American's simplest and commonest form of breakfast consists of coffee

and beefsteak; well, in Europe, coffee is an unknown beverage. You can get what the European
hotel-keeper thinks is coffee, but it resembles the
real thing as hypocrisy resembles holiness. It is a
feeble, characterless, uninspiring sort of stuff, and
almost as undrinkable as if it had been made in an
American hotel. The milk used for it is what the
French call "Christian" milk,— milk which has
been baptized.

After a few months' acquaintance with European
"coffee," one's mind weakens, and his faith with
it, and he begins to wonder if the rich beverage of
home, with its clotted layer of yellow cream on top
of it, is not a mere dream, after all, and a thing
which never existed.

Next comes the European bread,— fair enough,
good enough, after a fashion, but cold; cold and
tough, and unsympathetic; and never any change,
never any variety,— always the same tiresome thing.

Next, the butter,— the sham and tasteless butter;
no salt in it, and made of goodness knows what.

Then there is the beefsteak. They have it in
Europe, but they don't know how to cook it.
Neither will they cut it right. It comes on the table
in a small, round, pewter platter. It lies in the
center of this platter, in a bordering bed of grease-
soaked potatoes; it is the size, shape, and thickness
of a man's hand with the thumb and fingers cut
off. It is a little overdone, is rather dry, it tastes
pretty insipidly, it rouses no enthusiasm.

Q**

Imagine a poor exile contemplating that inert thing; and imagine an angel suddenly sweeping down out of a better land and setting before him a mighty porterhouse steak an inch and a half thick, hot and sputtering from the griddle; dusted with fragrant pepper; enriched with little melting bits of butter of the most unimpeachable freshness and genuineness; the precious juices of the meat trickling out and joining the gravy, archipelagoed with mushrooms; a township or two of tender, yellowish fat gracing an outlying district of this ample county of beefsteak; the long white bone which divides the sirloin from the tenderloin still in its place; and imagine that the angel also adds a great cup of American home-made coffee, with the cream a-froth on top, some real butter, firm and yellow and fresh, some smoking-hot biscuits, a plate of hot buckwheat cakes, with transparent syrup,— could words describe the gratitude of this exile?

The European dinner is better than the European breakfast, but it has its faults and inferiorities; it does not satisfy. He comes to the table eager and hungry; he swallows his soup,— there is an undefinable lack about it somewhere; thinks the fish is going to be the thing he wants,— eats it and isn't sure; thinks the next dish is perhaps the one that will hit the hungry place,— tries it, and is conscious that there was a something wanting about it, also. And thus he goes on, from dish to dish, like a boy after a butterfly which just misses getting caught every time it alights, but somehow doesn't get caught after all; and at the end the exile and the boy have fared about alike; the one is full, but grievously unsatisfied, the other has had plenty of exercise, plenty of interest, and a fine lot of hopes, but he hasn't got any butterfly. There is here and there an American who will say he can remember rising from a European table d'hôte perfectly satisfied; but we must not overlook the fact that there is also here and there an American who will lie.

The number of dishes is sufficient; but then it is such a monotonous variety of *unstriking* dishes. It is an inane dead level of " fair-to-middling." There is nothing to *accent* it. Perhaps if the roast of mutton or of beef,— a big, generous one,— were brought on the table and carved in full view of the client, that might give the right sense of earnestness and reality to the thing; but they don't do that, they pass the sliced meat around on a dish, and so you are perfectly calm, it does not stir you in the least. Now a vast roast turkey, stretched on the broad of his back, with his heels in the air and the rich juices oozing from his fat sides......but I may as well stop there, for they would not know how to cook him. They can't even cook a chicken respectably; and as for carving it, they do that with a hatchet.

This is about the customary table d'hôte bill in summer:

Soup (characterless).

Fish — sole, salmon, or whiting — usually toler-ably good.

Roast — mutton or beef — tasteless — and some last year's potatoes.

A pâté, or some other made dish — usually good —"considering."

One vegetable — brought on in state, and all alone — usually insipid lentils, or string beans, or indifferent asparagus.

Roast chicken, as tasteless as paper.

Lettuce-salad — tolerably good.

Decayed strawberries or cherries.

Sometimes the apricots and figs are fresh, but this is no advantage, as these fruits are of no account anyway.

The grapes are generally good, and sometimes there is a tolerably good peach, by mistake.

The variations of the above bill are trifling. After a fortnight one discovers that the variations are only apparent, not real; in the third week you get what you had the first, and in the fourth week you get what you had the second. Three or four months of this weary sameness will kill the robustest appetite.

It has now been many months, at the present writing, since I have had a nourishing meal, but I shall soon have one, — a modest, private affair, all to myself. I have selected a few dishes, and made out a little bill of fare, which will go home in the steamer that precedes me, and be hot when I arrive — as follows:

Radishes. Baked apples, with cream.

Fried oysters; stewed oysters. Frogs.

American coffee, with real cream.

American butter.

Fried chicken, Southern style.

Porter-house steak.

Saratoga potatoes.

Broiled chicken, American style.

Hot biscuits, Southern style.

Hot wheat-bread, Southern style.

Hot buckwheat cakes.

American toast. Clear maple syrup.

Virginia bacon, broiled.

Blue points, on the half shell.

Cherry-stone clams.

San Francisco mussels, steamed.

Oyster soup. Clam soup.

Philadelphia Terrapin soup.

Oysters roasted in shell — Northern style.

Soft-shell crabs. Connecticut shad.

Baltimore perch.

Brook trout, from Sierra Nevadas.

Lake trout, from Tahoe.

Sheephead and croakers from New Orleans.

Black bass from the Mississippi.

American roast beef.

Roast turkey, Thanksgiving style.

Cranberry sauce. Celery.

Roast wild turkey. Woodcock.

Canvasback-duck, from Baltimore.

Prairie hens, from Illinois.

Missouri partridges, broiled.

'Possum. Coon.

Boston bacon and beans.

Bacon and greens, Southern style.

Hominy. Boiled onions. Turnips.

Pumpkin. Squash. Asparagus.

Butter Beans. Sweet potatoes.

Lettuce. Succotash. String beans.

Mashed potatoes. Catsup.

Boiled potatoes, in their skins.

New potatoes, minus the skins.

Early rose potatoes, roasted in the ashes, Southern style, served hot.

Sliced tomatoes, with sugar or vinegar. Stewed tomatoes.

Green corn, cut from the ear and served with butter and pepper.

Green corn, on the ear.

Hot corn-pone, with chitlings, Southern style.

Hot hoe-cake, Southern style.

Hot egg-bread, Southern style.

Hot light-bread, Southern style.

Buttermilk. Iced sweet milk.

Apple dumplings, with real cream.

Apple pie. Apple fritters.

Apple puffs, Southern style.

Peach cobbler, Southern style.

Peach pie. American mince pie.

Pumpkin pie. Squash pie.

All sorts of American pastry.

Fresh American fruits of all sorts, including strawberries, which are not to be doled out as if they were jewelry, but in a more liberal way.

Ice-water — not prepared in the ineffectual goblet, but in the sincere and capable refrigerator.

Americans intending to spend a year or so in European hotels, will do well to copy this bill and carry it along. They will find it an excellent thing to get up an appetite with, in the dispiriting presence of the squalid table d'hôte.

Foreigners cannot enjoy our food, I suppose, any more than we can enjoy theirs. It is not strange; for tastes are made, not born. I might glorify my bill of fare until I was tired; but after all, the Scotchman would shake his head and say, "Where's your haggis?" and the Fijian would sigh and say, "Where's your missionary?"

I have a neat talent in matters pertaining to nourishment. This has met with professional recognition. I have often furnished recipes for cookbooks. Here are some designs for pies and things, which I recently prepared for a friend's projected cook-book, but as I forgot to furnish diagrams and perspectives, they had to be left out, of course.

### Recipe for an Ash-Cake.

Take a lot of water and add to it a lot of coarse Indian meal and about a quarter of a lot of salt. Mix well together, knead into the form of a "pone," and let the pone stand a while,— not on its edge, but the other way. Rake away a place among the embers, lay it there, and cover it an inch deep with hot ashes. When it is done, remove it; blow off all the ashes but one layer; butter that one and eat.

N. B. No household should ever be without this

talisman. It has been noticed that tramps never return for another ash-cake.

---

### Recipe for New England Pie.

To make this excellent breakfast dish, proceed as follows: Take a sufficiency of water and a sufficiency of flour, and construct a bullet-proof dough. Work this into the form of a disk, with the edges turned up some three-fourths of an inch. Toughen and kiln-dry it a couple of days in a mild but unvarying temperature. Construct a cover for this redoubt in the same way and of the same material. Fill with stewed dried apples; aggravate with cloves, lemon-peel, and slabs of citron; add two portions of New Orleans sugar, then solder on the lid and set in a safe place till it petrifies. Serve cold at breakfast and invite your enemy.

---

### Recipe for German Coffee.

Take a barrel of water and bring it to a boil; rub a chiccory berry against a coffee berry, then convey the former into the water. Continue the boiling and evaporation until the intensity of the flavor and aroma of the coffee and chiccory has been diminished to a proper degree; then set aside to cool. Now unharness the remains of a once cow from the plow, insert them in a hydraulic press, and when you shall have acquired a teaspoonful of that pale blue juice which a German superstition regards as milk, modify the malignity of its strength in a bucket of tepid water and ring up the breakfast. Mix the beverage in a cold cup, partake with moderation, and keep a wet rag around your head to guard against over-excitement.

---

### To Carve Fowls in the German Fashion.

Use a club, and avoid the joints.

# CHAPTER XXI.

I WONDER why some things are? For instance,
Art is allowed as much indecent license to-day
as in earlier times — but the privileges of Literature
in this respect have been sharply curtailed within
the past eighty or ninety years. Fielding and
Smollett could portray the beastliness of their day
in the beastliest language; we have plenty of foul
subjects to deal with in our day, but we are not
allowed to approach them very near, even with nice
and guarded forms of speech. But not so with Art.
The brush may still deal freely with any subject,
however revolting or indelicate. It makes a body
ooze sarcasm at every pore, to go about Rome and
Florence and see what this last generation has been
doing with the statues. These works, which had
stood in innocent nakedness for ages, are all fig-
leaved now. Yes, every one of them. Nobody
noticed their nakedness before, perhaps; nobody
can help noticing it now, the fig-leaf makes it so
conspicuous. But the comical thing about it all, is,
that the fig-leaf is confined to cold and pallid marble,
which would be still cold and unsuggestive without

this sham and ostentatious symbol of modesty, whereas warm-blooded paintings which do really need it have in no case been furnished with it.

At the door of the Uffizzi, in Florence, one is confronted by statues of a man and a woman, nose-less, battered, black with accumulated grime,— they hardly suggest human beings — yet these ridiculous creatures have been thoughtfully and conscientiously fig-leaved by this fastidious generation. You enter, and proceed to that most-visited little gallery that exists in the world — the Tribune — and there, against the wall, without obstructing rag or leaf, you may look your fill upon the foulest, the vilest, the obscenest picture the world possesses — Titian's Venus. It isn't that she is naked and stretched out on a bed — no, it is the attitude of one of her arms and hand. If I ventured to describe that attitude, there would be a fine howl — but there the Venus lies, for anybody to gloat over that wants to — and there she has a right to lie, for she is a work of art, and Art has its privileges. I saw young girls steal-ing furtive glances at her; I saw young men gaze long and absorbedly at her; I saw aged, infirm men hang upon her charms with a pathetic interest. How I should like to describe her — just to see what a holy indignation I could stir up in the world — just to hear the unreflecting average man deliver himself about my grossness and coarseness, and all that. The world says that no worded description of a moving spectacle is a hundredth part as moving as the same spectacle seen with one's own eyes—yet the world is willing to let its son and its daughter and itself look at Titian's beast, but won't stand a description of it in words. Which shows that the world is not as consistent as it might be.

There are pictures of nude women which suggest no impure thought — I am well aware of that. I am not railing at such. What I am trying to emphasize is the fact that Titian's Venus is very far from being one of that sort. Without any question it was painted for a bagnio and it was probably refused because it was a trifle too strong. In truth, it is too strong for any place but a public Art Gallery. Titian has two Venuses in the Tribune; persons who have seen them will easily remember which one I am referring to.

In every gallery in Europe there are hideous pictures of blood, carnage, oozing brains, putrefaction — pictures portraying intolerable suffering — pictures alive with every conceivable horror, wrought out in dreadful detail — and similar pictures are being put on the canvas every day and publicly exhibited — without a growl from anybody — for they are innocent, they are inoffensive, being works of art. But suppose a literary artist ventured to go into a painstaking and elaborate description of one of these grisly things — the critics would skin him alive. Well, let it go, it cannot be helped; Art retains her privileges, Literature has lost hers. Somebody else may cipher out the whys and the

18**

wherefores and the consistencies of it — I haven't got time.

Titian's Venus defiles and disgraces the Tribune, there is no softening that fact, but his "Moses" glorifies it. The simple truthfulness of this noble work wins the heart and the applause of every visitor, be he learned or ignorant. After wearying one's self with the acres of stuffy, sappy, expressionless babies that populate the canvases of the Old Masters of Italy, it is refreshing to stand before this peerless child and feel that thrill which tells you you are at last in the presence of the real thing. This is a human child, this is genuine. You have seen him a thousand times — you have seen him just as he is here — and you confess, without reserve, that Titian *was* a Master. The doll-faces of other painted babes may mean one thing, they may mean another, but with the "Moses" the case is different. The most famous of all the art critics has said, "There is no room for doubt, here — plainly this child is in trouble."

I consider that the ' Moses " has no equal among the works of the Old Masters, except it be the divine Hair Trunk of Bassano. I feel sure that if all the other Old Masters were lost and only these two preserved, the world would be the gainer by it.

My sole purpose in going to Florence was to see this immortal "Moses," and by good fortune I was just in time, for they were already preparing to remove it to a more private and better protected

place because a fashion of robbing the great galleries
was prevailing in Europe at the time.

I got a capable artist to copy the picture; Panne-
maker, the engraver of Doré's books, engraved it
for me, and I have the pleasure of laying it before
the reader in this volume.

We took a turn to Rome and some other Italian
cities — then to Munich, and thence to Paris —
partly for exercise, but mainly because these things
were in our projected program, and it was only
right that we should be faithful to it.

From Paris I branched out and walked through
Holland and Belgium, procuring an occasional lift
by rail or canal when tired, and I had a tolerably
good time of it "by and large." I worked Spain
and other regions through agents to save time and
shoe leather.

We crossed to England, and then made the
homeward passage in the Cunarder *Gallia*, a very
fine ship. I was glad to get home — immeasurably
glad; so glad, in fact, that it did not seem possible
that anything could ever get me out of the country
again. I had not enjoyed a pleasure abroad which
seemed to me to compare with the pleasure I felt in
seeing New York harbor again. Europe has many
advantages which we have not, but they do not
compensate for a good many still more valuable
ones which exist nowhere but in our own country.
Then we are such a homeless lot when we are over

there! So are Europeans themselves, for that matter. They live in dark and chilly vast tombs,— costly enough, maybe, but without conveniences. To be condemned to live as the average European family lives would make life a pretty heavy burden to the average American family.

On the whole, I think that short visits to Europe are better for us than long ones. The former preserve us from becoming Europeanized; they keep our pride of country intact, and at the same time they intensify our affection for our country and our people; whereas long visits have the effect of dulling those feelings,— at least in the majority of cases. I think that one who mixes much with Americans long resident abroad must arrive at this conclusion.

**THE END**

# APPENDIX

Nothing gives such weight and
dignity to a book as an Appendix.

*Herodotus.*

## A

### THE PORTIER

OMAR KHAYÁM, the poet-prophet of Persia, writing more than eight hundred years ago, has said:

"In the four parts of the earth are many that are able to write learned books, many that are able to lead armies, and many also that are able to govern kingdoms and empires; but few there be that can keep a hotel."

A word about the European hotel *portier*. He is a most admirable invention, a most valuable convenience. He always wears a conspicuous uniform; he can always be found when he is wanted, for he sticks closely to his post at the front door; he is as polite as a duke; he speaks from four to ten languages; he is your surest help and refuge in time of trouble or perplexity. He is not the clerk, he is not the landlord; he ranks above the clerk, and represents the landlord, who is seldom seen. Instead of going to the clerk for information, as we do at home, you go to the portier. It is the pride of our average hotel clerk to know nothing whatever; it is the pride of the portier to know everything. You ask the portier at what hours the trains leave,— he tells you instantly; or you ask him who is the best physician in town; or what is the hack tariff; or how many children the mayor has; or what days the galleries are open, and whether a permit is required, and where you are to get it, and what you must pay for it; or when the theaters

18                                                    (273)

open and close, what the plays are to be, and the price of seats; or
what is the newest thing in hats; or how the bills of mortality average;
or "who struck Billy Patterson." It does not matter what you ask
him: in nine cases out of ten he knows, and in the tenth case he will
find out for you before you can turn around three times. There is nothing he will not put his hand to. Suppose you tell him you wish to go
from Hamburg to Peking by the way of Jericho, and are ignorant of
routes and prices,— the next morning he will hand you a piece of paper
with the whole thing worked out on it to the last detail. Before you
have been long on European soil, you find yourself still *saying* you are
relying on Providence, but when you come to look closer you will see
that in reality you are relying on the portier. He discovers what is
puzzling you, or what is troubling you, or what your need is, before you
can get the half of it out, and he promptly says, "Leave that to me."
Consequently, you easily drift into the habit of leaving everything to him.
There is a certain embarrassment about applying to the average American
hotel clerk, a certain hesitancy, a sense of insecurity against rebuff; but
you feel no embarrassment in your intercourse with the portier; he
receives your propositions with an enthusiasm which cheers, and plunges
into their accomplishment with an alacrity which almost inebriates. The
more requirements you can pile upon him, the better he likes it. Of
course the result is that you cease from doing anything for yourself. He
calls a hack when you want one; puts you into it; tells the driver
whither to take you; receives you like a long lost child when you return;
sends you about your business, does all the quarreling with the hack-
man himself, and pays him his money out of his own pocket. He sends
for your theater tickets, and pays for them; he sends for any possible
article you can require, be it a doctor, an elephant, or a postage stamp;
and when you leave, at last, you will find a subordinate seated with the
cab driver who will put you in your railway compartment, buy your
tickets, have your baggage weighed, bring you the printed tags, and tell
you everything is in your bill and paid for. At home you get such
elaborate, excellent, and willing service as this only in the best hotels of
our large cities; but in Europe you get it in the mere back country
towns just as well.

What is the secret of the portier's devotion? It is very simple: he
gets *fees, and no salary*. His fee is pretty closely regulated, too. If
you stay a week in the house, you give him five marks — a dollar and a
quarter, or about eighteen cents a day. If you stay a month, you

reduce this average somewhat. If you stay two or three months or longer, you cut it down half, or even more than half. If you stay only one day, you give the portier a mark.

The head waiter's fee is a shade less than the portier's; the Boots, who not only blacks your boots and brushes your clothes, but is usually the porter and handles your baggage, gets a somewhat smaller fee than the head waiter; the chambermaid's fee ranks below that of the Boots. You fee only these four, and no one else. A German gentleman told me that when he remained a week in a hotel, he gave the portier five marks, the head waiter four, the Boots three, and the chambermaid two; and if he staid three months he divided ninety marks among them, in about the above proportions. Ninety marks make $22.50.

None of these fees are ever paid until you leave the hotel, though it be a year, — except one of these four servants should go away in the meantime; in that case he will be sure to come and bid you good-bye and give you the opportunity to pay him what is fairly coming to him. It is considered very bad policy to fee a servant while you are still to remain longer in the hotel, because if you gave him too little he might neglect you afterward, and if you gave him too much he might neglect somebody else to attend to you. It is considered best to keep his expectations "on a string" until your stay is concluded.

I do not know whether hotel servants in New York get any wages or not, but I do know that in some of the hotels there the feeing system in vogue is a heavy burden. The waiter expects a quarter at breakfast, — and gets it. You have a different waiter at luncheon, and so he gets a quarter. Your waiter at dinner is another stranger, — consequently he gets a quarter. The boy who carries your satchel to your room and lights your gas fumbles around and hangs around significantly, and you fee him to get rid of him. Now you may ring for ice water; and ten minutes later for a lemonade; and ten minutes afterwards, for a cigar; and by and by for a newspaper, — and what is the result? Why, a new boy has appeared every time and fooled and fumbled around until you have paid him something. Suppose you boldly put your foot down, and say it is the hotel's business to pay its servants? — and suppose you stand your ground and stop feeing? You will have to ring your bell ten or fifteen times before you get a servant there; and when he goes off to fill your order you will grow old and infirm before you see him again. You may struggle nobly for twenty-four hours, maybe, if you are an adamantine sort of person, but in the meantime you will have been so wretchedly served, and so insolently, that you will haul down your colors, and go to impoverishing yourself with fees.

It seems to me that it would be a happy idea to import the European feeing system into America. I believe it would result in getting even the bells of the Philadelphia hotels answered, and cheerful service rendered.

The greatest American hotels keep a number of clerks and a cashier, and pay them salaries which mount up to a considerable total in the course of a year. The great continental hotels keep a cashier on a trifling salary, and a portier *who pays the hotel a salary*. By the latter system both the hotel and the public save money and are better served than by our system. One of our consuls told me that the portier of a great Berlin hotel paid $5,000 a year for his position, and yet cleared $6,000 for himself. The position of portier in the chief hotels of Saratoga, Long Branch, New York, and similar centers of resort, would be one which the holder could afford to pay even more than $5,000 for, perhaps.

When we borrowed the feeing fashion from Europe a dozen years ago, the salary system ought to have been discontinued, of course. We might make this correction now, I should think. And we might add the portier, too. Since I first began to study the portier, I have had opportunities to observe him in the chief cities of Germany, Switzerland, and Italy; and the more I have seen of him the more I have wished that he might be adopted in America, and become there, as he is in Europe, the stranger's guardian angel.

Yes, what was true eight hundred years ago, is just as true to-day: "Few there be that can keep hotel." Perhaps it is because the landlords and their subordinates have in too many cases taken up their trade without first learning it. In Europe the trade of hotel-keeper is taught. The apprentice begins at the bottom of the ladder and masters the several grades one after the other. Just as in our country printing-offices the apprentice first learns how to sweep out and bring water; then learns to "roll"; then to sort "pi"; then to set type; and finally rounds and completes his education with job-work and press-work; so the landlord-apprentice serves as call-boy; then as under-waiter; then as a parlor waiter; then as head-waiter, in which position he often has to make out all the bills; then as clerk or cashier; then as portier. His trade is learned now, and by and by he will assume the style and dignity of landlord, and be found conducting a hotel of his own.

Now in Europe, the same as in America, when a man has kept a hotel so thoroughly well during a number of years as to give it a great reputation, he has his reward. He can live prosperously on that reputation. He can let his hotel run down to the last degree of shabbiness and yet have it full of people all the time. For instance, there is the Hôtel de Ville, in Milan. It swarms with mice and fleas, and if the rest of the world were destroyed it could furnish dirt enough to start another one with. The food would create an insurrection in a poor-house; and yet if you go outside to get your meals that hotel makes up its loss by over-charging you on all sorts of trifles, — and without making any denials or excuses about it, either. But the Hôtel de Ville's old excellent reputation still keeps its dreary rooms crowded with travelers who would be elsewhere if they had only had some wise friend to warn them.

B

## HEIDELBERG CASTLE

HEIDELBERG CASTLE must have been very beautiful before the French battered and bruised and scorched it two hundred years ago. The stone is brown, with a pinkish tint, and does not seem to stain easily. The dainty and elaborate ornamentation upon its two chief fronts is as delicately carved as if it had been intended for the interior of a drawing-room rather than for the outside of a house. Many fruit and flower-clusters, human heads and grim projecting lion's heads are still as perfect in every detail as if they were new. But the statues which are ranked between the windows have suffered. These are life-size statues of old-time emperors, electors, and similar grandees, clad in mail and bearing ponderous swords. Some have lost an arm, some a head, and one poor fellow is chopped off at the middle. There is a saying that if a stranger will pass over the drawbridge and walk across the court to the castle front without saying anything, he can make a wish and it will be fulfilled. But they say that the truth of this thing has never had a chance to be proved, for the reason that before any stranger can walk from the drawbridge to the appointed place, the beauty of the palace front will extort an exclamation of delight from him.

A ruin must be rightly situated, to be effective. This one could not have been better placed. It stands upon a commanding elevation, it is buried in green woods, there is no level ground about it, but, on the contrary, there are wooded terraces upon terraces, and one looks down through shining leaves into profound chasms and abysses where twilight reigns and the sun cannot intrude. Nature knows how to garnish a ruin to get the best effect. One of these old towers is split down the middle, and one half has tumbled aside. It tumbled in such a way as to establish itself in a picturesque attitude. Then all it lacked was a fitting drapery, and Nature has furnished that; she has robed the rugged mass in flowers and verdure, and made it a charm to the eye. The standing half exposes its arched and cavernous rooms to you, like open, toothless mouths; there, too, the vines and flowers have done their work of grace. The rear portion of the tower has not been neglected, either, but is clothed with a clinging garment of polished ivy which hides the wounds and stains of time. Even the top is not left bare, but is crowned with a flourishing group of trees and shrubs. Misfortune has done for this old tower what it has done for the human character sometimes — improved it.

A gentleman remarked, one day, that it might have been fine to live in the castle in the day of its prime, but that we had one advantage which its vanished inhabitants lacked — the advantage of having a charming ruin to visit and muse over. But that was a hasty idea. Those people had the advantage of *us*. They had the fine castle to live in, and they could cross the Rhine valley and muse over the stately ruin of Trifels besides. The Trifels people, in their day, five hundred years ago, could go and muse over majestic ruins which have vanished, now, to the last stone. There have always been ruins, no doubt; and there have always been pensive people to sigh over them, and asses to scratch upon them their names and the important date of their visit. Within a hundred years after Adam left Eden, the guide probably gave the usual general flourish with his hand and said: "Place where the animals were named, ladies and gentlemen; place where the tree of the forbidden fruit stood; exact spot where Adam and Eve first met; and here, ladies and gentlemen, adorned and hallowed by the names and addresses of three generations of tourists, we have the crumbling remains of Cain's altar, — fine old ruin!" Then, no doubt, he taxed them a shekel apiece and let them go.

An illumination of Heidelberg Castle is one of the sights of Europe. The Castle's picturesque shape; its commanding situation, midway up the steep and wooded mountain side; its vast size, — these features combine to make an illumination a most effective spectacle. It is necessarily an expensive show, and consequently rather infrequent. Therefore whenever one of these exhibitions is to take place, the news goes about in the papers and Heidelberg is sure to be full of people on that night. I and my agent had one of these opportunities, and improved it.

About half past seven on the appointed evening we crossed the lower bridge, with some American students, in a pouring rain, and started up the road which borders the Neunheim side of the river. This roadway was densely packed with carriages and foot passengers; the former of all ages, and the latter of all ages and both sexes. This black and solid mass was struggling painfully onward, through the slop, the darkness, and the deluge. We waded along for three-quarters of a mile, and finally took up a position in an unsheltered beer garden directly opposite the Castle. We could not *see* the Castle, — or anything else, for that matter, — but we could dimly discern the outlines of the mountain over the way, through the pervading blackness, and knew whereabouts the Castle was located. We stood on one of the hundred benches in the garden, under our umbrellas; the other ninety-nine were occupied by standing men and women, and they also had umbrellas. All the region round about, and up and down the river-road, was a dense wilderness of humanity hidden under an unbroken pavement of carriage tops and umbrellas. Thus we stood during two drenching hours. No rain fell on my head, but the converging whalebone points of a dozen neighboring umbrellas poured little cooling streams of water down my neck, and sometimes into my ears, and thus kept me from getting hot and impatient. I had the rheumatism, too, and had heard that this was good for it. Afterward, however, I was led to believe that the water treatment is *not* good for rheumatism. There were even little girls in that dreadful place. A man held one in his arms, just in front of me, for as much as an hour, with umbrella-drippings soaking into her clothing all the time.

In the circumstances, two hours was a good while for us to have to wait, but when the illumination did at last come, we felt repaid. It came unexpectedly, of course, — things always do, that have been long looked and longed for. With a perfectly breath-taking suddenness several vast sheaves of varicolored rockets were vomited skyward out of the black throats of the castle towers, accompanied by a thundering crash of sound, and instantly every detail of the prodigious ruin stood revealed against the mountain side and glowing with an almost intolerable splendor of fire and color. For some little time the whole building was a blinding crimson mass, the towers continued to spout thick columns of rockets aloft, and overhead the sky was radiant with arrowy bolts which clove their way to the zenith, paused, curved gracefully downward, then burst into brilliant fountain sprays of richly-colored sparks. The red fires died slowly down, within the castle, and presently the shell grew nearly black outside; the angry glare that shone out through the broken arches and innumerable sashless windows, now, reproduced the aspect which the Castle must have borne in the old time when the French spoilers saw the monster bonfire which they had made there fading and smouldering toward extinction.

While we still gazed and enjoyed, the ruin was suddenly enveloped in rolling and tumbling volumes of vaporous green fire; then in dazzling purple ones; then a mixture of many colors followed, and drowned the great fabric in its blended splendors. Meantime the nearest bridge had been illuminated, and from several rafts anchored in the river, meteor showers of rockets, Roman candles, bombs, serpents, and Catharine wheels were being discharged in wasteful profusion into the sky,—a marvelous sight indeed to a person as little used to such spectacles as I was. For a while the whole region about us seemed as bright as day, and yet the rain was falling in torrents all the time. The evening's entertainment presently closed, and we joined the innumerable caravan of half-drowned spectators, and waded home again.

The Castle grounds are very ample and very beautiful; and as they joined the Hotel grounds, with no fences to climb, but only some nobly shaded stone stairways to descend, we spent a part of nearly every day in idling through their smooth walks and leafy groves. There was an attractive spot among the trees where were a great many wooden tables and benches; and there one could sit in the shade and pretend to sip at his foamy beaker of beer while he inspected the crowd. I say pretend, because I only pretended to sip, without really sipping. That is the polite way; but when you are ready to go, you empty the beaker at a draught. There was a brass band, and it furnished excellent music every afternoon. Sometimes so many people came that every seat was occupied, every table filled. And never a rough in the assemblage,— all nicely dressed fathers and mothers, young gentlemen and ladies and children; and plenty of university students and glittering officers; with here and there a gray professor, or a peaceful old lady with her knitting; and always a sprinkling of gawky foreigners. Everybody had his glass of beer before him, or his cup of coffee, or his bottle of wine, or his hot cutlet and potatoes; young ladies chatted, or fanned themselves, or wrought at their crotcheting or embroidering; the students fed sugar to their dogs, or discussed duels, or illustrated new fencing-tricks with their little canes; and everywhere was comfort and enjoyment, and everywhere peace and good-will to men. The trees were jubilant with birds, and the paths with rollicking children. One could have a seat in that place and plenty of music, any afternoon, for about eight cents, or a family ticket for the season for two dollars.

For a change, when you wanted one, you could stroll to the castle, and burrow among its dungeons, or climb about its ruined towers, or visit its interior shows, — the great Heidelberg Tun, for instance. Everybody has heard of the great Heidelberg Tun, and most people have seen it, no doubt. It is a wine cask as big as a cottage, and some traditions say it holds eighteen hundred thousand bottles, and other traditions say it holds eighteen hundred million barrels. I think it likely that one of these statements is a mistake, and the other one a lie. However, the mere matter of capacity is a thing of no sort of consequence, since the cask is empty, and indeed has always been empty, history says. An empty cask the size of a cathedral could excite but little emotion in me. I do not see any wisdom in building a monster cask to hoard up emptiness in, when you can get a better quality, outside, any day, free of expense. What could this cask have been built for? The more one studies over that, the more uncertain and unhappy he becomes. Some historians say that thirty couples, some say thirty thousand couples, can dance on the head of this cask at the same time. Even this does not seem to me to account for the building of it. It does not even throw light on it. A profound and scholarly Englishman, — a specialist, — who had made the great Heidelberg Tun his sole study for fifteen years, told me he had at last satisfied himself that the ancients built it to make German cream in. He said that the average German cow yielded from one to two and a half teaspoonfuls of milk, when she was not worked in the plow or the hay wagon more than eighteen or nineteen hours a day. This milk was very sweet and good, and of a beautiful transparent bluish tint; but in order to get cream from it in the most economical way, a peculiar process was necessary. Now he believed that the habit of the ancients was to collect several milkings in a teacup, pour it into the Great Tun, fill up with water, and then skim off the cream from time to time as the needs of the German Empire demanded.

This began to look reasonable. It certainly began to account for the German cream which I had encountered and marveled over in so many hotels and restaurants. But a thought struck me, —

" Why did not each ancient dairyman take his own teacup of milk and his own cask of water, and mix them, without making a government matter of it ? "

" Where could he get a cask large enough to contain the right proportion of water? "

Very true. It was plain that the Englishman had studied the matter from all sides. Still I thought I might catch him on one point; so I asked him why the modern empire did not make the nation's cream in the Heidelberg Tun, instead of leaving it to rot away unused. But he answered as one prepared, —

" A patient and diligent examination of the modern German cream has satisfied me that they do not use the Great Tun now, because they have got a *bigger* one hid away somewhere. Either that is the case or they empty the spring milkings into the mountain torrents and then skim the Rhine all summer."

There is a museum of antiquities in the castle, and among its most treasured relics are ancient manuscripts connected with German history. There are hundreds of these, and their dates stretch back through many centuries. One of them is a decree signed and sealed by the hand of a successor of Charlemagne, in the year 896. A signature made by a hand which vanished out of this life near a thousand years ago, is a more impressive thing than even a ruined castle. Luther's wedding ring was shown me; also a fork belonging to a time anterior to our era, and an early bootjack. And there was a plaster cast of the head of a man who was assassinated about sixty years ago. The stab-wounds in the face were duplicated with unpleasant fidelity. One or two real hairs still remained sticking in the eyebrows of the cast. That trifle seemed to almost change the counterfeit into a corpse.

There are many aged portraits, — some valuable, some worthless; some of great interest, some of none at all. I bought a couple, — one a gorgeous duke of the olden time, and the other a comely blue-eyed damsel, a princess, maybe. I bought them to start a portrait gallery of my ancestors with. I paid a dollar and a half for the duke and two and a half for the princess. One can lay in ancestors at even cheaper rates than these, in Europe, if he will mouse among old picture shops and look out for chances.

# C

## THE COLLEGE PRISON

It seems that the student may break a good many of the public laws without having to answer to the public authorities. His case must come before the University for trial and punishment. If a policeman catches him in an unlawful act and proceeds to arrest him, the offender proclaims that he is a student, and perhaps shows his matriculation card, whereupon the officer asks for his address, then goes his way, and reports the matter at headquarters. If the offense is one over which the city has no jurisdiction, the authorities report the case officially to the University, and give themselves no further concern about it. The University court send for the student, listen to the evidence, and pronounce judgment. The punishment usually inflicted is imprisonment in the University prison. As I understand it, a student's case is often tried without his being present at all. Then something like this happens: A constable in the service of the University visits the lodgings of the said student, knocks, is invited to come in, does so, and says politely, —

"If you please, I am here to conduct you to prison."

"Ah," says the student, "I was not expecting it. What have I been doing?"

"Two weeks ago the public peace had the honor to be disturbed by you."

"It is true; I had forgotten it. Very well: I have been complained of, tried, and found guilty — is that it?"

"Exactly. You are sentenced to two days' solitary confinement in the College prison, and I am sent to fetch you."

*Student.* "O, I can't go to-day!"

*Officer.* "If you please, — why?"

*Student.* "Because I've got an engagement."

*Officer.* "To-morrow, then, perhaps?"

*Student.* "No, I am going to the opera, to-morrow."

*Officer.* "Could you come Friday?"

*Student.* (Reflectively.) "Let me see,—Friday—Friday. I don't seem to have anything on hand Friday."

*Officer.* "Then, if you please, I will expect you on Friday."

*Student.* "All right, I'll come around Friday."

*Officer.* "Thank you. Good day, sir."

*Student.* "Good day."

So on Friday the student goes to the prison of his own accord, and is admitted.

It is questionable if the world's criminal history can show a custom more odd than this. Nobody knows, now, how it originated. There have always been many noblemen among the students, and it is presumed that all students are gentlemen; in the old times it was usual to mar the convenience of such folk as little as possible; perhaps this indulgent custom owes its origin to this.

One day I was listening to some conversation upon this subject when an American student said that for some time he had been under sentence for a slight breach of the peace and had promised the constable that he would presently find an unoccupied day and betake himself to prison. I asked the young gentleman to do me the kindness to go to jail as soon as he conveniently could, so that I might try to get in there and visit him, and see what college captivity was like. He said he would appoint the very first day he could spare.

His confinement was to endure twenty-four hours. He shortly chose his day, and sent me word. I started immediately. When I reached the University Place, I saw two gentlemen talking together, and, as they had portfolios under their arms, I judged they were tutors or elderly students; so I asked them in English to show me the college jail. I had learned to take it for granted that anybody in Germany who knows anything, knows English, so I had stopped afflicting people with my German. These gentlemen seemed a trifle amused,—and a trifle confused, too,—but one of them said he would walk around the corner with me and show me the place. He asked me why I wanted to get in there, and I said to see a friend,—and for curiosity. He doubted if I would be admitted, but volunteered to put in a word or two for me with the custodian.

He rang the bell, a door opened, and we stepped into a paved way and then into a small living-room, where we were received by a hearty

19**

and good-natured German woman of fifty. She threw up her hands with a surprised "Ach Gott, Herr Professor!" and exhibited a mighty deference for my new acquaintance. By the sparkle in her eye I judged she was a good deal amused, too. The "Herr Professor" talked to her in German, and I understood enough of it to know that he was bringing very plausible reasons to bear for admitting me. They were successful. So the Herr Professor received my earnest thanks and departed. The old dame got her keys, took me up two or three flights of stairs, unlocked a door, and we stood in the presence of the criminal. Then she went into a jolly and eager description of all that had occurred downstairs, and what the Herr Professor had said, and so forth and so on. Plainly, she regarded it as quite a superior joke that I had waylaid a Professor and employed him in so odd a service. But I wouldn't have done it if I had known he was a Professor; therefore my conscience was not disturbed.

Now the dame left us to ourselves. The cell was not a roomy one; still it was a little larger than an ordinary prison cell. It had a window of good size, iron-grated; a small stove; two wooden chairs: two oaken tables, very old and most elaborately carved with names, mottoes, faces, armorial bearings, etc., — the work of several generations of imprisoned students; and a narrow wooden bedstead with a villainous old straw mattress, but no sheets, pillows, blankets, or coverlets, — for these the student must furnish at his own cost if he wants them. There was no carpet, of course.

The ceiling was completely covered with names, dates, and monograms, done with candle smoke. The walls were thickly covered with pictures and portraits (in profile), some done with ink, some with soot, some with a pencil, and some with red, blue, and green chalks; and wherever an inch or two of space had remained between the pictures, the captives had written plaintive verses, or names and dates. I do not think I was ever in a more elaborately frescoed apartment.

Against the wall hung a placard containing the prison laws. I made a note of one or two of these. For instance: The prisoner must pay, for the "privilege" of entering, a sum equivalent to 20 cents of our money; for the privilege of leaving, when his term has expired, 20 cents; for every day spent in the prison, 12 cents; for fire and light, 12 cents a day. The jailer furnishes coffee, mornings, for a small sum; dinners and suppers may be ordered from outside if the prisoner chooses, — and he is allowed to pay for them, too.

**Here and there**, on the walls, appeared the names of American students, and in one place the American arms and motto were displayed in colored chalks.

With the help of my friend I translated many of the inscriptions. Some of them were cheerful, others the reverse. I will give the reader a few specimens:

"In my tenth semestre (my best one), I am cast here through the complaints of others. Let those who follow me take warning."

"III Tage ohne Grund angeblich aus Neugierde." Which is to say, he had a curiosity to know what prison life was like; so he made a breach in some law and got three days for it. It is more than likely that he never had the same curiosity again.

(*Translation.*) "E. Glinicke, four days for being too eager a spectator of a row."

"F. Graf Bismarck, — 27-29, II, '74." Which means that Count Bismarck, son of the great statesman, was a prisoner two days in 1874.

(*Translation.*) "R. Diergandt, — for Love, — 4 days." Many people in this world have caught it heavier than that for the same indiscretion.

This one is terse. I translate:

"Four weeks for *misinterpreted gallantry.*"

I wish the sufferer had explained a little more fully. A four-weeks term is a rather serious matter.

There were many uncomplimentary references, on the walls, to a certain unpopular college dignitary. One sufferer had got three days for not saluting him. Another had "here two days slept and three nights lain awake," on account of this same "Dr. K." In one place was a picture of Dr. K. hanging on a gallows.

Here and there, lonesome prisoners had eased the heavy time by altering the records left by predecessors. . Leaving the name standing, and the date and length of the captivity, they had erased the description of the misdemeanor, and written in its place, in staring capitals, "FOR THEFT!" or "FOR MURDER!" or some other gaudy crime. In one place, all by itself, stood this blood-curdling word:

"RACHE !" *

There was no name signed, and no date. It was an inscription well calculated to pique curiosity. One would greatly like to know the

---

* "Revenge!"

nature of the wrong that had been done, and what sort of vengeance was wanted, and whether the prisoner ever achieved it or not. But there was no way of finding out these things.

Occasionally, a name was followed simply by the remark, "II days, for disturbing the peace," and without comment upon the justice or injustice of the sentence.

In one place was a hilarious picture of a student of the green-cap corps with a bottle of champagne in each hand; and below was the legend: "These make an evil fate endurable."

There were two prison cells, and neither had space left on walls or ceiling for another name or portrait or picture. The inside surfaces of the two doors were completely covered with cartes de visite of former prisoners, ingeniously let into the wood and protected from dirt and injury by glass.

I very much wanted one of the sorry old tables which the prisoners had spent so many years in ornamenting with their pocket-knives, but red tape was in the way. The custodian could not sell one without an order from a superior; and that superior would have to get it from *his* superior; and this one would have to get it from a higher one, — and so on up and up until the faculty should sit on the matter and deliver final judgment. The system was right, and nobody could find fault with it; but it did not seem justifiable to bother so many people, so I proceeded no further. It might have cost me more than I could afford, anyway; for one of those prison tables, which was at that time in a private museum in Heidelberg, was afterwards sold at auction for two hundred and fifty dollars. It was not worth more than a dollar, or possibly a dollar and a half, before the captive students began their work on it. Persons who saw it at the auction said it was so curiously and wonderfully carved that it was worth the money that was paid for it.

Among the many who have tasted the college prison's dreary hospitality was a lively young fellow from one of the Southern States of America, whose first year's experience of German university life was rather peculiar. The day he arrived in Heidelberg he enrolled his name on the college books, and was so elated with the fact that his dearest hope had found fruition and he was actually a student of the old and renowned university, that he set to work that very night to celebrate the event by a grand lark in company with some other students. In the course of his lark he managed to make a wide breach in one of the university's most stringent laws. Sequel: before noon, next day, he was in the college prison,— booked for three months. The twelve long weeks dragged slowly by, and the day of deliverance came at last. A great crowd of sympathizing fellow-students received him with a rousing demonstration as he came forth, and of course there was another grand lark,— in the course of which he managed to make a wide breach in one of the *city's* most stringent laws. Sequel: before noon, next day, he was safe in the city lockup,— booked for three months. This second tedious captivity drew to an end in the course of time, and again a great crowd of sympathizing fellow-students gave him a rousing reception as he came forth; but his delight in his freedom was so boundless that he could not proceed soberly and calmly, but must go hopping and skipping and jumping down the sleety street from sheer excess of joy. Sequel: he slipped and broke his leg, and actually lay in the hospital during the next three months!

When he at last became a free man again, he said he believed he would hunt up a brisker seat of learning; the Heidelberg lectures might be good, but the opportunities of attending them were too rare, the educational process too slow; he said he had come to Europe with the idea that the acquirement of an education was only a matter of time, but if he had averaged the Heidelburg system correctly, it was rather a matter of eternity.

19

## THE AWFUL GERMAN LANGUAGE

A little learning makes the whole world kin.— Proverbs xxxii, **7.**

I WENT often to look at the collection of curiosities in Heidelberg Castle, and one day I surprised the keeper of it with my German. I spoke entirely in that language. He was greatly interested; and after I had talked awhile he said my German was very rare, possibly a "unique"; and wanted to add it to his museum.

If he had known what it had cost me to acquire my art, he would also have known that it would break any collector to buy it. Harris and I had been hard at work on our German during several weeks at that time, and although we had made good progress, it had been accomplished under great difficulty and annoyance, for three of our teachers had died in the meantime. A person who has not studied German can form no idea of what a perplexing language it is.

Surely there is not another language that is so slipshod and systemless, and so slippery and elusive to the grasp. One is washed about in it, hither and hither, in the most helpless way; and when at last he thinks he has captured a rule which offers firm ground to take a rest on amid the general rage and turmoil of the ten parts of speech, he turns over the page and reads, "Let the pupil make careful note of the following *exceptions*." He runs his eye down and finds that there are more exceptions to the rule than instances of it. So overboard he goes again, to hunt for another Ararat and find another quicksand. Such has been, and continues to be, my experience. Every time I think I have got one of these four confusing "cases" where I am master of it, a seemingly insignificant preposition intrudes itself into my sentence, clothed with an awful and unsuspected power, and crumbles the ground from under me. For instance, my book inquires after a certain bird—

(it is always inquiring after things which are of no sort of consequence to anybody): "Where is the bird?" Now the answer to this question, — according to the book, — is that the bird is waiting in the blacksmith shop on account of the rain. Of course no bird would do that, but then you must stick to the book. Very well, I begin to cipher out the German for that answer. I begin at the wrong end, necessarily, for that is the German idea. I say to myself, "*Regen* (rain) is masculine — or maybe it is feminine — or possibly neuter — it is too much trouble to look now. Therefore, it is either *der* (the) Regen, or *die* (the) Regen, or *das* (the) Regen, according to which gender it may turn out to be when I look. In the interest of science, I will cipher it out on the hypothesis that it is masculine. Very well — then *the* rain is *der* Regen, if it is simply in the quiescent state of being *mentioned*, without enlargement or discussion — Nominative case; but if this rain is lying around, in a kind of a general way on the ground, it is then definitely located, it is *doing something* — that is, *resting* (which is one of the German grammar's ideas of doing something), and this throws the rain into the Dative case, and makes it *dem* Regen. However, this rain is not resting, but is doing something *actively*, — it is falling, — to interfere with the bird, likely, — and this indicates *movement*, which has the effect of sliding it into the Accusative case and changing *dem* Regen into *den* Regen." Having completed the grammatical horoscope of this matter, I answer up confidently and state in German that the bird is staying in the blacksmith shop "wegen (on account of) *den* Regen." Then the teacher lets me softly down with the remark that whenever the word "wegen" drops into a sentence, it *always* throws that subject into the *Genitive* case, regardless of consequences — and that therefore this bird staid in the blacksmith shop "wegen *des* Regens."

N. B. I was informed, later, by a higher authority, that there was an "exception" which permits one to say "wegen *den* Regen" in certain peculiar and complex circumstances, but that this exception is not extended to anything *but* rain.

There are ten parts of speech, and they are all troublesome. An average sentence, in a German newspaper, is a sublime and impressive curiosity; it occupies a quarter of a column; it contains all the ten parts of speech — not in regular order, but mixed; it is built mainly of compound words constructed by the writer on the spot, and not to be found in any dictionary — six or seven words compacted into one, without joint or seam — that is, without hyphens; it treats of fourteen or fifteen different subjects, each enclosed in a parenthesis of its own, with here and there extra parentheses which re-enclose three or four of the minor parentheses, making pens within pens: finally, all the parentheses and reparentheses are massed together between a couple of king-parentheses, one of which is placed in the first line of the majestic sentence and the other in the middle of the last line of it — *after which comes the* VERB, and you find out for the first time what the man has been talking about; and after the verb — merely by way of ornament, as far as I can make out, — the writer shovels in " *haben sind gewesen gehabt haben geworden sein,*" or words to that effect, and the monument is finished. I suppose that this closing hurrah is in the nature of the flourish to a man's signature — not necessary, but pretty. German books are easy enough to read when you hold them before the looking-glass or stand on your head, — so as to reverse the construction, — but I think that to learn to read and understand a German newspaper is a thing which must always remain an impossibility to a foreigner.

Yet even the German books are not entirely free from attacks of the Parenthesis distemper — though they are usually so mild as to cover only a few lines, and therefore when you at last get down to the verb it carries some meaning to your mind because you are able to remember a good deal of what has gone before.

Now here is a sentence from a popular and excellent German novel, — with a slight parenthesis in it. I will make a perfectly literal translation, and throw in the parenthesis-marks and some hyphens for the assistance of the reader, — though in the original there are no parenthesis-marks or hyphens, and the reader is left to flounder through to the remote verb the best way he can:

"But when he, upon the street, the (in-satin-and-silk-covered-now-very-unconstrainedly-after-the-newest-fashion-dressed) government counsellor's wife *met,*" etc., etc.*

That is from " The Old Mamselle's Secret," by Mrs. Marlitt. And that sentence is constructed upon the most approved German model. You observe how far that verb is from the reader's base of operations; well, in a German newspaper they put their verb away over on the next page; and I have heard that sometimes after stringing along on exciting preliminaries and parentheses for a column or two, they get in a hurry

---

* Wenn er aber auf der Strasse der in Sammt und Seide gehüllten jetz sehr ungenirt nach der neusten mode gekleideten Regierungsrathin begegnet."

and have to go to press without getting to the verb at all.  Of course, then, the reader is left in a very exhausted and ignorant state.

We have the Parenthesis disease in our literature, too; and one may see cases of it every day in our books and newspapers: but with us it is the mark and sign of an unpracticed writer or a cloudy intellect, whereas with the Germans it is doubtless the mark and sign of a practiced pen and of the presence of that sort of luminous intellectual fog which stands for clearness among these people.  For surely it is *not* clearness,— it necessarily can't be clearness.  Even a jury would have penetration enough to discover that.  A writer's ideas must be a good deal confused, a good deal out of line and sequence, when he starts out to say that a man met a counsellor's wife in the street, and then right in the midst of this so simple undertaking halts these approaching people and makes them stand still until he jots down an inventory of the woman's dress. That is manifestly absurd.  It reminds a person of those dentists who secure your instant and breathless interest in a tooth by taking a grip on it with the forceps, and then stand there and drawl through a tedious anecdote before they give the dreaded jerk.  Parentheses in literature and dentistry are in bad taste.

The Germans have another kind of parenthesis, which they make by splitting a verb in two and putting half of it at the beginning of an exciting chapter and the *other half* at the end of it.  Can any one conceive of anything more confusing than that?  These things are called " separable verbs."  The German grammar is blistered all over with separable verbs; and the wider the two portions of one of them are spread apart, the better the author of the crime is pleased with his performance.  A favorite one is *reiste ab*,— which means *departed*.  Here is an example which I culled from a novel and reduced to English:

" The trunks being now ready, he DE- after kissing his mother and sisters, and once more pressing to his bosom his adored Gretchen, who, dressed in simple white muslin, with a single tuberose in the ample folds of her rich brown hair, had tottered feebly down the stairs, still pale from the terror and excitement of the past evening, but longing to lay her poor aching head yet once again upon the breast of him whom she loved more dearly than life itself, PARTED."

However, it is not well to dwell too much on the separable verbs. One is sure to lose his temper early; and if he sticks to the subject, and will not be warned, it will at last either soften his brain or petrify it. Personal pronouns and adjectives are a fruitful nuisance in this language, and should have been left out. For instance, the same sound, *sie,* means *you,* and it means *she,* and it means *her,* and it means *it,* and it means *they,* and it means *them.* Think of the ragged poverty of a language which has to make one word do the work of six,— and a poor little weak thing of only three letters at that. But mainly, think of the exasperation of never knowing which of these meanings the speaker is trying to convey. This explains why, whenever a person says *sie* to me, I generally try to kill him, if a stranger.

Now observe the Adjective. Here was a case where simplicity would have been an advantage; therefore, for no other reason, the inventor of this language complicated it all he could. When we wish to speak of our " good friend or friends," in our enlightened tongue, we stick to the one form and have no trouble or hard feeling about it; but with the German tongue it is different. When a German gets his hands on an adjective, he declines it, and keeps on declining it until the common sense is all declined out of it. It is as bad as Latin. He says, for instance:

SINGULAR.

*Nominative* — Mein gut*er* Freund, my good friend.
*Genitive* — Mein*es* gu*ten* Freund*es,* of my good friend.
*Dative* — Mein*em* gu*ten* Freund, to my good friend.
*Accusative* — Mein*en* gu*ten* Freund, my good friend.

PLURAL.

N.— Mein*e* gut*en* Freund*e,* my good friends.
G.— Mein*er* gut*en* Freund*e,* of my good friends.
D.— Mein*en* gut*en* Freund*en,* to my good friends.
A.— Mein*e* gut*en* Freund*e,* my good friends.

Now let the candidate for the asylum try to memorize those variations, and see how soon he will be elected. One might better go without friends in Germany than take all this trouble about them. I have shown what a bother it is to decline a good (male) friend; well this is only a third of the work, for there is a variety of new distortions of the adjective to be learned when the object is feminine, and still another when the object is neuter. Now there are more adjectives in this language than there are black cats in Switzerland, and they must all be as elaborately declined as the examples above suggested. Difficult? — troublesome? — these words cannot describe it. I heard a Californian student in Heidelberg say, in one of his calmest moods, that he would rather decline two drinks than one German adjective.

The inventor of the language seems to have taken pleasure in complicating it in every way he could think of. For instance, if one is casually referring to a house, *Haus*, or a horse, *Pferd*, or a dog, *Hund*, he spells these words as I have indicated; but if he is referring to them in the Dative case, he sticks on a foolish and unnecessary *e* and spells them Hause, Pferde, Hunde. So, as an added *e* often signifies the plural, as the *s* does with us, the new student is likely to go on for a month making twins out of a Dative dog before he discovers his mistake; and on the other hand, many a new student who could ill afford loss, has bought and paid for two dogs and only got one of them, because he ignorantly bought that dog in the Dative singular when he really supposed he was talking plural,— which left the law on the seller's side, of course, by the strict rules of grammar, and therefore a suit for recovery could not lie.

In German, all the Nouns begin with a capital letter. Now that is a good idea; and a good idea, in this language, is necessarily conspicuous from its lonesomeness. I consider this capitalizing of nouns a good idea, because by reason of it you are almost always able to tell a noun the minute you see it. You fall into error occasionally, because you mistake the name of a person for the name of a thing, and waste a good deal of time trying to dig a meaning out of it. German names almost always do mean something, and this helps to deceive the student. I translated a passage one day, which said that "the infuriated tigress broke loose and utterly ate up the unfortunate fir-forest" (*Tannenwald*). When I was girding up my loins to doubt this, I found out that Tannenwald in this instance, was a man's name.

Every noun has a gender, and there is no sense or system in the distribution; so the gender of each must be learned separately and by heart. There is no other way. To do this one has to have a memory like a memorandum book. In German, a young lady has no sex, while a turnip has. Think what overwrought reverence that shows for the turnip, and what callous disrespect for the girl. See how it looks in print — I translate this from a conversation in one of the best of the German Sunday-school books:

"*Gretchen*. Wilhelm, where is the turnip?

"*Wilhelm*. She has gone to the kitchen.

"*Gretchen*. Where is the accomplished and beautiful English maiden?

"*Wilhelm*. It has gone to the opera."

To continue with the German genders: a tree is male, its buds are female, its leaves are neuter; horses are sexless, dogs are male, cats are female,— Tom-cats included, of course; a person's mouth, neck, bosom, elbows, fingers, nails, feet, and body, are of the male sex, and his head is male or neuter according to the word selected to signify it, and *not* according to the sex of the individual who wears it,— for in Germany all the women wear either male heads or sexless ones; a person's nose, lips, shoulders, breast, hands, hips, and toes are of the female sex; and his hair, ears, eyes, chin, legs, knees, heart, and conscience, haven't any sex at all. The inventor of the language probably got what he knew about a conscience from hearsay.

Now, by the above dissection, the reader will see that in Germany a man may *think* he is a man, but when he comes to look into the matter closely, he is bound to have his doubts; he finds that in sober truth he is a most ridiculous mixture; and if he ends by trying to comfort himself with the thought that he can at least depend on a third of this mess as being manly and masculine, the humiliating second thought will quickly remind him that in this respect he is no better off than any woman or cow in the land.

In the German it is true that by some oversight of the inventor of the language, a Woman is a female; but a Wife (*Weib*) is not,— which is unfortunate. A Wife, here, has no sex; she is neuter; so, according to the grammar, a fish is *he*, his scales are *she*, but a fishwife is neither. To describe a wife as sexless may be called under-description; that is bad enough, but over-description is surely worse. A German speaks of an Englishman as the *Engländer ;* to change the sex, he adds *inn*, and that stands for Englishwoman,— *Engländerinn*. That seems descriptive enough, but still it is not exact enough for a German; so he precedes the word with that article which indicates that the creature to follow is feminine, and writes it down thus: "*die* Engländer*inn*," — which means "the *she-Englishwoman*." I consider that that person is over-described.

Well, after the student has learned the sex of a great number of nouns, he is still in a difficulty, because he finds it impossible to persuade his tongue to refer to things as "*he*" and "*she*," and "*him*" and "*her*," which it has been always accustomed to refer to as "*it*." When he even frames a German sentence in his mind, with the hims and hers in the right places, and then works up his courage to the utterance-point, it is no use,— the moment he begins to speak his tongue flies the track and all those labored males and females come out as "*its*." And even when he is reading German to himself, he always calls those things "*it*", whereas he ought to read in this way:

## TALE OF THE FISHWIFE AND ITS SAD FATE *

It is a bleak Day. Hear the Rain, how he pours, and the Hail, how he rattles; and see the Snow, how he drifts along, and oh the Mud, how deep he is! Ah the poor Fishwife, it is stuck fast in the Mire ; it has dropped its Basket of Fishes; and its Hands have been cut by the Scales as it seized some of the falling Creatures; and one Scale has even got into its Eye, and it cannot get her out. It opens its Mouth to cry for Help; but if any Sound comes out of him, alas he is drowned by the raging of the Storm. And now a Tomcat has got one of the Fishes and she will surely escape with him. No, she bites off a Fin, she holds her in her Mouth,—will she swallow her ? No, the Fishwife's brave Mother-dog deserts his Puppies and rescues the Fin,—which he eats, himself, as his Reward. O, horror, the Lightning has struck the Fish-basket; he sets him on Fire; see the Flame, how she licks the doomed Utensil with her red and angry Tongue; now she attacks the helpless Fishwife's Foot,—she burns him up, all but the big Toe, and even *she* is partly consumed; and still she spreads, still she waves her fiery Tongues; she attacks the Fishwife's Leg and destroys *it ;* she attacks its Hand and destroys *her ;* she attacks its poor worn Garment and destroys *her* also; she attacks its Body and consumes *him ;* she wreathes herself about its Heart and *it* is consumed; next about its Breast, and in a Moment *she* is a Cinder; now she reaches its Neck, — *he* goes; now its Chin,— *it* goes; now its Nose,— *she* goes. In another Moment, except Help come, the Fishwife will be no more. Time presses,—is there none to succor and save? Yes! Joy, joy, with flying Feet the she-Englishwoman comes! But alas, the generous she-Female is too late: where now is the fated Fishwife? It has ceased from its Sufferings, it has gone to a better Land; all that is left of it for its loved Ones to lament over, is this poor smouldering Ash-heap. Ah, woful, woful Ash-heap! Let us take him up tenderly, reverently, upon the lowly Shovel, and bear him to his long Rest, with the Prayer that when he rises again it will be in a Realm where he will have one good

---

* I capitalize the nouns, in the German (and ancient English) fashion.

square responsible Sex, and have it all to himself, instead of having a
mangy lot of assorted Sexes scattered all over him in Spots.

---

There, now, the reader can see for himself that this pronoun business is a very awkward thing for the unaccustomed tongue.

I suppose that in all languages the similarities of look and sound
between words which have no similarity in meaning are a fruitful source
of perplexity to the foreigner. It is so in our tongue, and it is notably
the case in the German. Now there is that troublesome word *vermählt:*
to me it has so close a resemblance,— either real or fancied,— to three
or four other words, that I never know whether it means despised,
painted, suspected, or married; until I look in the dictionary, and then
I find it means the latter. There are lots of such words and they are a
great torment. To increase the difficulty there are words which *seem* to
resemble each other, and yet do not; but they make just as much
trouble as if they did. For instance, there is the word *vermiethen* (to
let, to lease, to hire); and the word *verheirathen* (another way of saying to *marry*). I heard of an Englishman who knocked at a man's
door in Heidelberg and proposed, in the best German he could command, to "verheirathen" that house. Then there are some words
which mean one thing when you emphasize the first syllable, but mean
something very different if you throw the emphasis on the last syllable.
For instance, there is a word which means a runaway, or the act of
glancing through a book, according to the placing of the emphasis; and
another word which signifies to *associate* with a man, or to *avoid* him,
according to where you put the emphasis,— and you can generally
depend on putting it in the wrong place and getting into trouble.

There are some exceedingly useful words in this language. *Schlag,*
for example; and *Zug.* There are three-quarters of a column of Schlags
in the dictionary, and a column and a half of Zugs. The word Schlag
means Blow, Stroke, Dash, Hit, Shock, Clap, Slap, Time, Bar, Coin,
Stamp, Kind, Sort, Manner, Way, Apoplexy, Wood-Cutting, Enclosure,
Field, Forest-Clearing. This is its simple and *exact* meaning,— that is
to say, its restricted, its fettered meaning; but there are ways by which
you can set it free, so that it can soar away, as on the wings of the
morning, and never be at rest. You can hang any word you please to
its tail, and make it mean anything you want to. You can begin with
*Schlag-ader*, which means artery, and you can hang on the whole

dictionary, word by word, clear through the alphabet to *Schlag-wasser*, which means bilge-water,— and including *Schlag-mutter*, which means mother-in-law.

Just the same with *Zug*. Strictly speaking, Zug means Pull, Tug, Draught, Procession, March, Progress, Flight, Direction, Expedition, Train, Caravan, Passage, Stroke, Touch, Line, Flourish, Trait of Character, Feature, Lineament, Chess-move, Organ-stop, Team, Whiff, Bias, Drawer, Propensity, Inhalation, Disposition: but that thing which it does *not* mean,— when all its legitimate pendants have been hung on, has not been discovered yet.

One cannot over-estimate the usefulness of Schlag and Zug. Armed just with these two, and the word *Also*, what cannot the foreigner on German soil accomplish? The German word *Also* is. the equivalent of the English phrase " You know," and does not mean anything at all,— in *talk*, though it sometimes does in print. Every time a German opens his mouth an *Also* falls out; and every time he shuts it he bites one in two that was trying to *get* out.

Now, the foreigner, equipped with these three noble words, is master of the situation. Let him talk right along, fearlessly; let him pour his indifferent German forth, and when he lacks for a word, let him heave a *Schlag* into the vacuum; all the chances are that it fits it like a plug, but if it doesn't let him promptly heave a *Zug* after it; the two together can hardly fail to bung the hole; but if, by a miracle, they *should* fail, let him simply say *Also !* and this will give him a moment's chance to think of the needful word. In Germany, when you load your conversational gun it is always best to throw in a *Schlag* or two and a *Zug* or two, because it doesn't make any difference how much the rest of the charge may scatter, you are bound to bag something with *them*. Then you blandly say *Also*, and load up again. Nothing gives such an air of grace and elegance and unconstraint to a German or an English conversation as to scatter it full of " Also's " or " You-knows."

In my note-book I find this entry:

*July* 1.— In the hospital yesterday, a word of thirteen syllables was successfully removed from a patient,—a North-German from near Hamburg; but as most unfortunately the surgeons had opened him in the wrong place, under the impression that he contained a panorama, he died. The sad event has cast a gloom over the whole community.

That paragraph furnishes a text for a few remarks about one of the most curious and notable features of my subject,— the length of German

words. Some German words are so long that they have a perspective.
Observe these examples:

Freundschaftsbezeigungen.

Dilettantenaufdringlichkeiten.

Stadtverordnetenversammlungen.

These things are not words, they are alphabetical processions. And
they are not rare; one can open a German newspaper any time and see
them marching majestically across the page,—and if he has any imagination he can see the banners and hear the music, too. They impart a
martial thrill to the meekest subject. I take a great interest in these
curiosities. Whenever I come across a good one, I stuff it and put it in
my museum. In this way I have made quite a valuable collection.
When I get duplicates, I exchange with other collectors, and thus
increase the variety of my stock. Here are some specimens which I
lately bought at an auction sale of the effects of a bankrupt bric-a-brac
hunter:

GENERALSTAATSVERORDNETENVERSAMMLUNGEN。

ALTERTHUMSWISSENSCHAFTEN.

KINDERBEWAHRUNGSANSTALTEN.

UNABHAENGIGKEITSERKLAERUNGEN.

WIEDERERSTELLUNGSBESTREBUNGEN.

WAFFENSTILLSTANDSUNTERHANDLUNGEN.

Of course when one of these grand mountain ranges goes stretching
across the printed page, it adorns and ennobles that literary landscape,
—but at the same time it is a great distress to the new student, for it
blocks up his way; he cannot crawl under it, or climb over it, or tunnel
through it. So he resorts to the dictionary for help, but there is no
help there. The dictionary must draw the line somewhere,—so it
leaves this sort of words out. And it is right, because these long things
are hardly legitimate words, but are rather combinations of words, and
the inventor of them ought to have been killed. They are compound
words with the hyphens left out. The various words used in building
them are in the dictionary, but in a very scattered condition; so you can
hunt the materials out, one by one, and get at the meaning at last, but
it is a tedious and harassing business. I have tried this process upon
some of the above examples. "Freundschaftsbezeigungen" seems to
be "Friendship demonstrations," which is only a foolish and clumsy
way of saying "demonstrations of friendship." "Unabhaengigkeitserklaerungen" seems to be "Independencedeclarations," which is no

improvement upon "Declarations of Independence," so far as I can see. "Generalstaatsverordnetenversammlungen" seems to be "Generalstatesrepresentativesmeetings," as nearly as I can get at it,— a mere rhythmical, gushy euphuism for "meetings of the legislature," I judge. We used to have a good deal of this sort of crime in our literature, but it has gone out now. We used to speak of a thing as a "never-to-be-forgotten" circumstance, instead of cramping it into the simple and sufficient word "memorable" and then going calmly about our business as if nothing had happened. In those days we were not content to embalm the thing and bury it decently, we wanted to build a monument over it.

But in our newspapers the compounding-disease lingers a little to the present day, but with the hyphens left out, in the German fashion. This is the shape it takes: instead of saying "Mr. Simmons, clerk of the county and district courts, was in town yesterday," the new form puts it thus: "Clerk of the County and District Court Simmons was in town yesterday." This saves neither time nor ink, and has an awkward sound besides. One often sees a remark like this in our papers:" Mrs. Assistant District Attorney Johnson returned to her city residence yesterday for the season." That is a case of really unjustifiable compounding; because it not only saves no time or trouble, but confers a title on Mrs. Johnson which she has no right to. But these little instances are trifles indeed, contrasted with the ponderous and dismal German system of piling jumbled compounds together. I wish to submit the following local item, from a Mannheim journal, by way of illustration:

"In the daybeforeyesterdayshortlyaftereleveno'clock Night, the inthistownstandingtavern called 'The Wagoner' was downburnt. When the fire to the onthedownburninghouseresting Stork's Nest reached, flew the parent Storks away. But when the bytheraging, firesurrounded Nest *itself* caught Fire, straightway plunged the quickreturning Mother Stork into the Flames and died, her Wings over her young ones outspread."

Even the cumbersome German construction is not able to take the pathos out of that picture,— indeed, it somehow seems to strengthen it. This item is dated away back yonder months ago. I could have used it sooner, but I was waiting to hear from the Father-Stork. I am still waiting.

"*Also !*" If I have not shown that the German is a difficult language, I have at least intended to do it. I have heard of an American student who was asked how he was getting along with his German, and

20**

who answered promptly: "I am not getting along at all. I have worked at it hard for three level months, and all I have got to show for it is one solitary German phrase,—'Zwei glas,'" (two glasses of beer). He paused a moment, reflectively; then added with feeling: "But I've got that *solid!*"

And if I have not also shown that German is a harassing and infuriating study, my execution has been at fault, and not my intent. I heard lately of a worn and sorely-tried American student who used to fly to a certain German word for relief when he could bear up under his aggravations no longer,—the only word in the whole language whose sound was sweet and precious to his ear and healing to his lacerated spirit. This was the word *Damit*. It was only the *sound* that helped him, not the meaning;* and so, at last, when he learned that the emphasis was not on the first syllable, his only stay and support was gone, and he faded away and died.

I think that a description of any loud, stirring, tumultuous episode must be tamer in German than in English. Our descriptive words of this character have such a deep, strong, resonant sound, while their German equivalents do seem so thin and mild and energyless. Boom, burst, crash, roar, storm, bellow, blow, thunder, explosion; howl, cry, shout, yell, groan; battle, hell. These are magnificent words; they have a force and magnitude of sound befitting the things which they describe. But their German equivalents would be ever so nice to sing the children to sleep with, or else my awe-inspiring ears were made for display and not for superior usefulness in analyzing sounds. Would any man want to die in a battle which was called by so tame a term as a *Schlacht?* Or would not a consumptive feel too much bundled up, who was about to go out, in a shirt collar and a seal ring, into a storm which the bird-song word *Gewitter* was employed to describe? And observe the strongest of the several German equivalents for explosion,—*Ausbruch*. Our word Toothbrush is more powerful than that. It seems to me that the Germans could do worse than import it into their language to describe particularly tremendous explosions with. The German word for hell,—Hölle,—sounds more like *helly* than anything else; therefore, how necessarily chipper, frivolous, and unimpressive it is. If a man were told in German to go there, could he really rise to the dignity of feeling insulted?

---

* It merely means, in its general sense, "*herewith.*"

Having now pointed out, in detail, the several vices of this language, I now come to the brief and pleasant task of pointing out its virtues. The capitalizing of the nouns I have already mentioned. But far before this virtue stands another, — that of spelling a word according to the sound of it. After one short lesson in the alphabet, the student can tell how any German word is pronounced without having to ask; whereas in our language if a student should inquire of us, "What does B, O, W, spell?" we should be obliged to reply, "Nobody can tell what it spells when you set it off by itself; you can only tell by referring to the context and finding out what it signifies, — whether it is a thing to shoot arrows with, or a nod of one's head, or the forward end of a boat."

There are some German words which are singularly and powerfully effective. For instance, those which describe lowly, peaceful, and affectionate home life; those which deal with love, in any and all forms, from mere kindly feeling and honest good will toward the passing stranger, clear up to courtship; those which deal with outdoor Nature, in its softest and loveliest aspects, — with meadows and forests, and birds and flowers, the fragrance and sunshine of summer, and the moonlight of peaceful winter nights; in a word, those which deal with any and all forms of rest, repose, and peace; those also which deal with the creatures and marvels of fairyland; and lastly and chiefly, in those words which express pathos, is the language surpassingly rich and effective. There are German songs which can make a stranger to the language cry. That shows that the *sound* of the words is correct, — it interprets the meanings with truth and with exactness; and so the ear is informed, and through the ear, the heart.

The Germans do not seem to be afraid to repeat a word when it is the right one. They repeat it several times, if they choose. That is wise. But in English, when we have used a word a couple of times in a paragraph, we imagine we are growing tautological, and so we are weak enough to exchange it for some other word which only approximates exactness, to escape what we wrongly fancy is a greater blemish. Repetition may be bad, but surely inexactness is worse.

---

There are people in the world who will take a great deal of trouble to point out the faults in a religion or a language, and then go blandly about their business without suggesting any remedy. I am not that kind

of a person.  I have shown that the German language needs reforming
Very well, I am ready to reform it.    At least I am ready to make the
proper suggestions.    Such a course as this might be immodest in an·
other; but I have devoted upwards of nine full weeks, first and last, to
a careful and critical study of this tongue, and thus have acquired a
confidence in my ability to reform it which no mere superficial culture
could have conferred upon me.

In the first place, I would leave out the Dative Case.   It confuses
the plurals ;  and, besides, nobody ever knows when he is in the Dative
Case, except he discover it by accident, — and then he does not know
when or where it was that he got into it, or how long he has been in it,
or how he is ever going to get out of it again.    The Dative Case is but
an ornamental folly, — it is better to discard it.

In the next place, I would move the Verb further up to the front.
You may load up with ever so good a Verb, but I notice that you never
really bring down a subject with it at the present German range, — you
only cripple it.   So I insist that this important part of speech should be
brought forward to a position where it may be easily seen with the
naked eye.

Thirdly, I would import some strong words from the English tongue,
— to swear with, and also to use in describing all sorts of vigorous
things in a vigorous way.*

Fourthly, I would reorganize the sexes, and distribute them accord·
ing to the will of the Creator.    This as a tribute of respect, if nothing
else.

Fifthly, I would do away with those great long compounded words ;

----

* " *Verdammt*," and its variations and enlargements, are words
which have plenty of meaning, but the *sounds* are so mild and in·
effectual that German ladies can use them without sin.   German ladies
who could not be induced to commit a sin by any persuasion or com-
pulsion, promptly rip out one of these harmless little words when they
tear their dresses or don't like the soup.    It sounds about as wicked as
our " My gracious."    German ladies are constantly saying, "Ach !
Gott !" "Mein Gott !" "Gott in Himmel !" "Herr Gott !" "Der
Herr Jesus !" etc.    They think our ladies have the same custom, per·
haps ; for I once heard a gentle and lovely old German lady say to a
sweet young American girl:    "The two languages are so alike — how
pleasant that is ; we say 'Ach ! Gott !' you say ' *Goddam*.' "

or require the speaker to deliver them in sections, with intermissions for refreshments. To wholly do away with them would be best, for ideas are more easily received and digested when they come one at a time than when they come in bulk. Intellectual food is like any other; it is pleasanter and more beneficial to take it with a spoon than with a shovel.

Sixthly, I would require a speaker to stop when he is done, and not hang a string of those useless "haben sind gewesen gehabt haben geworden seins" to the end of his oration. This sort of gew-gaws undignify a speech, instead of adding a grace. They are, therefore, an offense, and should be discarded.

Seventhly, I would discard the Parenthesis. Also the re-parenthesis, the re-re-parenthesis, and the re-re-re-re-re-re-parentheses, and likewise the final wide-reaching all-enclosing King-parenthesis. I would require every individual, be he high or low, to unfold a plain straightforward tale, or else coil it and sit on it and hold his peace. Infractions of this law should be punishable with death.

And eighthly and last, I would retain *Zug* and *Schlag*, with their pendants, and discard the rest of the vocabulary. This would simplify the language.

I have now named what I regard as the most necessary and important changes. These are perhaps all I could be expected to name for nothing; but there are other suggestions which I can and will make in case my proposed application shall result in my being formally employed by the government in the work of reforming the language.

My philological studies have satisfied me that a gifted person ought to learn English (barring spelling and pronouncing) in thirty hours, French in thirty days, and German in thirty years. It seems manifest, then, that the latter tongue ought to be trimmed down and repaired. If it is to remain as it is, it ought to be gently and reverently set aside among the dead languages, for only the dead have time to learn it.

A FOURTH OF JULY ORATION IN THE GERMAN TONGUE, DELIVERED AT A BANQUET OF THE ANGLO-AMERICAN CLUB OF STUDENTS BY THE AUTHOR OF THIS BOOK.

GENTLEMEN: Since I arrived, a month ago, in this old wonderland, this vast garden of Germany, my English tongue has so often proved a useless piece of baggage to me, and so troublesome to carry around, in a country where they haven't the checking system for luggage, that I finally set to work, last week, and learned the German language. Also! Es freut mich dass dies so ist, denn es muss, in ein hauptsächlich degree, höflich sein, dass man auf ein occasion like this, sein Rede in die Sprache des Landes worin he boards, aussprechen soll. Dafür habe ich, aus reinische Verlegenheit, — no, Vergangenheit, — no, I mean Höf-lichkeit, — aus reinische Höflichkeit habe ich resolved to tackle this business in the German language, um Gottes willen! Also! Sie müssen so freundlich sein, und verzeih mich die interlarding von ein oder zwei Englischer Worte, hie und da, denn ich finde dass die deutsche is not a very copious language, and so when you've really got anything to say, you've got to draw on a language that can stand the strain.

Wenn aber man kann nicht meinem Rede verstehen, so werde ich ihm später dasselbe übersetz, wenn er solche Dienst verlangen wollen haben werden sollen sein hätte. (I don't know what wollen haben werden sollen sein hätte means, but I notice they always put it at the end of a German sentence — merely for general literary gorgeousness, I sup-pose.)

This is a great and justly honored day, — a day which is worthy of the veneration in which it is held by the true patriots of all climes and nationalities, — a day which offers a fruitful theme for thought and speech; und meinem Freunde, — no, meinen Freunden, — meines Freun-des, — well, take your choice, they're all the same price; I don't know which one is right, — also! ich habe gehabt haben worden gewesen sein, as Goethe says in his Paradise Lost, — ich, — ich, — that is to say, — ich, — but let us change cars.

Also! Die Anblick so viele Grossbrittanischer und Amerikanischer hier zusammengetroffen in Bruderliche concord, ist zwar a welcome and inspiriting spectacle. And what has moved you to it? Can the terse German tongue rise to the expression of this impulse? Is it Freund-schaftsbezeigungenstadtverordnetenversammlungenfamilieneigenthüm-lichkeiten? Nein, o nein! This is a crisp and noble word, but it fails to pierce the marrow of the impulse which has gathered this friendly meeting and produced diese Anblick, — eine Anblick welche ist gut zu sehen, — gut für die Augen in a foreign land and a far country, — eine Anblick solche als in die gewöhnliche Heidelberger phrase nennt man ein "schönes Aussicht!" Ja, freilich natürlich wahrscheinlich ebensowohl! Also! Die Aussicht auf dem Königsstuhl mehr grösserer ist, aber geist-lische sprechend nicht so schön, lob' Gott! Because sie sind hier zusammengetroffen, in Bruderlichem concord, ein grossen Tag zu feiern, whose high benefits were not for one land and one locality only, but have conferred a measure of good upon all lands that know liberty to-day, and love it. Hundert Jahre vorüber, waren die Engländer und die Amerikaner Feinde; aber heute sind sie herzlichen Freunde, Gott sei Dank! May this good fellowship endure; may these banners here blended in amity so remain; may they never any more wave over opposing hosts, or be stained with blood which was kindred, is kindred, and always will be kindred, until a line drawn upon a map shall be able to say: " *This* bars the ancestral blood from flowing in the veins of the descendant!"

# LEGEND OF THE CASTLES

CALLED THE "SWALLOW'S NEST" AND "THE BROTHERS," AS CON-
DENSED FROM THE CAPTAIN'S TALE

In the neighborhood of three hundred years ago the Swallow's Nest
and the larger castle between it and Neckarsteinach were owned and
occupied by two old knights who were twin brothers, and bachelors.
They had no relatives. They were very rich. They had fought through
the wars and retired to private life — covered with honorable scars.
They were honest, honorable men in their dealings, but the people had
given them a couple of nicknames which were very suggestive, — Herr
Givenaught and Herr Heartless. The old knights were so proud of
these names that if a burgher called them by their right ones they
would correct them.

The most renowned scholar in Europe, at that time, was the Herr
Doctor Franz Reikmann, who lived in Heidelberg. All Germany was
proud of the venerable scholar, who lived in the simplest way, for great
scholars are always poor. He was poor, as to money, but very rich in
his sweet young daughter Hildegarde and his library. He had been all
his life collecting his library, book by book, and he loved it as a miser
loves his hoarded gold. He said the two strings of his heart were
rooted, the one in his daughter, the other in his books; and that if
either were severed he must die. Now in an evil hour, hoping to win a
marriage portion for his child, this simple old man had entrusted his
small savings to a sharper to be ventured in a glittering speculation.
But that was not the worst of it: he signed a paper, — without reading
it. That is the way with poets and scholars; they always sign without
reading. This cunning paper made him responsible for heaps of things.

( 208 )

The result was that one night he found himself in debt to the sharper eight thousand pieces of gold!— an amount so prodigious that it simply stupefied him to think of it. It was a night of woe in that house.

"I must part with my library,— I have nothing else. So perishes one heartstring," said the old man.

"What will it bring, father?" asked the girl.

"Nothing! It is worth seven hundred pieces of gold; but by auction it will go for little or nothing."

"Then you will have parted with the half of your heart and the joy of your life to no purpose, since so mighty a burden of debt will remain behind."

"There is no help for it, my child. Our darlings must pass under the hammer. We must pay what we can."

"My father, I have a feeling that the dear Virgin will come to our help. Let us not lose heart."

"She cannot devise a miracle that will turn *nothing* into eight thousand gold pieces, and lesser help will bring us little peace."

"She can do even greater things, my father. She will save us, I know she will."

Toward morning, while the old man sat exhausted and asleep in his chair where he had been sitting before his books as one who watches by his beloved dead and prints the features on his memory for a solace in the aftertime of empty desolation, his daughter sprang into the room and gently woke him, saying,—

"My presentiment was true! She will save us. Three times has she appeared to me in my dreams, and said, 'Go to the Herr Givenaught, go to the Herr Heartless, ask them to come and bid. There, did I not tell you she would save us, the thrice blessed Virgin!"

Sad as the old man was, he was obliged to laugh.

"Thou mightest as well appeal to the rocks their castles stand upon as to the harder ones that lie in those men's breasts, my child. *They* bid on books writ in the learned tongues!— they can scarce read their own."

But Hildegarde's faith was in no wise shaken. Bright and early she was on her way up the Neckar road, as joyous as a bird.

Meantime Herr Givenaught and Herr Heartless were having an early breakfast in the former's castle,— the Sparrow's Nest,— and flavoring it with a quarrel; for although these twins bore a love for each other which almost amounted to worship, there was one subject upon which they could not touch without calling each other hard names,— and yet it was the subject which they oftenest touched upon.

"I tell you,' said Givenaught, "you will beggar yourself yet with your insane squanderings of money upon what you choose to consider poor and worthy objects. All these years I have implored you to stop this foolish custom and husband your means, but all in vain. You are always lying to me about these secret benevolences, but you never have managed to deceive me yet. Every time a poor devil has been set upon his feet I have detected your hand in it — incorrigible ass!"

"Every time you didn't set him on his feet yourself, you mean. Where I give one unfortunate a little private lift, you do the same for a dozen. The idea of *your* swelling around the country and petting yourself with the nickname of Givenaught,— intolerable humbug! Before I would be such a fraud as that, I would cut my right hand off. Your life is a continual lie. But go on, I have tried *my* best to save you from beggaring yourself by your riotous charities,— now for the thousandth time I wash my hands of the consequences. A maundering old fool! that's what you are."

"And you a blethering old idiot!" roared Givenaught, springing up.

"I won't stay in the presence of a man who has no more delicacy than to call me such names. Mannerless swine!"

So saying, Herr Heartless sprang up in a passion. But some lucky accident intervened, as usual, to change the subject, and the daily quarrel ended in the customary daily loving reconciliation. The gray-headed old eccentrics parted, and Herr Heartless walked off to his own castle.

Half an hour later, Hildegarde was standing in the presence of Herr Givenaught. He heard her story, and said,—

"I am sorry for you, my child, but I am very poor, I care nothing for bookish rubbish, I shall not be there."

He said the hard words kindly, but they nearly broke poor Hildegarde's heart, nevertheless. When she was gone the old heart-breaker muttered, rubbing his hands,—

"It was a good stroke. I have saved my brother's pocket this time, in spite of him. Nothing else would have prevented his rushing off to rescue the old scholar, the pride of Germany, from his troubles. The poor child won't venture near *him* after the rebuff she has received from his brother the Givenaught."

But he was mistaken. The Virgin had commanded, and Hildegarde would obey. She went to Herr Heartless and told her story. But he said coldly,—

"I am very poor, my child, and books are nothing to me. I wish you well, but I shall not come."

When Hildegarde was gone, he chuckled and said,—

"How my fool of a soft-headed soft-hearted brother would rage if he knew how cunningly I have saved his pocket. How he would have flown to the old man's rescue! But the girl won't venture near him now."

When Hildegarde reached home, her father asked her how she had prospered. She said,—

"The Virgin has promised, and she will keep her word; but not in the way I thought. She knows her own ways, and they are best."

The old man patted her on the head, and smiled a doubting smile, but he honored her for her brave faith, nevertheless.

## II

Next day the people assembled in the great hall of the Ritter tavern, to witness the auction,— for the proprietor had said the treasure of Germany's most honored son should be bartered away in no meaner place. Hildegarde and her father sat close to the books, silent and sorrowful, and holding each other's hands. There was a great crowd of people present. The bidding began,—

"How much for this precious library, just as it stands, all complete?" called the auctioneer.

"Fifty pieces of gold!"

"A hundred!"

"Two hundred!"

"Three!"

"Four!"

"Five hundred!"

"Five twenty-five!"

A brief pause.

"Five forty!"

A longer pause, while the auctioneer redoubled his persuasions.

"Five forty-five!"

A heavy drag — the auctioneer persuaded, pleaded, implored,— it was useless, everybody remained silent,—

"Well, then,— going, going,— one,— two,— "

" Five hundred and fifty ! "

This in a shrill voice, from a bent old man, all hung with rags, and with a green patch over his left eye. Everybody in his vicinity turned and gazed at him. It was Givenaught in disguise. He was using a disguised voice, too.

" Good ! " cried the auctioneer. " Going, going,— one,— two,— "

" Five hundred and sixty ! "

This, in a deep harsh voice, from the midst of the crowd at the other end of the room. The people near by turned, and saw an old man, in a strange costume, supporting himself on crutches. He wore a long white beard, and blue spectacles. It was Herr Heartless, in disguise, and using a disguised voice.

" Good again ! Going, going,— one,— "

" Six hundred ! "

Sensation. The crowd raised a cheer, and some one cried out, "Go it, Green-patch ! " This tickled the audience and a score of voices shouted, " Go it, Green-patch ! "

" Going,— going,— going,— third and last call,— one,—two,— "

" Seven hundred ! "

" Huzzah ! — well done, Crutches ! " cried a voice. The crowd took it up, and shouted altogether, " Well done, Crutches ! "

" Splendid, gentlemen ! you are doing magnificently. Going, going,— "

" A thousand ! "

"Three cheers for Green-patch ! Up and at him, Crutches ! "

" Going,— going,— "

" Two thousand ! "

And while the people cheered and shouted, " Crutches " muttered, " Who can this devil be that is fighting so to get these useless books? — But no matter, he shan't have them. The pride of Germany shall have his books if it beggars me to buy them for him."

" Going, going, going,— "

" Three thousand ! "

" Come, everybody — give a rouser for Green-patch ! "

And while they did it, " Green-patch " muttered, " This cripple is plainly a lunatic; but the old scholar shall have his books, nevertheless, though my pocket sweat for it."

" Going,— going,— "

" Four thousand ! "

"Huzza!'

"Five thousand!"

"Huzza!"

"Six thousand!"

"Huzza!"

"Seven thousand!"

"Huzza!"

"*Eight* thousand!"

"We are saved, father! I told you the Holy Virgin would keep her word!" "Blessed be her sacred name;" said the old scholar, with emotion. The crowd roared, "Huzza, huzza, huzza,— at him again, Green-patch!"

"Going,— going,—"

"TEN thousand!" As Givenaught shouted this, his excitement was so great that he forgot himself and used his natural voice. His brother recognized it, and muttered, under cover of the storm of cheers,—

"Aha, you are there, are you, besotted old fool? Take the books, I know what you'll do with them!"

So saying, he slipped out of the place and the auction was at an end. Givenaught shouldered his way to Hildegarde, whispered a word in her ear, and then he also vanished. The old scholar and his daughter embraced, and the former said, "Truly the Holy Mother has done more than she promised, child, for she has given you a splendid marriage portion,— think of it, two thousand pieces of gold!"

"And more still," cried Hildegarde, "for she has given you back your books; the stranger whispered me that he would none of them,— 'the honored son of Germany must keep them,' so he said. I would I might have asked his name and kissed his hand and begged his blessing; but he was Our Lady's angel, and it is not meet that we of earth should venture speech with them that dwell above."

# F

## GERMAN JOURNALS

THE daily journals of Hamburg, Frankfort, Baden, Munich, and Augsburg are all constructed on the same general plan. I speak of these because I am more familiar with them than with any other German papers. They contain no "editorials" whatever; no "personals,"— and this is rather a merit than a demerit, perhaps; no funny-paragraph column; no police court reports; no reports of proceedings of higher courts; no information about prize fights or other dog fights, horse races, walking matches, yachting contests, rifle matches, or other sporting matters of any sort; no reports of banquet-speeches; no department of curious odds and ends of floating fact and gossip; no "rumors" about anything or anybody; no prognostications or prophecies about anything or anybody; no lists of patents granted or sought, or any reference to such things; no abuse of public officials, big or little, or complaints against them, or praises of them; no religious columns Saturdays, no rehash of cold sermons Mondays; no "weather indications"; no "local item" unveilings of what is happening in town,— nothing of a local nature, indeed, is mentioned, beyond the movements of some prince, or the proposed meeting of some deliberative body.

After so formidable a list of what one can't find in a German daily, the question may well be asked, What *can* be found in it ? It is easily answered: A child's handful of telegrams, mainly about European national and international political movements; letter-correspondence about the same things; market reports. There you have it. That is what a German daily is made of. A German daily is the slowest and saddest and dreariest of the inventions of man. Our own dailies infuriate the reader, pretty often; the German daily only stupefies him. Once a week the German daily of the highest class lightens up its heavy columns,— that is, it thinks it lightens them up,— with a profound, an abysmal, book criticism; a criticism which carries you down, down, down into the scientific bowels of the subject,— for the German critic is nothing if not scientific,— and when you come up at last and scent the fresh air and see the bonny daylight once more, you resolve without a dissenting voice that a book criticism is a mistaken way to lighten up a German daily. Sometimes, in place of the criticism, the first-class daily gives you what it thinks is a gay and chipper essay,— about ancient Grecian funeral customs, or the ancient Egyptian method of tarring a mummy, or the reasons for believing that some of the peoples who existed before the flood did not approve of cats. These are not unpleasant subjects; they are not uninteresting subjects; they are even exciting subjects,— until one of these massive scientists gets hold of them. He soon convinces you that even these matters can be handled in such a way as to make a person low-spirited.

As I have said, the average German daily is made up solely of correspondence, — a trifle of it by telegraph, the rest of it by mail. Every paragraph has the side-head, " London," " Vienna," or some other town, and a date. And always, before the name of the town, is placed a letter or a sign, to indicate who the correspondent is, so that the authorities can find him when they want to hang him. Stars, crosses, triangles, squares, half-moons, suns, — such are some of the signs used by correspondents.

Some of the dailies move too fast, others too slowly. For instance, my Heidelberg daily was always twenty-four hours old when it arrived at the hotel ; but one of my Munich evening papers used to come a full twenty-four hours before it was due.

Some of the less important dailies give one a tablespoonful of a continued story every day ; it is strung across the bottom of the page, in the French fashion. By subscribing for the paper for five years I judge that a man might succeed in getting pretty much all of the story.

If you ask a citizen of Munich which is the best Munich daily journal, he will always tell you that there is only one good Munich daily, and that it is published in Augsburg, forty or fifty miles away. It is like saying that the best daily paper in New York is published out in New Jersey somewhere. Yes, the Augsburg *Allgemeine Zeitung* is " the best Munich paper," and it is the one I had in my mind when I was describing a " first-class German daily " above. The entire paper, opened out, is not quite as large as a single page of the New York

*Herald.* It is printed on both sides, of course; but in such large type that its entire contents could be put, in *Herald* type, upon a single page of the *Herald*, — and there would still be room enough on the page for the *Zeitung's* "supplement" and some portion of the *Zeitung's* next day's contents.

Such is the first-class daily. The dailies actually printed in Munich are all called second-class by the public. If you ask which is the best of these second-class papers they say there is no difference: one is as good as another. I have preserved a copy of one of them; it is called the *Münchener Tages-Anzeiger*, and bears date January 25, 1879. Comparisons are odious, but they need not be malicious; and without any malice I wish to compare this journal, published in a German city of 170,000 inhabitants, with journals of other countries. I know of no other way to enable the reader to "size" the thing.

A column of an average daily paper in America contains from 1,800 to 2,500 words; the reading matter in a single issue consists of from 25,000 to 50,000 words. The reading matter in my copy of the Munich journal consists of a total of 1,654 words, — for I counted them. That would be nearly a column of one of our dailies. A single issue of the bulkiest daily newspaper in the world — the London *Times* — often contains 100,000 words of reading matter. Considering that the *Daily Anzeiger* issues the usual twenty-six numbers per month, the reading matter in a single number of the London *Times* would keep it in "copy" two months and a half!

The *Anzeiger* is an eight-page paper; its page is one inch wider and one inch longer than a foolscap page; that is to say, the dimensions of its page are somewhere between those of a schoolboy's slate and a lady's pocket handkerchief. One-fourth of the first page is taken up with the heading of the journal; this gives it a rather top-heavy appearance; the rest of the first page is reading matter; all of the second page is reading matter; the other six pages are devoted to advertisements.

The reading matter is compressed into two hundred and five small pica lines, and is lighted up with eight pica head-lines. The bill of fare is as follows: First, under a pica head-line, to enforce attention and respect, is a four-line sermon urging mankind to remember that, although they are pilgrims here below, they are yet heirs of heaven; and that "When they depart from earth they soar to heaven." Perhaps a four-line sermon in a Saturday paper is the sufficient German equivalent of the eight or ten columns of sermons which the New

Yorkers get in their Monday morning papers. The latest news (two days old) follows the four-line sermon, under the pica head-line "Telegrams," — these are "telegraphed" with a pair of scissors out of the *Augsburger Zeitung* of the day before. These telegrams consist of fourteen and two-thirds lines from Berlin, fifteen lines from Vienna, and two and five-eighths lines from Calcutta. Thirty-three small pica lines of telegraphic news in a daily journal in a King's Capital of 170,000 inhabitants is surely not an overdose. Next we have the pica heading, "News of the Day," under which the following facts are set forth: Prince Leopold is going on a visit to Vienna, six lines; Prince Arnulph is coming back from Russia, two lines; the Landtag will meet at ten o'clock in the morning and consider an election law, three lines and one word over; a city government item, five and one-half lines; prices of tickets to the proposed grand Charity Ball, twenty-three lines, — for this one item occupies almost one-fourth of the entire first page; there is to be a wonderful Wagner concert in Frankfurt-on-the-Main, with an orchestra of one hundred and eight instruments, seven and one-half lines. That concludes the first page. Eighty-five lines, altogether, on that page, including three headlines. About fifty of those lines, as one perceives, deal with local matters; so the reporters are not overworked.

Exactly one-half of the second page is occupied with an opera criticism, fifty-three lines (three of them being headlines), and "Death Notices," ten lines.

The other half of the second page is made up of two paragraphs under the head of "Miscellaneous News." One of these paragraphs tells about a quarrel between the Czar of Russia and his eldest son, twenty-one and a half lines; and the other tells about the atrocious destruction of a peasant child by its parents, forty lines, or one-fifth of the total of the reading matter contained in the paper.

Consider what a fifth part of the reading matter of an American daily paper issued in a city of 170,000 inhabitants amounts to! Think what a mass it is. Would any one suppose I could so snugly tuck away such a mass in a chapter of this book that it would be difficult to find it again if the reader lost his place? Surely not. I will translate that child murder word for word, to give the reader a realizing sense of what a fifth part of the reading matter of a Munich daily actually is when it comes under measurement of the eye:

"From Oberkreuzberg, January 21, the *Donau Zeitung* receives a long account of a crime, which we shorten as follows: In Rametuach,

21**

a village near Eppenschlag, lived a young married couple with two children, one of which, a boy aged five, was born three years before the marriage. For this reason, and also because a relative at Iggensbach had bequeathed M400 ($100) to the boy, the heartless father considered him in the way; so the unnatural parents determined to sacrifice him in the cruelest possible manner. They proceeded to starve him slowly to death, meantime frightfully maltreating him, — as the village people now make known, when it is too late. The boy was shut up in a hole, and when people passed by he cried, and implored them to give him bread. His long-continued tortures and deprivations destroyed him at last, on the third of January. The sudden (*sic*) death of the child created suspicion, the more so as the body was immediately clothed and laid upon the bier. Therefore the coroner gave notice, and an inquest was held on the 6th. What a pitiful spectacle was disclosed then! The body was a complete skeleton. The stomach and intestines were utterly empty; they contained nothing whatever. The flesh on the corpse was not as thick as the back of a knife, and incisions in it brought not a drop of blood. There was not a piece of sound skin the size of a dollar on the whole body; wounds, scars, bruises, discolored extravasated blood, everywhere, — even on the soles of the feet there were wounds. The cruel parents asserted that the boy had been so bad that they had been obliged to use severe punishments, and that he finally fell over a bench and broke his neck. However, they were arrested two weeks after the inquest and put in the prison at Deggendorf."

Yes, they were arrested "two weeks after the inquest." What a home sound that has. That kind of police briskness rather more reminds me of my native land than German journalism does.

I think a German daily journal doesn't do any good to speak of, but at the same time it doesn't do any harm. That is a very large merit, and should not be lightly weighed nor lightly thought of.

The German humorous papers are beautifully printed upon fine paper, and the illustrations are finely drawn, finely engraved, and are not vapidly funny, but deliciously so. So also, generally speaking, are the two or three terse sentences which accompany the pictures. I remember one of these pictures: A most dilapidated tramp is ruefully contemplating some coins which lie in his open palm. He says: "Well, begging is getting played out. Only about five marks ($1.25) for the whole day; many an official makes more!" And I call to mind a picture of a commercial traveler who is about to unroll his samples:

*Merchant* (pettishly). — No, don't. I don't want to buy anything!

*Drummer.* — If you please, I was only going to show you —

*Merchant.* — But I don't wish to see them!

*Drummer* (after a pause, pleadingly). — But do you mind letting *me* look at them! I haven't seen them for three weeks!

COM